Your Towns and Cities in

Chelmsford

in the Great War

To my wife Rebecca, for her unfailing support and enthusiasm throughout the whole process of researching and writing this book.

And to Jack and Jeremy, for their polite indifference.

Your Towns and Cities in the Great War

Chelmsford
in the Great War

Jonathan Swan

Pen & Sword
MILITARY

First published in Great Britain in 2015 by
PEN & SWORD MILITARY
an imprint of
Pen and Sword Books Ltd
47 Church Street
Barnsley
South Yorkshire S70 2AS

ISBN 978 1 47382 114 9

Printed and bound in England
by CPI Group (UK) Ltd, Croydon, CR0 4YY

Typeset in Times New Roman by Chic Graphics

Pen & Sword Books Ltd incorporates the imprints of
Pen & Sword Archaeology, Atlas, Aviation, Battleground, Discovery,
Family History, History, Maritime, Military, Naval, Politics, Railways,
Select, Social History, Transport, True Crime, Claymore Press,
Frontline Books, Leo Cooper, Praetorian Press, Remember When,
Seaforth Publishing and Wharncliffe.

For a complete list of Pen and Sword titles please contact
Pen and Sword Books Limited
47 Church Street, Barnsley, South Yorkshire, S70 2AS, England
E-mail: enquiries@pen-and-sword.co.uk
Website: www.pen-and-sword.co.uk

Contents

Introduction

Chelmsford, as we survey it in 1914, is a small, prosperous provincial town. According to the recent 1911 census it has a population of 18,008, including those in the workhouse, industrial school and the prison. Although in the centre of a large agricultural region with an important market and milling, corn and seed concerns such as Marriage's, as well as a number of breweries such as Wells & Perry, the town is home to some very modern industrial factories. The Hoffman Manufacturing Company produces ball bearings to an astonishing level of precision and in vast quantities for the machines and engines of the Empire. Crompton & Co, electric light and power contractors, provides lighting systems used to illuminate whole towns. The Christy Brothers & Co and Christy & Norris also manufacture electrical lighting and power systems along with pumps, milling equipment and other machinery. And the jewel in the crown is the Marconi Wireless Telegraph Company, working at the leading edge of radio communication. These firms, and others like them, employ large numbers of skilled workers and these they draw in from the surrounding area. To satisfy the demand for intelligent young people the town is well provided with good schools – King Edward VI Grammar School, already over three hundred years old, and the new County High School for Girls, along with the seven public elementary schools: Trinity Road, Friar's, Victoria in Church Street (boys) with Victoria in New Street (girls and infants), St. John's, St. Peter's, Springfield Green, and New London Road Catholic school. Technical and cultural education is provided at the Chelmsford School of Science and Art and agricultural and horticultural skills are developed at the East Anglian Institute of Agriculture.

To handle the increase in population brought by these major

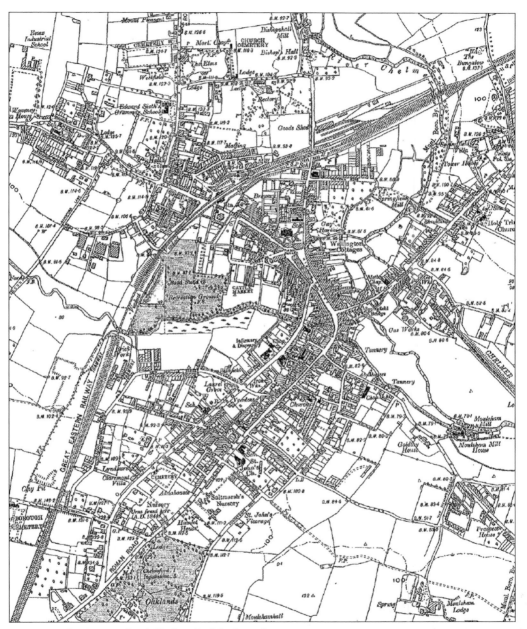

The Borough of Chelmsford before the war.

employers, the town corporation has plans for growth: the recent (1907) addition of the parish of Springfield brings opportunities for more housing to the north west of the town, whilst the small community of Great Baddow is already growing and will continue to do so once the roads are improved. The council is having little trouble finding tenants for the new working class housing in Rainsford Road and there are new homes for the middle classes in Swiss Avenue and in Braemar and Rothesay Avenues. Economic growth is fuelled by good transport links – the Great Eastern Railway, with fast access to London and the rest of the region, and also by the Chelmer & Blackwater Canal Navigation, which brings in coal and other supplies to the heart of the town at Springfield Basin and the Chelmsford Gas Light & Coke Company.

A considerable amount of investment in public infrastructure has taken place in the last decade. The Post Office, Police Station, County Education Committee offices, Chelmsford Rural District Council offices, Public Library and Museum, and School of Art have all been built and opened between 1904 and 1913.

Health is, as always, the subject of much attention and opinion. There is the Chelmsford and Essex Hospital and Dispensary on New London Road, which has just (1909) been considerably enlarged, and

Shire Hall. [Spalding, author's collection]

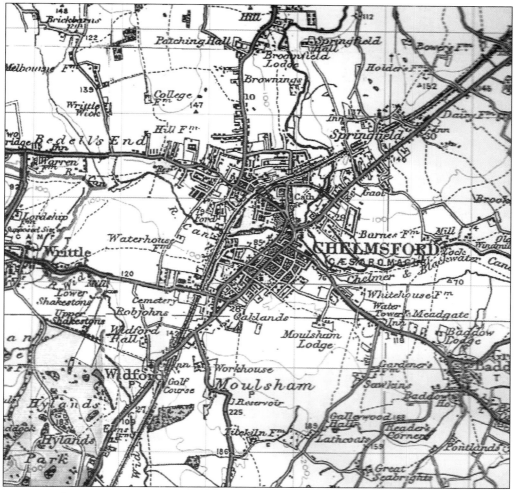

The Chelmsford district.

there is an infectious diseases isolation hospital in Great Baddow. The 1911 National Insurance Act has helped extend medical care to the working classes of the borough, which is surprisingly healthy despite the heavy industry. The hospitals and the general practitioners working alone or in panels under the Act, still rely on fees from the wealthier patients and on charitable giving. Social care is also provided by the Chelmsford Union Workhouse, on Wood Street, and with a number of charitable homes for orphaned boys and girls, perhaps the best known being the Essex Industrial School & Home for Destitute Boys on Rainsford Road.

The Shire Hall, with the Crimean War gun on a plinth in front, is one of the grandest buildings in Chelmsford and is home to the Crown Court and magistrates' court, as well as being used for meetings of borough council and the venue for many aspects of civic life in the borough (curiously, many of the meetings of the Essex County Council committees are held in River Plate House in Finsbury Square in London, close to Liverpool Street Station). Chelmsford as a parish includes Moulsham, to the south, and parts of Springfield and Writtle, added in 1907. Chelmsford as a borough is comprised of three wards: North, South and Springfield. The surrounding parishes are organized into the Chelmsford Union, which largely corresponds to the Chelmsford Rural District Council, comprising Boreham, Broomfield, Buttsbury, Chelmsford, Chignal, Danbury, the East, West and South Hanningfields, Great and Little Baddows, Great and Little Leighs, Great and Little Walthams, Ingatestone and Fryerning, Margaretting, Mashbury, Pleshey, Rettendon, Roxwell, Runwell, Sandon, Springfield, Stock, Widford, Woodham Ferrers, and Writtle.

Chelmsford civic life is dominated by a group of influential individuals. The Mayor of the Corporation of Chelmsford is Alderman George Taylor JP and the deputy Mayor is Alderman Frank Whitmore. John Ockelford Thompson, the proprietor of the *Essex Chronicle*, is an alderman, as is the architect Frederick Chancellor JP, and Frederick Spalding, the photographer and owner of the Assembly Rooms. The men of the Quaker dynasties of the Marriages and the Christys are well represented on the many charitable bodies in the town.

St Mary's Church, to the immense pride of the community, has just been consecrated as the Cathedral of the new Diocese of Chelmsford on 23 January this year; the first Bishop, the Rt. Rev. JE Watts-Ditchfield, was enthroned on 23 April.

Our narrative begins in early August, 1914. The town watched the war clouds developing in Europe, unsure if Britain would become involved. As late as Sunday 2 August there was hope for peace. Mr Newbery of the Adult School organised a peace meeting in front of Shire Hall, proposing that:

This meeting of the inhabitants of Chelmsford expresses its strongest sympathy with you [the Prime Minister] and His Majesty's ministers in the awful responsibility which rests upon

St Mary's Church, now the new Cathedral. [author's collection]

you at this time. It prays that you may strenuously work for the maintenance of peaceful relations with all European nations and for the preservation of our freedom to act for peace as opportunity offers.

At the very time they passed this resolution the 5th Battalion Essex Regiment was under orders in their summer camp at Clacton. Each man was issued with twenty rounds of ammunition and the commanding officer, Lieutenant Colonel Welch, led his men to Harwich on anti-invasion duties.

The next morning saw the annual Children's Day in the Recreation Ground in Chelmsford, with around 2,200 children taking part in a range of serious and not-so-serious athletics events and games; in total 104 races with 300 prizes. The champion boy and girl received a watch and a medal; but no one went away disappointed as three thousand bags of sweets were handed out. The shadow of war was felt even here – the band of the Somerset Light Infantry was due to perform but the men had been called away, and their place was filled by the Essex Industrial School boys' band.

The Great Eastern Railway was able to report that holiday

The Recreation Ground and Viaduct. [Valentine's, author's collection]

bookings over the weekend had held up well, with over four thousand Chelmsford day trippers heading off to Southend, Clacton and London.

The *Essex Chronicle* carried a report that Mrs Brooks of Downham, formerly Writtle, was still 'going strong' at the grand old age of 102. In her childhood she claimed to have seen Napoleon and had spoken to the Duke of Wellington. Elsewhere the 'Farm and Garden' column suggested that the week's work should include potting up early bulbs in the greenhouse, taking dahlia cuttings from the flower garden, layering strawberries in the fruit garden, and planting up late spring broccoli.

War was declared at 11 pm on Tuesday 4 August 1914. The first *Essex Chronicle* of

THE GREAT WAR.

BRITAIN UNDER ARMS.

Germany's Disgraceful Bid for Britain's Neutrality.

German Ultimatum to Italy.

£100,000,000 VOTED.

ACTIONS IN THE NORTH SEA.

WOUNDED AT HARWICH.

German Mine-layer Sunk.

HALF A MILLION MORE MEN FOR ENGLAND.

Essex Chronicle *reports the outbreak of war.*

the war was published on Friday 7 August. The initial reaction was a little muted, with the simple headline 'CHELMSFORD CALM. FINE RECRUITING RESPONSE'. Major Hilder of the Essex Royal Horse Artillery had begun requisitioning horses at the Cattle Market. The

Hon. C H Strutt wrote to the Editor, imploring the people of Chelmsford not to panic, not to lay up stores of money or goods, nor to neglect ordinary business. Despite this the prices of basic goods shot up, with sugar rising from 4d to 5d a pound, bacon by 2d and cheese by a penny three farthings, bringing about complaints that the well-to-do were being catered to by the shopkeepers at the expense of the poor (a theme that would be returned to throughout the war). But on the other side incredible generosity was also being demonstrated: Dr HW Newton offered his house, Fairfield (near the railway station), as a twenty bed hospital; the Corn Exchange was offered to the Chelmsford Voluntary Aid Detachment (VAD) as a hospital. Marconi's had around seventy men called up, and the management issued a statement that 'every man in the company's employ who is called to serve in His Majesty's Navy or Army will have his position in the Company reserved for him, and during such service his salary will be dealt with until further notice as he may direct'. Hoffmann's had around two hundred men called up, about one hundred went from the Arc Works, and the National Steam Car Company sent about forty.

On Saturday afternoon the 5th Battalion of the Essex Regiment deposited their Colours in the Cathedral for safe custody for the duration of hostilities. An honour guard of twelve privates marched from the Market Road Drill Hall to the Cathedral and the flags were furled and placed on the chancel screen. This was followed later the same day by a large public service outside the Shire Hall on Saturday evening, with a crowd of over three thousand participating as the band of the Salvation Army played '*O God, our help in ages past*'. On Sunday 9 August a solemn 'Service of Humble Supplication, for our country in this time of war' was held at the Cathedral. The congregation, under Canon Lake (the Bishop was away in Llandudno at this critical time), sang three hymns: No 165, '*To whom but thee, O God of grace*', No 376, '*O thou, the contrite sinner's Friend*', and No 290, '*In stature grows the heavenly child*', and they finished with the National Anthem.

By the next issue, 14 August, the real war stories were emerging. Harold Boreham, son of ER Boreham of Sunnyside, Bouverie Road, was serving as a 1st Class Stoker on the *Oceanic* which left New York on 1 August. It was carrying £3 million and a number of German and Austrian passengers. They learned of the outbreak of war on 5 August and were alarmed by news that the German battleship *Dresden* was in the area. After a 21 knot race across the Atlantic they rendezvoused with British warships off Land's End on the Saturday morning and eventually docked at Southampton.

The rapid increase in the price of food caused concern to many in the town. Chelmsford Labour Council asked the Chelmsford Star Co-operative Society to take a lead in keeping food prices down and a vigilance committee was set up to monitor the prices charged by shopkeepers. The Chelmsford Board of Guardians, entrusted with the management of the Workhouse and other institutions, was concerned that suppliers should honour the terms and prices of the contracts they had originally undertaken to provide. There was a request that all in possession of gardens or plots of land should sow turnips, carrots, beetroot, onions and cabbage. The government was concerned that people were taking money and gold out of the banks and in order to support the currency the first one pound notes and ten shilling notes were issued over the weekend of the 8 and 9 of August. Some Chelmsford workmen, on being paid with paper money, tore them up in the belief that they were wage tickets.

The first meeting of the town council since the outbreak of war was reported in the same issue. Under consideration was the proposal for the paving of Duke Street from Threadneedle Street to the Railway Arch with wooden blocks, rather than the granite ballast used elsewhere. The poor road conditions were being worsened by the increased use from military traffic. The large military population newly billeted on the town was also seen as a sanitary risk, and there was a request to hose down the High Street each day. It was noted that the Isolation Hospital in Baddow Road had been issued with an emergency tent in case of a typhoid outbreak. Subsequently a notice was issued to all inhabitants that 'owing to the Importation of some Thousands of Troops, clean surroundings and a systematic cleaning of yards and the thorough removal of all house, stable and yard refuse at frequent intervals' was obligatory. Particular attention was to be paid to the destruction of flies, and residents were to show moderation in the use of water. By mid-September the water supply was becoming a major concern because of the massive increase in the population and arrangements were made with the Broomfield Waterworks to provide water to the town at 5d per thousand gallons.

The council clerk was asked to confirm that Councillor Baker, absent on service with the 5th Essex, was not disqualified from office. It was noted that two council employees had so far joined the Army. Half wages were to be paid to their dependents. The Essex Education Committee anticipated problems if too many teachers were called up. As with the Council, they agreed that existing reservists and Territorials could join, but otherwise teachers and education officials should seek permission at the County level; head teachers would be automatically refused. The records show that they believed that there should be no difficulty in getting women to take the vacant places 'for a time'.

The Bishop of Chelmsford was also dealing with requests to serve in the military. He had already refused permission to a number of priests and deacons and he held that the undertaking given at the Ordination Service to forsake all else other than the purely spiritual prohibited them from taking up arms.

A poignant letter to the Editor was published in the *Chronicle* on 28 August 1914:

Sir, – We are asking you to publish the news of the death of the "A" Company mascot, a little kitten, which died at 3.30 Saturday morning. Chelmsford people do not know we had a mascot, and we should like them to know, as we are a Chelmsford Company, and we should be very pleased if any lady or gentleman could send us one to carry through the war. Our other little kitten had the utmost care. It was seen by the battalion doctor when it was ill.

I hope you will publish this for the Company. We miss our kitten very much.

THE CHELMSFORD COMPANY OF TERRITORIALS
"A" Company, 5th Batt. Essex Regiment
Drayton Station, Norfolk

On the evening of Monday 7 September a major demonstration was held in the Recreation Ground. The Mayor was joined by a number of dignitaries, including Mr Pretyman MP and General Heath, commanding the South Midland Division. Several eloquent speeches were given on the call for more troops, and it was announced that in the week or so up until 2 pm on Sunday 1,060 men had enlisted at the

Chelmsford depot for Lord Kitchener's new army, of whom 609 were to join the Essex Regiment. The assembly passed a resolution:

> That this meeting of the inhabitants of Chelmsford, profoundly believing that we are fighting a just cause, for the vindication of the rights of small States and the public law of Europe, pledges itself unswervingly to support the Prime Minister's appeal to the nation, and all measures necessary for the prosecution of the war to a victorious conclusion, whereby alone the lasting peace of Europe can be assured.

And then the *Chronicle* of Friday 25 September brought news of the first casualties.

'Lieutenant James Seabrook, the talented son of Mr and Mrs W. Seabrook, of the Bungalow, Arbour Lane, was killed in France on the 10th inst. At the outbreak of war he volunteered as a motor cycle dispatch rider and was accepted for service, being granted a lieutenant's commission and attached to the 5th Cavalry Brigade. He left England on August 12th and since his departure his relatives had only received three letters from him, one so recently as Wednesday last. He was 30 years of age, and was associated with his father in the well-known horticultural business of Messrs. W. Seabrook and Sons. He was very popular and highly esteemed among a large circle of friends. An amateur actor of acknowledged ability, Lieut. Seabrook took a leading part in the productions of the Chelmsford Amateur Dramatic Club, of which he was honorary treasurer. The news of his death was conveyed to his father in a telegram from the Intelligence Department of the 5th Cavalry Brigade advanced base.'

LIEUT. J. H. SEABROOK,
Intelligence Department,
Son of Mr. W. Seabrook, Springfield,
Chelmsford, killed on duty.

Lieutenant James Seabrook.

This level of detail in an obituary was rarely seen as the list of casualties grew. Lieutenant Seabrook is commemorated on the Chelmsford War Memorial; his grave is in Gandelu Communal Cemetery in France.

This is the story of Chelmsford and its people as they faced up to the realities of a new form of warfare. In the early days it was enough to put a few pennies in the Red Cross collection box, or to knit socks or balaclavas for the boys at the Front – the sort of thing that might result in a letter from a grateful Tommy. But then the pressure on manpower grew as the years passed, and those men who weren't engaged in munitions work in the big factories found themselves conscripted into military service. Small businesses were put under tremendous pressure, at a time when economic pressures forced prices on an endless upwards spiral. The incessant demand for more and more men could only be relieved by older men and, increasingly, women taking over their jobs. The voluntary services such as the Volunteer Aid Detachments and the Volunteer Regiments even assumed some of the duties of the regular forces to free them to serve in France and Flanders. By 1917 food shortages were a serious concern although rationing was not imposed until early 1918. The final months of the war were bleak and every man, woman and child in Chelmsford was under no doubt that they each had a real and personal contribution to make to the national war effort.

This book has drawn on many sources. It would not have been possible without the superb resources of the British Newspaper Archive website (www.britishnewspaperarchive.co.uk) which provides searchable access to the *Essex Chronicle* and the *Essex Newsman* for the entire First World War. These provided the stories and anecdotes that were validated and expanded using a number of references from our wonderful Essex Records Office (ERO), the staff of which so patiently withstood my regular Saturday raids on their archives and who proved so helpful in locating the few photographs and images of Chelmsford from that period. They also have an extensive collection of contemporary Ordnance Survey maps which have proved essential in trying to understand the layout of the old town; the impact of the Parkway and post-World War 2 developments has been substantial and I have included an appendix which lists the roads and streets of each municipal ward. The map extracts used in this book are from the 25" County Series 3rd Edition maps (1915-1924). The ERO holds a comprehensive collection of the minutes of all town council, committee and subcommittee meetings of the period, all printed and bound. The 1911 census records on the www.ancestry.co.uk website have been helpful in matching names to addresses, along with the 1918 Electoral Register recently put online by the ERO (C/E 2/1/1). Although this book is primarily about the people of Chelmsford and not about battles or military campaigns, the staff at the Essex Regiment Museum have responded to questions with great speed and efficiency. Kelly's Directory 1914 is an invaluable document which provides a fascinating insight into the civic and business life of the town and its spectacular growth prior to the war. A very important source has been the notebook and papers of Special Constable Herbert Gripper (ERO D/Z 137/1, copyright Essex Police Museum) – his handwriting is appalling, but well worth the effort. The memoirs of Basil Harrison, published as *A Duke Street Childhood*, along with Richard Godfrey's *Rambling Reminiscences: the autobiography of a nobody* (Essex Records Office T/Z 318/1) are referred to many times. And a final mention must be given to the anonymous author of the weekly column in the *Essex Newsman*, under the by-line 'Reflexions by Reflex'. Initially I found his musings rather whimsical and irrelevant, but after a while it became apparent that Reflex was an ascerbic commentator on Chelmsford life, providing some idiosyncratic insights into the issues of the day – although unfortunately tempered by a taste for appalling poetry.

At the time of the Great War Britain used the imperial system of measurements and currency. Rather than translating each reference as it occurs, it may be helpful to refer to the tables opposite.

The conversion of Great War prices to their modern equivalents is not straightforward, as the standard measure of inflation used today – the Retail Price Index – was introduced in 1947; and according to the Bank of England around 60 per cent of the 1914 family budget was spent on food, where today it is more like 11 per cent. There is a useful inflation calculator at the Bank of England website (http://www. bankofengland. co.uk/education/Pages/inflation/calculator/ index1.aspx).

Using this calculator we can get the following very approximate values for the penny, shilling and pound; note the substantial fall in the value of money over the four years of the war.

Imperial unit	Abbreviation	Metric equivalent
LENGTH		
Inch	" or in	2.54 cm
Foot	' or ft	30.48 cm
Yard	yd	91.44 cm
Mile	m	1.6 km
WEIGHT		
Ounce	oz	28.35g
Pound	lb	453 g
Stone	st	6.35 kg
Hundredweight	cwt	50.8 kg
VOLUME		
Pint	pt	0.57 litres
Gallon	gal	4.55 litres
AREA		
acre	a.	4046.9 m2

	Abbreviation	Modern value (approximate)	
CURRENCY		1914	1918
Penny	d	41p	20p
Shilling	s 12 d = 1 s	£4.89	£2.41
Pound	£ 20 s = £1	£97.71	£48.12

Invasion

'Each for all, and all for each'
Motto, Chelmsford War Emergency Committee, 1915

With a century of hindsight the fears of a German invasion of England seem quite groundless but throughout the First World War it was given serious attention by the military authorities. The idea of a continental or naval war involving the two nations had engaged the interest of a number of authors, playwrights and even early film makers and a direct German assault on England was a recurrent theme. In Le Queux's *The Invasion of 1910*, serialised in the *Daily Mail* in 1906, the East Coast was overrun by German forces and it even featured the Battle of Chelmsford:

> 'The enemy were fast closing in upon us. It was a terrible night in Chelmsford. There was panic on every hand. A man mounted the Tindal statue and harangued the crowd, urging the people to rise and compel the Government to stop the war. A few young men endeavoured to load the old Crimean cannon in front of the Shire Hall, but found it clogged with rust and useless. People fled from the villa residences in the Brentwood Road into the town for safety, now that the enemy were upon them. The banks in the High Street were being barricaded, and the stores still remaining in the various grocers' shops, Luckin Smith's, Martin's, Cramphorn's, and Pearke's, were rapidly being concealed from the invaders. All the ambulance waggons entering the town were filled with wounded, although as many

as possible were sent south by train. By one o'clock in the morning, however, most of the civilian inhabitants had fled. The streets were empty, but for the bivouacking troops and the never-ending procession of wounded men. The General and his staff were deliberating to a late hour in the Shire Hall, at which he had established his headquarters. The booming of the guns waxed and waned till dawn, when a furious outburst announced that the second act of the tragedy was about to open.' (*The Invasion of England, Ch XI*)

The fictional Germans launched a three-pronged assault from the direction of Little Waltham to the north, Partridge Green (Basildon) to the south, and along the railway from the east, forcing the evacuation of the town and a military withdrawal to Widford and Moulsham, then to Writtle and defeat.

Perhaps in response to these hypothetical scenarios a large-scale naval and military exercise involving two divisions – 12,000 men – under the leadership of General Sir John French simulated a seaborne assault between Clacton and Holland-on-Sea in 1904. The invaders advanced as far as Witham before they were repelled and pushed back to the sea. A local exercise took place in May 1911, with the Essex Royal Engineers joining up with the 5th Battalion of the Essex Regiment (part of the new Territorial Force) to form the Red force against the rest of the Essex Territorials (the Blue force). In this scenario the Blue force had landed on the coast and occupied Chelmsford but the Red force had marched up from London. The Blue transport route to the coast was cut off by a force from Braintree. The invaders retired from Chelmsford along the Springfield Road, and battle was joined at Sandford Mill, with fighting between Barnes Mill and the Rifle Butts at Sandford. No outcome was recorded.

Looking at the map, Essex would appear to be a logical landing site for a force crossing the North Sea (or German Ocean, as it was often known at the time) from ports in occupied Belgium and Germany, but anyone with local sailing experience would probably point out that the shallow waters and extensive sandbanks, mudflats and marshlands along the Thames, Crouch and Blackwater estuaries and the Walton Backwater, along with the bleak exposed shoreline of Clacton, together comprise a formidable and valuable natural defence.

But with the outbreak of war these fears returned and paranoia set in, with spies to be found everywhere. Anti-German feeling was present in Chelmsford but with none of the attacks and looting of shops that occurred in London and elsewhere. James Thompson, a baker, of 5 Broomfield Road, and Mr. Isaac Bryman, a Ladies' and Gentlemen's Tailor, of 13a Duke Street, both felt it necessary to publish declarations that they were not of German or Austrian origin. Under the first Defence of the Realm Act (1914), ports, railways and military and naval installations were placed firmly out of bounds. The English coast from Dorset to Northumberland was declared a Prohibited Zone and restrictions were placed on travel. Local authorities in Essex, Suffolk and Norfolk were discouraged from taking Belgian refugees. The summer season was ruined for many seaside resorts. The local Territorials were mobilised, with the Chelmsford contingent of the Essex Fortress Royal Engineers being sent to Harwich even as the first rumours of war began. Within the next few weeks many other Regular and Territorial troops were deployed in Essex, and units such as the 8th (Cyclist) Battalion of the Essex Regiment carried out patrols of the

The Essex Regiment parading on the High Street before the war.
[Reproduced by courtesy of the Essex Record Office ERO T/Z 297/1]

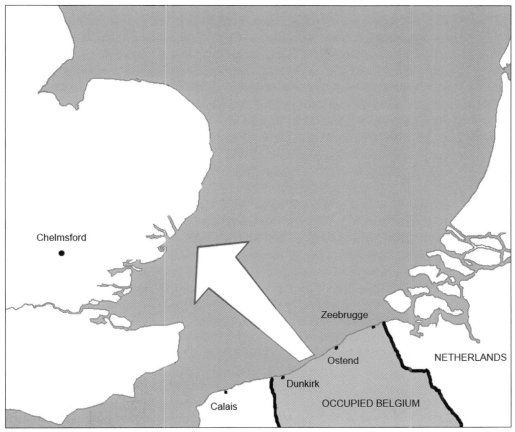

The route across the German Ocean from occupied Belgium.

coastline. The South Midland Division, which was to have such a big impact on Chelmsford, was deployed at various locations across Essex for training and defence purposes. The Essex diarist, Dr Salter, recorded an invasion scare on 14 November 1914, when several submarines were supposedly seen at the entrance to the Blackwater.

The chief concern of the civil authorities in the event of an invasion would be the protection and welfare of the civilian population. This problem was given to the newly formed war emergency committees, and the County of Essex Central Emergency Committee first met on 22 October 1914 under the chairmanship of the Lord Lieutenant of

Essex, the Earl of Warwick. Membership was drawn from the military authorities, the police, and the various local authorities in the county, including the Mayor of Chelmsford. It was obvious that the enormity of the task would take some time to resolve and in particular the focus for the Essex committee would be the control of the civilian community in the event of an enemy landing. The workings of the committee were shrouded in secrecy 'to allay undue alarm', and the minutes were handwritten (virtually every other county and borough council committee had its records printed). Subsequently, at an informal meeting of Chelmsford Town Council on Tuesday 2 March 1915, the military representative, Mr R Magor, explained the purpose of the committee at county and at local level and the council resolved to form a Local Emergency Committee, subject to the approval of the Lord Lieutenant.

The minutes record that the official duties of the Emergency Committee were:

1. To arrange for the removal of horses, motors, vehicles, etc.
2. To make arrangements for the movements of civil population, keeping off the military roads [evacuation became voluntary from October 1916].
3. To arrange the supply of spades, pick axes, tools etc. required by the military authorities, and for placing at their disposal physically fit people.

Despite a clear awareness on the part of the committee and the authorities that an invasion was highly unlikely an early decision was to plan for the mass evacuation of the entire county. The rationale was that it would be easier to break down a county-wide scheme into smaller components operated by the district committees, each of which could be coordinated by the central committee, than it would be to allow the proliferation of local evacuation plans. Local Emergency Committees were under the guidance of the Essex committee, with the Chelmsford & District Emergency Committee comprised of local dignitaries, the Mayor and the Town Clerk, and the chairman was Lieutenant Colonel Kemble. In December the Lord Lieutenant issued a notice to householders in the county of Essex:

Whereas a state of war at present exists between Great Britain and Germany, I have to state that precautionary arrangements have been made to safeguard the civil population of this County in the event of a hostile attack on our shores.

To prevent any alarm or panic amongst the community, I wish to point out that such an attack is not regarded as imminent or probable; but on the other hand the contingency cannot be ignored. A system of Emergency Committees has been established throughout the County; such Committees will have the assistance of the Police and Special Constables. These Committees will, I trust, receive the loyal support of the inhabitants of the County.

Instructions will be given to the inhabitants whenever and wherever it is thought advisable that they should leave any particular district and by what means and in what direction they should proceed.

I desire to record my earnest hope that all those who have not joined recognised Volunteer Corps will refrain from the attack on the enemy, and will remember that such action might mean terrible reprisals and punishment on an innocent community.

Warwick
Lord Lieutenant
Dunmow
2nd December 1914

In October 1916 the Emergency Committees were issued with the approved declaration of emergency, to be printed and posted around the designated area, and a stock of these notices was held by the Town Clerk:

County of Essex: Emergency Notice
Instructions to the Civil Population
The Military Authorities have declared that a state of
emergency has arisen in this parish: -
The Orders of the Local Emergency Committee are to be
carried out with all possible speed.
The main roads must be kept clear for the movement of troops.

NOTHING is to be DESTROYED without definite orders
from the Military Authorities.
ALL ORDERS of the Military and Police must be
immediately obeyed.
By order of the Lord Lieutenant
J. A. Unett, Capt. Chief Constable
God Save the King

The military authorities identified the roads by which they intended to move troops to the coast in response to an invasion; these were designated Military Roads and would be strictly out of bounds to civilians. In the Chelmsford area these were:

London to Colchester road (the modern A12)
Chelmsford to Dunmow (B1008)
Chelmsford to Southend (now the A114)
Chelmsford to Stock (B1007)
Chelmsford to Ongar (A414)
Chelmsford to Leaden Roding and Sawbridgeworth (A1060)
Chelmsford to Maldon (A414)

An inspection of the Ordnance Survey map will show that this would leave very little choice for an evacuation route and the path decided upon is best understood using a contemporary map. It was proposed that the ultimate objective for Chelmsford would be Welwyn in Hertfordshire, and a route was identified that would allow the refugees to keep to the back roads and out of the way of the military. According to the instructions of February 1915, Chelmsford residents of North Ward, on the orders of the Military Authorities, would firstly make their way to the assembly area in Admiral's Park on Rainsford Road.

Here they would be formed into groups by the appointed Leader, and assigned a Guide, who had been previously selected, and had 'made themselves fully acquainted with the line of route' from the official maps and wore the official armlet. Inspired by the official motto 'each for all, and all for each', the Guides would then lead their parties to Rainsford Road and turn up the Chignall Road, past Writtle Wick, out along the Mashbury Road to Chignall St James, on to Mashbury, Good Easter and up to Dunmow. The next leg, for which no directions

DISCOVER MORE ABOUT MARITIME AND NAVAL HISTORY

Seaforth PUBLISHING is probably the country's leading maritime book publisher, producing the very best reference books, narrative histories, ship monographs and modelling books, all reflecting the latest research and designed and printed to the highest standards.

Keep up to date with our new releases by completing and returning the form below (no stamp required if posting in the UK).

Alternatively, please enter your details online at **www.seaforthpublishing.com**

All those subscribing to our mailing list via our website will receive a free e-book, *HMS Victory, First Rate 1765.* Please enter code number ACC2 when subscribing to receive your free e-book.

Mr/Mrs/Ms ....

Address...

Postcode.................... Email address..

Website: www.seaforthpublishing.com – Email: enquiries@seaforthpublishing.com
Telephone: 01226 734555

Freepost Plus RTKE-RGRJ-KTTX
Pen & Sword Books Ltd
47 Church Street
BARNSLEY
S70 2AS

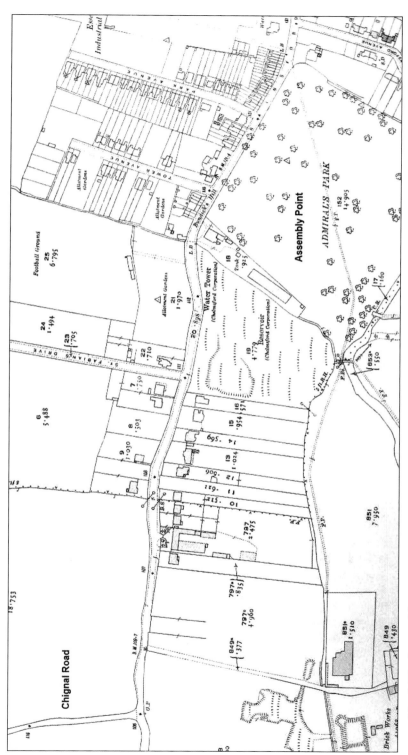

North Ward assembly point.

Evacuation route.

were provided, would be to Welwyn. By May 1916 the route was changed: proceed to Mashbury, then High Easter, Aythorpe Roding, White Roding, and on to Welwyn. The distance was around forty miles.

For residents of South Ward, the assembly point was the Recreation Ground, then moving on to Rainsford Road. The Mayor, the Town Clerk, and Mr W Hilliard and Mr F Collins were leaders for the North and South Wards. The Springfield Ward leader was Mr R Magor, assisted by H Coward, SL Bolingbroke, and G Wray, and they and their residents assembled at Church Lane, near Springfield Rectory, and followed a convoluted route along Lawn Lane, Little Waltham Road, taking Mill Lane across to Broomfield, and so to Chignall St James. Those closer into town gathered near the Gaol and went to Lawn Lane via Arbour Lane.

Evacuees would be restricted to taking only those belongings necessary for the journey, including food and water for two days. Clothes, blankets, money and jewellery were allowed, but furniture and furnishings were strictly forbidden. The use of prams, handcarts and bicycles was permitted and encouraged, but the use of motor and horse-drawn vehicles was subject to military requirements, it being likely that such vehicles would be requisitioned very early on. It was agreed that owners of cars and carts could use them to transport their families and property 'a reasonable distance' so that the vehicle could be returned, if required, within twenty-four hours. The majority of the people would make their way on foot. The calculation allowed for a movement of two miles per hour, with women and children making ten miles per day, given 1,000 refugees per mile of road. Wheeled traffic was assumed to travel twenty miles a day. This would mean that they could reach Dunmow by the first night; but there is a fundamental assumption that the order to evacuate would be given early in the day otherwise movement to plan would be compromised. The guides were instructed to find accommodation for their groups wherever they could, with women, children and the elderly having priority for shelter. Guides were also instructed that their first responsibility was to the group and that they were not to stay behind if anyone should drop out. There were very strict instructions to ensure that groups remained together and adhered to the specified route; shortcuts and breakaway groups were not to be allowed. Following the allegations of German atrocities on the civilian populations in France and Belgium the

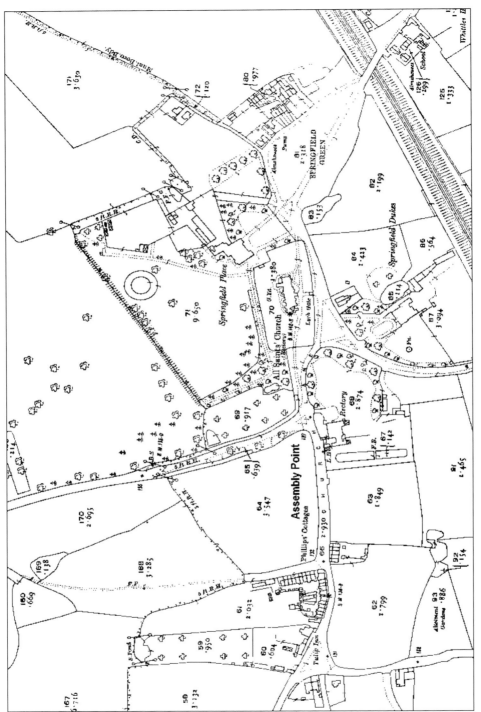

Springfield Ward assembly point.

authorities were determined to stamp out the possibility of spontaneous guerrilla-style attacks by civilians on German forces, which would inevitably incur drastic reprisals, and so under the evacuation order all firearms were to be handed over to the police.

In its earliest forms the scheme required the compulsory evacuation of all able bodied civilians. The sick, aged and infirm were to be left at home; their details were to be given to the Town Clerk who would maintain a register. Every effort would be made to provide assistance should an evacuation take place but, ominously, 'no guarantee can be given'. The Emergency Measures in the Event of a Hostile Landing included provisions for the removal and/or destruction of livestock, foodstuffs and machinery and equipment, but from October 1916 onwards evacuation was no longer mandatory, and individuals could choose to remain behind at their own risk. Private property, furnishings and fittings were clearly at risk of damage or destruction in any hostilities; livestock could be appropriated by either side and moved or slaughtered as needed. Each parish police constable was required to maintain an inventory of horses, cattle, etc. and it was recommended that animals should be branded on the hind quarter, with the letters SX to indicate Essex, and CH for Chelmsford. Full instructions concerning property and equipment were issued in mid-1916:

Instructions for the Guidance of Civil Populations in the Event of a Landing by the Enemy in this Country

1. All motors, bicycles, horses, mules, donkeys, carts, carriages and other vehicles, harness, petrol, launches and lighters should be removed away from military operations. If they cannot be removed immediately, they should be destroyed.
2. No attempt should be made to remove livestock.
3. Food supplies and forage are not to be destroyed.
4. No attempt should be made to… burn, cut or destroy:
    bridges   waterworks
    railway rolling stock   sluices or locks
    electric light or power stations   piers or jetties
    telegraph or telephone wires   ferries
    wireless stations

Each town and district in Essex had its own evacuation route. Given that Chelmsford had a population of about 20,000 at this time, a successful countywide evacuation would have been a spectacular feat of logistics. The Emergency Committees had regular communication with their counterparts in the region: the chairman of the Suffolk committee sought to reassure Essex that their routes did not enter into the county, and they would not therefore require supplies or accommodation. Although the evacuees were expected to bring provisions of their own and the guides were supposed to know where the water supplies were, the committees were concerned about additional provisions. There was a prolonged and robust correspondence with the Lord Lieutenant of Cambridgeshire, who was very clear about the fact that they were not going to provide any food or supplies to the Essex refugees who were to be evacuated to or through his county. It took until July 1918 for the Home Office and War Office to introduce a combined scheme for refugees from the East Coast in which stores of cocoa and Army biscuits were laid down in the county depot in Anchor Street, Chelmsford. It was anticipated that there would be 150,000 refugees and so sixty-seven tons of biscuits and four tons of Admiralty cocoa were allocated. This works out at 1lb of biscuits and 1 oz. of cocoa per person, to last them two days on the road. This scheme was primarily intended for those evacuating from a coastal zone which extended ten miles inland, at which point responsibility for provisions passed on to the Local Food Committees. Incredibly, the Emergency Committees were still revising their evacuation plans as the end of the war approached. In July 1918 a Note on Emergency Measures was circulated, setting out the three warning phases: the First Emergency Warning 'Special Vigilance', the Second Warning 'Prepare to Move', and the Third and Final Warning 'Move'. These had a military significance but for the civilian authorities, especially the police, they entailed specific actions. With the Special Vigilance notification the Chief Constable put the constabulary on standby and notified the Honorary Secretary of the Central Organising Committee. Prepare to Move triggered the posting of picquets (guards) on the designated military roads, transport was prepared, and work gangs were put on standby. With the Emergency Order to Move, all prearranged measures were put into action in the named area.

The movement of the population posed substantial problems for the authorities and at various times the Chelmsford and District Emergency Committee discussed some form of practical exercise or rehearsal, but there is no record that it was ever carried out (perhaps unsurprising, given the Council's ambivalent attitude to other non-mandatory services such as the provision of public air raid shelters, food kitchens, or the keeping of pigs). The legal authority of the Emergency Committee was the Defence of the Realm Act, and its executive powers were devolved to the Chief Constable of Essex, Captain Showers (until his retirement in March, 1915, later Captain Unett), and his police officers. The police force had insufficient manpower to take on these additional responsibilities, and so the burden fell upon the volunteer special constables. In the event of an invasion the special constables were to assist the police in protecting and evacuating the civilian population. In the absence of a formal military response, the defence of the county was in the hands of another group of men: the Essex Volunteer Regiment.

The invasion never materialised; but the war did come to Chelmsford, from the air.

CHAPTER 2

Air Raids

These Instructions are of an entirely Precautionary character,
and while there is no reason for expecting attacks by means
of Aircraft, the possibility cannot be ignored.
Notice, Mayor of Chelmsford, 1915

German Zeppelin air ships and, later in the war, Gotha heavy bombers flew from their bases in Germany and occupied Belgium directly across the North Sea, making landfall over the Essex coast and following the rivers or using the railway lines to navigate their way to London or on into the Midlands. Southend in particular suffered from aerial bombing on many occasions, whilst Maldon suffered a heavy raid in 1915; but for a town with such significant industrial concerns producing material of great strategic value to the Allied war effort, Chelmsford received very little attention from the enemy.

At the start of the war little thought was given to the risks of air attack. Zeppelins were used in support of the first German offensives but primarily in a reconnaissance role. Although capable of long distance flight and able to carry a considerable load the first daylight bombing missions, in Belgium, were risky and the airships had to fly at high altitude to avoid artillery fire, which with the primitive bomb sighting equipment produced very poor results. On 9 January 1915 the Kaiser gave permission to commence air raids on military targets in England. The use of the airship as a strategic weapon began with a raid on Norfolk on the night of 19th January. A Little Waltham man, Private Poulton of 5th Essex, was injured in the chest by a bomb fragment in the attack on Great Yarmouth.

The raids took place at night and navigation was assisted by the light from streets, houses and factories. At this time Chelmsford was illuminated by the Electric Supply Corporation, which had a formal contract to provide electricity and lighting to the North and South wards of the borough and they provided twenty-one arc lamps (on Moulsham Street, High Street, Tindal Street, and Duke Street), and 344 incandescent lamps, with two additional lamps at Parker Road and Wood Street, another in Admiral Road (Rainsford Road estate, now

Rainsford Estate.

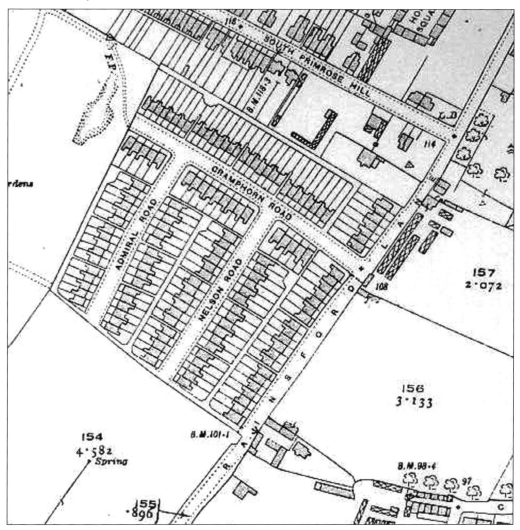

gone), and two lamps at the public convenience on the High Street. There were eighty-three gas lamps in Springfield Ward, supplied by Chelmsford Gas Light & Coke Company, with two additional lamps opposite Trinity Road and Weight Road, and two more at Meadside (now Meadowside) and at Oak Lea on Springfield Road. In October 1914 the Council considered an order issued by the General Officer Commanding (GOC) of the South Midland Division to control the lighting of the borough between the hours of sunset and sunrise. After consultation with Mr Eustace, the manager of the Electric Supply Corporation, it was agreed that they would extinguish each alternate arc lamp and 'blacken the globes of the remainder with the exception of a small portion of the bottom thereof, so only sufficient light may be given as necessary to illuminate the street below, and so that the lamps are, as far as possible, invisible from above'. It was further agreed to extinguish alternate incandescent lamps other than those at street corners. This pragmatic agreement was to cause problems later in the war, as the Council had entered into a long-term contract for electric lighting services with the Electric Supply Corporation and the borough continued to pay for lighting at the full rate until the contract was renegotiated in 1916.

The issue of lighting restrictions caused considerable confusion. On 18 February 1915 Herbert Taylor, a clothier's manager, failed to extinguish the lights in his shop window at 226 Moulsham Street and became the first person in the town to be prosecuted for this offence. The court clerk advised the bench that a conviction carried a fine of up to £100 or six months' imprisonment. The Mayor, in the chair, imposed a fine of 40s with 4s costs. Alderman Frederick Spalding, the noted photographer, found himself in court in March 1915, along with three other Chelmsford tradesmen, for the same offence. Although pleading guilty, Spalding pointed out that the first sunrise-sunset lighting order introduced at the start of the war had been amended in November, permitting screened lights, but then at the end of January another order prohibited any visible light from 6 pm to 6 am. It was not clear which version of the order was current at the time; and it was further noted that in Essex there were three relevant 'military authorities': one covering the Metropolitan area (the part of Essex now in London), the Third Army, and at that time the South Midland Division. Following representations from the police and the military the magistrates put aside the guilty pleas and took no further action. On 1 June 1915 the Chief Constable resolved the problem with an order under Regulation 11 of the Defence of the Realm Act, directing that no street lamps were to be lit in Chelmsford from one hour after sunset to one hour before sunrise.

Street lighting continued to engage the attention of the Council and the military authorities; the Council even had a Lighting Committee. At their meeting in October 1915, with the approval of the Chief Constable and the Assistant Provost Marshal of the South Midland Division they agreed to the installation of coloured, shaded lamps in the interests of public safety at the following locations:

Junction of	Moulsham Street and London Road
	Writtle Road and London Road
	High Street and London Road
	Baddow Road and Moulsham Street
Near Shire Hall	
Under railway arch at	Duke Street
	New Street
On the Conduit	High Street
Junction of	Broomfield Road and Rainsford Road
Springfield Road	opposite Rosling's Garage

It was also decided to paint the lower portions of the street lamp standards white, and similarly to whiten the edges of footpaths in the principal streets and at all street crossings and corners, following an experiment in Duke Street from the railway station to Shire Hall. Further lights were added in December 1916, outside the Post Office and Railway Station, outside the Police Station on New Street, and one at the junction of New Street and Duke Street. The lower parts of trees were also painted white at this time.

By October 1917 the Chief Constable had realised that lighting restrictions were hazardous and he wrote to the Council:

A real danger exists (particularly in New Street) owing to the almost total absence of any lighting in some of the streets in Chelmsford. Nights are becoming very long and dark and large numbers of people, chiefly from the works, make use of New

The junction of Rainsford Road with Broomfield Road (on right). [Spalding, reproduced by courtesy of the Essex Record Office ERO SCN 32]

Street, both in the evenings and early mornings… is it possible to light certain streets to some extent and at the same time avoid the possibility of indicating the position of the town to hostile aircraft?

Recent experience points to hostile aircraft approaching on moonlit nights, whereas in the past the darkest nights were generally selected for the purpose. Conditions have therefore changed to some extent, and I am of the opinion that the question of lights requires some reconsideration.

The management of Marconi's also wrote to the council about the dire lighting in New Street, with the result that three new lights were installed.

Police officers with whistles and bugles provided the earliest form of air raid warning but for the civilian population it was not immediately apparent as to the action that should be taken in the event. Zeppelins could be heard more often than they could be seen, but unless bombs were actually falling a raid, particularly at night with the searchlights playing across the skies, was more of a public spectacle and people would watch from their windows or gather in the streets. In February 1915 the Mayor of Chelmsford, George Taylor, issued a notice in the *Essex Chronicle*:

DEFENCE OF THE REALM
Borough of Chelmsford

The WAR OFFICE, with the concurrence of the ADMIRALTY, recommend that the FOLLOWING PRECAUTIONS should be OBSERVED by the INHABITANTS OF TOWNS in the possible event of a BOMBARDMENT by AIRCRAFT:

1. Inhabitants of Houses should go into the Cellars or Lower Rooms.
2. Gathering into crowds or watching the Bombardment from an exposed position may lead to unnecessary loss of life.
3. If an Aircraft is seen or heard overhead, crowds should disperse, and all persons should if possible take shelter.
4. Unexploded Shells or Bombs should not be touched, as they may burst if moved; the Local Military Authorities, or the Police, should be informed where they are as soon as this can be done safely.

In the event of the Police Authorities receiving intimation of an impending attack by Aircraft they will issue instructions for the Firehorn at the Gasworks to be sounded intermittently for periods of about thirty seconds for ten minutes as a warning to the general Public.

These Instructions are of an entirely Precautionary character, and while there is no reason for expecting attacks by means of Aircraft, the possibility cannot be ignored.

The optimism of the Council was to be short lived, as on 26 February a German aircraft, flying at 'great speed, quite sixty miles an hour', flew around the county and dropped bombs in fields outside Braintree, in Coggeshall, and a high explosive bomb landed on Colchester. The route of the raider was tracked by listeners on the ground: it was first heard at Brightlingsea at 7.45 pm, at Coggeshall at 8.25 pm, Braintree 8.30, Coggeshall again at 8.35, Colchester at 8.40 and then away over Harwich. Other than a few frightened horses and a number of broken windows, there was no damage or injury caused, but the general reaction was of indignation and, rather tellingly, there was no mention of any anti-aircraft or artillery fire, nor of any British aircraft. Unsurprisingly, perhaps, by the time of the first raid on London on 31 May, our capital was protected by four 6-pounder Hotchkiss guns, six 1-pounder pom-poms, and two 3-inch naval guns.

A second raid followed on 16 April when, just after midnight, a Zeppelin followed the Blackwater estuary to Maldon and dropped five incendiary bombs on Maldon and six on Heybridge, with the flashes and explosions seen and heard across a wide area, shaking the windows of houses in Chelmsford. According to one eyewitness the population turned out 'as if they were going to see the pictures at a picture

'Take Air Raid Action'. [courtesy Essex Police Museum]

palace'. Post-war figures suggest that there were actually four high explosive and thirty incendiary bombs dropped in this attack. A more serious raid struck Southend on 10 May, with sixty bombs falling; one woman was killed and her husband severely injured. This time there was anti-aircraft fire from a battery at Cliffe and eleven Royal Flying Corps aircraft were sent up, although the airship evaded them.

Following further raids on London additional guidance was issued by Captain Unett, the Chief Constable of Essex, in June 1915.

'Resume Normal Conditions'. [courtesy Essex Police Museum]

In all probability if an air raid is made it will take place at a time when most people are in bed. The only intimation the public are likely to get will be the reports of the anti-aircraft guns or the noise of falling bombs.

The public are advised not to go into the streets, where they might be struck by falling missiles, moreover, the streets being required for the passage of fire engines, etc. should not be obstructed by pedestrians.

In many houses there are no facilities for procuring water on the upper floors. It is suggested, therefore, that a supply of water and sand might be kept there, so that any fire breaking out on a small scale can at once be dealt with. Everyone should know the position of the fire post nearest the house.

All windows and doors on the lower floor should be closed, to prevent the admission of noxious gases. An indication that poison gas is being used will be that a peculiar and irritating smell may be noticed following the dropping of a bomb.

Many enquiries have been made as to the best respirator. To this question there is no really satisfactory answer, as, until the specific poison being used is known, an antidote cannot be indicated. There are many forms of respirator on the market for which special advantages are claimed, but the Commissioner is advised by competent experts that in all probability a pad of cotton waste contained in gauze to tie round the head saturated with a strong solution of washing soda would be effective as a filtering medium for noxious gases, and could be improvised at home at trifling cost. It should be damped when required for use, and must be large enough to protect the nose as well as the mouth, the gauze being so adjusted as to protect the eyes.

Gas should not be turned off at the meter at night, as this practice involves a risk of subsequent fire and of explosion from burners left on when the meter was shut off. This risk outweighs any advantages that might accrue from the gas being shut off at the time of a night air raid by aircraft.

Persons purchasing portable chemical fire extinguishers should require a written guarantee that they comply with the specifications of the Board of Trade, Office of Works, Metropolitan Police, or some approved Fire Prevention Committee.

No bomb of any description should be handled unless it has shown itself to be of incendiary type. In this case it may be possible to remove it without undue risk. In all other cases a bomb should be left alone and the police informed.

Apart from the lack of an air raid warning system, this guidance is remarkably comprehensive, bearing in mind that the Germans had first used gas on the Western Front only three months previously. According to a House of Commons statement, by this time there had been fourteen air raids on England, with fifty-six deaths and 138 wounded.

On the night of 17 August 1915 the Zeppelin L10 crossed the Suffolk coast and picked up the railway south of Ipswich, following it down to Chelmsford and on to North London. After dropping bombs on Walthamstow and Leyton, killing ten people, it turned back and, flying over Chelmsford a second time, it dropped two bombs. One exploded in Admiral's Park, the Germans presumably aiming at either the Roxwell Road military camp or the adjacent waterworks. Cecil Campen, of Chignall Road, was on the scene the next morning and recalled a crater two feet deep by six feet across. The other bomb went through the roof of 7 Glebe Road, smashing through the bedroom floor and through the sofa in the living room below. It failed to explode. Mrs Maisie Felton was an infant at the time and only a few moments before had been lying on the pillows on the sofa before being taken to bed, but remembered the story for an article in the *Chronicle* in 1986. The objective of the Glebe Road bomb was the Marconi Wireless Telegraph Company's works. One of its two 450 foot wireless masts stood less than eighty yards from the house; a hit on such a target would have been a major propaganda coup for the Germans.

As a result of the bomb damage, Maisie's father, Harry Childs, was one of the first to put in a claim for assistance from the Chelmsford committee of the Prince of Wales' War Relief Fund and in October he was awarded £10 towards the cost of furniture repairs 'damaged by the dropping of a bomb from a hostile aircraft'. Although the story of the Chelmsford bombs was not reported by the local newspapers, the Secretary of the Admiralty that week announced that 'Zeppelins visited the Eastern Counties last night and dropped bombs... some houses and other buildings were damaged.' The incident attracted a lot of local attention and is mentioned in a number of written and oral accounts of the war.

The responsibility for repairs for bomb damage was a recurrent theme throughout the war, and it was never clear whether the local authorities or central government should bear the brunt of the costs, or whether individuals and organisations should take out insurance.

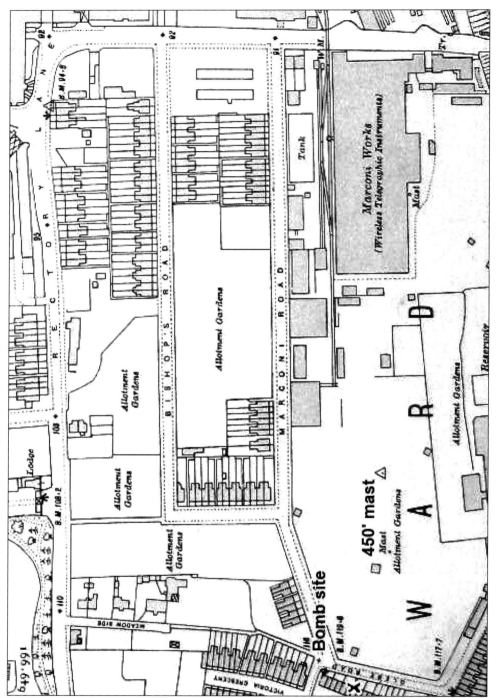

Glebe Road and Marconi's.

Advertisements appeared in the local newspapers concerning the *Daily Mail* scheme: readers who submitted a signed order requesting a daily copy of the *Daily Mail* would qualify for compensation in the event of an air raid, receiving £200 in the event of death; £100 for the loss of two limbs or both eyes; £50 for the loss of one eye or one limb; and up to £100 for damage to property of any description. The Government subsequently introduced a national scheme of insurance against 'German Air Raids or Bombardment', with the caveat that following the establishment of the scheme, 'no liability can be accepted by the Government, and no claim can be entertained, in respect to damage to property ... unless the property has been insured under the scheme'. For each £100 of cover, the following premiums were due:

	Against aircraft	Against aircraft and bombardment
1. Building, rent and contents of private dwelling houses and buildings in which no trade or manufacture is carried on	2s	3s
2. All other buildings and their rents	3s	4s 6d
3. Farming stock (live and dead)	3s	4s 6d

The insurance against bombardment followed German naval attacks on east coast towns such as Great Yarmouth, Hartlepool, Scarborough, and Whitby in November and December the previous year. The insurance scheme was welcomed by the public, who could take out the policies through their Fire Insurance companies, but Chelmsford Council, along with a number of other public bodies, seemed never to resolve whether the costs were worth bearing.

Over the next few months the enemy developed the air offensive by launching attacks which involved sending over several airships at a time. The Zeppelin L14 was one of five raiders on 31 March 1916 which attacked various targets in London and the eastern counties. The airship pursued an erratic course across Essex and dropped bombs on Sudbury, Braintree, Blackmore, Doddinghurst, Stanford-le-Hope and

Thames Haven, before making away over Ipswich and the Orwell. One of the L14's bombs landed just off Springfield Road, at Springfield Tyrells, and Richard Godfrey later recalled seeing a crater about four feet deep and eight feet wide in a field. The big event that night, however, was the destruction of the L14's sister ship, the L15, by a combination of anti-aircraft fire over Rainham and an aerial attack over Brentwood by Second Lieutenant Alfred de Bathe Brandon, 19 Squadron, Royal Flying Corps. The damaged airship foundered and came down in the sea off the Kentish Knock lightship in the Thames estuary.

Outside the big cities the population continued to view air raids as an entertainment, as a report in the *Essex Chronicle* of the five Zeppelin assault in April 1916 records:

> It was noted as a curious circumstance that during the whole time of the raid [of 25 April] the railway trains were running and traffic was not disorganised or stopped in any way, thus showing how little importance was attached to the attack... Passengers homeward bound through Essex had exciting experiences. For nearly ten minutes the passengers of one train crowded on the footboards and watched the practice of the guns at the airship, and saw what many of them described as 'a grand fireworks display'.

The behaviour of the public during air raids left a lot to be desired in the opinion of the Chief Constable and in the same month he saw fit to publish a gentle reminder:

> The Police and Military are empowered in the case of sudden emergency to order all lights to be extinguished, but with the short time at disposal this cannot always be done.
>
> It therefore behoves everyone to always be extremely careful that as little indication as possible of inhabited areas is given.
>
> In spite of the loss of life already sustained, the Chief Constable still continues to receive constant reports of bright lights, burning rubbish heaps, and other instances of carelessness with regard to lights, which might easily be the means of causing further loss of life.

The Chief Constable wishes to draw attention in particular to the exercise of extreme care on occasions when, by the sound of falling bombs, or the firing of guns, Zeppelins are known to be about. It is on such occasions that especial care must be exercised, and disturbed civilians must refrain from using any lights, and must not light a lamp or open the windows to see what is going on, as is found to have been the case. The civil population must also keep quiet, as a babble of voices and other noises prevent the sound of the engine of a Zeppelin being heard, with the result that those whose duty it is to deal with it by gunfire may lose their target.

The safe and proper course to pursue is to keep quiet, keep indoors, and to ensure no light being visible from outside. It is only by precautions being taken and care being exercised by individuals that great loss of life and danger to property can to some extent be guarded against. It is therefore hoped that everyone will treat the matter as being a personal responsibility in the interests of the lives of others.

The Postmaster General was also concerned about the enthusiasm with which the public overwhelmed the telephone system during air raids, with trivial calls to the police and other public officials, and in February 1916 published a warning, threatening to 'curtail the facilities afforded to private persons' if such telephone calls continued to be made.

Air raids generated considerable amounts of shell and bomb fragments and Zeppelins in difficulties would often throw weaponry, ammunition and other material overboard in an attempt to lighten the load. Downed aircraft were magnets for souvenir collectors and in July 1916 the Chief Constable had to issue a further notice under the Defence of the Realm regulations that the public must notify the police or military authorities at once on finding any 'bomb or projectile or fragment thereof, or any other article discharged, dropped or lost from any enemy aircraft or vehicle'. Indeed the amount of material falling from the skies during raids was so substantial that there were unsubstantiated claims that there were more civilian casualties caused by shrapnel than by enemy bombs.

Basil Harrison, in his *Duke Street Childhood*, remembered one raid as being particularly heavy:

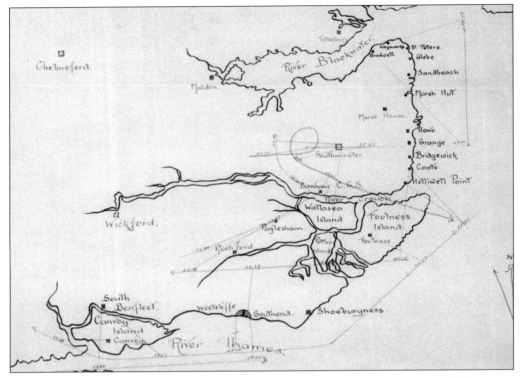

The track of German aircraft over Essex in 1918. [National Archives MPI 1/621/5]

The firing I heard that night was the closest and heaviest I had so far experienced in Chelmsford. It seemed to be coming from the south but from how far away it was impossible to tell. The next day I heard that a Zeppelin had been shot down in Billericay, only nine miles away. That day was a Saturday and, although I longed to go to the scene of the action, I had to go to work in London for the morning. At the first possible opportunity, on my arrival home from work, I cycled over to Billericay to see for myself the remains of the Zeppelin still lying where it had crashed. I picked up a small piece of fabric and a tiny fragment of metal as a reminder of that dreadful night.

Harrison dates this event as Friday 29 September 1917 but it was actually 23 September 1916, and the airship was the L32. He appears to be one of the few people in Essex who did not actually see the Zeppelin lighting up the night sky as it was shot down; there are many other accounts from the southern and central parts of the county. The L32 was apparently on course for London but was put off by heavy anti-aircraft fire. Second Lieutenant Frederick Sowrey RFC spotted the airship as it was picked out by searchlights. He fired three drums of incendiary bullets and the Zeppelin caught fire, sinking to the earth and crashing in Snail's Farm, South Green, Great Burstead. All twenty-two crewmen were killed. Richard Godfrey remembered that 'the Billericay one appeared like a large cigar in the sky with the ends alight and finally finishing with a big flash.' At the time there was an unobstructed view from Sandford Road to Billericay and many people enjoyed a grandstand view of the destruction of the L32. Special Constable Gripper, on patrol on New London Road, recorded the event in his log book: '8.30 preliminary [warning]. 9.35 Take action. 12.30 Zep passes SW to NE. Guns fired and bombs dropped. At 1.20 SW saw a Zep on fire which came down at Billericay. Great flame of light. Wonderful sight. At 1.30 another red flame due east. Zep went down at Great Wigborough.'

The same night saw the destruction of the L33. As it was approaching Chelmsford it was attacked by Second Lieutenant Brandon in a sustained twenty minute engagement. The stricken airship flew out to Mersea but turned back inland as the crew realised escape was impossible. The diarist Dr Salter, from his bedroom window in Tolleshunt D'Arcy, saw both airships go down within minutes of each other.

The original air raid signal in Chelmsford was the horn at the Gas Works and was more of a fire alarm. The Fire Brigade Committee of the Council discussed this at a meeting in October 1915, when it was reported that there was sometimes a delay in sounding the alarm because the button that sounded the horn also rang a bell at the Threadneedle Street fire station and this caused some degree of confusion. It took the Borough Engineer to suggest putting in a second line, one for the fire alarm and one for the air raid alert. As late as April 1916 there was still no organised borough-wide air raid warning system, with the Mayor reporting to Council that the matter was in the hands of the military, who claimed that alarms would frighten people and bring them out of their houses.

The Chief Constable published an updated notice for action to be taken in case of daylight air raids in June 1917:

> As there is always a possibility of an Essex town being the objective of a hostile air raid by day, the following arrangements have been made to give such warning as is possible to the inhabitants.
>
> One or more sirens will be sounded, or other forms of warning, at the following towns on information that the Hostile Aircraft are approaching:
>
> | | | | |
> |---|---|---|---|
> | Chelmsford | Brentwood | Romford | Grays |
> | Halstead | Clacton | Maldon | Saffron Walden |
> | Harwich | Braintree | Epping | |
>
> The warning of approach will consist of a series of THREE SHORT BLASTS followed by a CONTINUOUS BLAST for 15 seconds.
>
> The Warning will be sounded for three minutes.
>
> On hearing the Warning the civil population are urged, for their own safety, to seek the nearest possible shelter, and under no circumstances to congregate in the streets. After the danger of attack has passed the sirens will sound a series of short blasts for one minute.
>
> In places where there is no siren, warnings by fire bell or otherwise will be given.
>
> Even if hostile aircraft are known to be approaching it will not necessarily mean that any particular town is sure to be attacked, so that warnings may be sounded without an attack actually taking place.

To avoid confusion the regulations stipulated that only one person in the town, the Superintendent of Police H Mules, could initiate an air raid warning and it was an offence to raise a false report of a raid. The Mayor, JO Thompson, also published a notice to the people of Chelmsford in which he advised that the siren would only be sounded 'when Hostile Aircraft are seen or heard to be about to pass directly over the town and when danger appears... to be imminent'. He added his own suggestions for action to be taken, where people in the streets should take immediate cover but on the grounds of national interest, workers in factories should continue at their work 'and so continue what the Germans want to prevent them from doing'.

Under Unett's new system a chain of whistles and horns was set up across the town. The works horn at Hoffmann's covered the northern part of the town and Springfield, Clarkson's National Steam Car horn at Anchor Street the town centre and Moulsham, and there was another at Crompton's Arc Works for the south of the borough. These were not sirens as might be associated with the Blitz of the Second World War, but normal industrial whistles routinely used to mark the start and end of each work shift. To avoid confusion the Council invoked the 1872 Steam Whistles Act and the companies had to formally apply to use their horns 'for summoning and dismissing their workmen', to be sounded at the proper times and for no more than fifteen seconds. Permission was granted to Marconi's, Hoffmann's, Chelmsford Gas Company, Christy & Norris, Chelmsford Model Laundry, and the National Steam Car Company. In the latter case it was reported that the Moulsham works used 'an electric hooter' that apparently took time to get up to full volume and then it took a while to fade away, but this was soon solved to the Council's satisfaction.

The Bishop of Chelmsford was also concerned with the impact of air raids on his diocese, and on 9 July 1917 had a letter published in the *Times*, in which he was strongly critical about the apparent impunity with which the bombers went about their destructive business, and he asked the following questions:

1. Is the method of communicating [the raiders] approach the best that can be devised?
2. Is the coordination of naval and land aircraft satisfactory?
3. Are our different air stations around London so connected that rapidity of co-operation can be secured?

The Fire Brigade were also concerned about their ability to deal with air raids and drew the attention of the Council to the fact that in May

ESSEX COUNTY CONSTABULARY.

Air Raid Precautions.

The following official document from the Home Office in regard to Air Raid Precautions is circulated for the information of the public, who are urged to act carefully in compliance with the suggestions made should circumstances arise calling for such action.

J. A. UNETT, Capt.,
Chief Constable.

Headquarters, Chelmsford, Oct. 12, 1917.

AIR RAID PRECAUTIONS.

SUMMARY OF OFFICIAL RECOMMENDATIONS ISSUED FOR THE GUIDANCE OF THE PUBLIC.

NOTE.—It is not possible to provide within the compass of a leaflet detailed instructions to meet all circumstances that may arise. The following recommendations are to be read as general rules to be followed by each person so far as they apply to the circumstances in which he finds himself.

TAKING COVER.

1.—Do not pay heed to mere rumours of a raid, but as soon as you know, whether from a public warning or from the anti-aircraft guns coming into action or from the explosion of bombs, that an attack is imminent or has begun, take the best cover near at hand.

2.—Do not wait till you see the aircraft nearly overhead or hear the explosion of a bomb near you. You cannot tell how near the next bomb may fall, especially at night, and, apart from the danger from bombs, fragments of shells may fall a long way from the guns. To stay in the open involves needless risk even if the attack seems a long way off.

3.—If you are in the open, go into the nearest available building. A doorway or open archway, though better than remaining in the open, is not good cover, as it affords little protection against fragments of a bomb exploding on the ground.

4.—If bombs are being dropped and there is no building near, it is better to lie down on the ground in the best ditch or hole you can find near at hand, or behind a strong wall or tree, than to remain standing in the open.

5.—If you are in a building on the top floor, go downstairs where you will have the best available cover overhead, avoiding lift wells, open stairways and parts of the building under skylights.

6.—Do not look out of windows, but keep in a part of a room or passage where you will be out of the line of fragments of metal or débris which may enter by a window or door if a bomb should explode outside.

7.—Do not crowd in a basement with only a single means of exit. The fumes from all bombs are injurious if breathed in any quantity, and it is advisable to have a second means of exit in case fumes should enter, or a gas pipe be broken, or rapid escape be necessary for any other reason.

8.—Horses, if left unattended, should be secured sufficiently to prevent their running away.

FIRE PRECAUTIONS.

9.—Water is far the best extinguisher for general use against fires caused by incendiary bombs and should be applied as promptly as possible. Keep a supply of water ready in buckets or cans, some on each floor if possible. See that they are kept filled.

10.—Liquid fire extinguishers and hand pumps for directing the water on to the flames are very useful, though more expensive.

11.—You are advised not to buy an extinguisher without a written guarantee that it complies with the specifications of the Board of Trade, Office of Works, Metropolitan Police, or some approved Fire Prevention Committee.

12.—A supply of fine dry sand or soil may be kept ready, in pails or scuttles, in addition to water, especially where there are inflammable liquids which might be set alight. See that the sand or soil does not cake.

13.—If the gas is turned off at the meter see that all burners are turned off as well, otherwise there will be serious risk of fire and explosion when the gas is turned on again.

14.—Make a note of the quickest means of summoning the Fire Brigade—whether by telephone or the nearest fire alarm post.

UNEXPLODED BOMBS AND SHELLS.

15.—Do not move or touch any unexploded bomb or shell. The Police should be informed at once where any such missile is lying and steps should be taken to prevent its being interfered with meanwhile.

16.—If the bomb and powdered explosive has been scattered about, do not bring a naked light near.

17.—If it is necessary to handle the powder or any articles covered with it, take precautions as recommended in the Note below, specially as to cleansing the hands.

FUMES FROM BOMBS.

18.—Be careful not to breathe fumes given off by bombs. Do not go near where any bomb has fallen unless it is necessary to do so for rescue purposes or to extinguish a fire, or unless you are sure all fumes have cleared away.

19.—If a bomb falls near you, get away from the place where it has fallen as quickly as possible and keep away until the air has cleared. If you are indoors and fumes have entered the building, go out into the open away from where the bomb has fallen; and if the raid is not over find other shelter.

20.—While good cover is the point of most importance, choose, if you can, rooms, corridors, &c., where, in addition to cover overhead there are alternative means of exit, so that fumes should enter from one direction you may be able to escape the other way.

21.—It is better to avoid going near the place where any bomb has fallen than to trust to respirators. If, however, you desire to keep a respirator available for use in case it should be necessary to enter a room where there may be noxious fumes, make sure that the respirator is guaranteed by the maker to comply in all essential points with War Office specification. Do not on any account rely on a respirator offered for sale unless it is accompanied by such a guarantee.

USE' OF THE TELEPHONE.

22.—Do not use the telephone during, or immediately after, a raid except for the most necessary and urgent calls.

FALSE REPORTS OF AIR RAIDS.

23.—Remember it is an offence punishable by fine or imprisonment under the Defence of the Realm Regulations to spread false reports of an air raid warning having been issued or an air raid having taken place.

HOME OFFICE,
September, 1917.

NOTE.

PRECAUTIONS TO BE TAKEN IN HANDLING THE POWDER FROM BOMBS.

(1.) To remove the powdered explosive from surfaces on which it has fallen it is best to use a brush, wetted with a weak alkaline solution—one teaspoonful of soda (bicarbonate or ordinary washing soda) to a quart of water. If the powder can be washed down with water from a hose, this would suffice.

(2.) The powder, when collected, should not be mixed with ordinary dust, as it might be sent to a destructor and possibly cause damage. If there is only a small quantity it may be mixed with earth and buried. When there is much of it the Military Authorities should be consulted.

(3.) It is better to use moist rags rather than gloves to handle articles covered with the powder, as a glove soon becomes penetrated with the powder, and the skin is more easily irritated, whereas the rags can be thrown away and clean ones taken as often as necessary.

(4.) If the hands become stained an endeavour should be made to remove the stain at once with pumice stone and the soda solution. It may be found impossible to remove the stain entirely, but no ill results are likely to follow if the hands are carefully cleansed.

(5.) At the first sign of inflammation of the skin (e.g. irritation or small swellings containing fluid), a doctor should be consulted.

Air raid precautions leaflet issued to the public in October 1917. [ERO D/Z 137/1, courtesy Essex Police Museum]

1915 they had sufficient men and equipment to deal with two fires at the same time but would not be able to cope with multiple fires from an incendiary raid. Fifteen volunteer firemen were recruited and arrangements were made for them to have fire bells fitted in their homes, so that they could be summoned at night without using the fire horn at the fire station.

Special Constable Gripper (of whom more in Chapter 4) had orders concerning night air raids. On receipt of the warning from the military authority, as a section leader he was to turn out as many of his group as he thought sufficient and ensure that precautions had been taken, especially that lights had been subdued, not extinguished. If no further warning arrived within an hour he could disband his men, but was to keep himself in readiness for the 'Take Air Raid Action' or the 'Resume Normal Conditions' order. He was also to ensure that road traffic was to keep moving during a raid, as abandoned vehicles would cause obstruction to fire engines and the military. Drivers who wished to take cover were to park on the side roads. Those driving at night had to use low power headlights or sidelights and nothing that could possibly be used as a searchlight. Horse and motor vehicles were required to have a single red light mounted on the rear. Military and naval motor cars were distinguished with a red and a green light fitted to the offside of the vehicle. Gripper was also instructed that volunteer and regular firemen on their way to the fire station in response to a call were not to be stopped.

The County Constabulary published further orders concerning daylight air raids in July 1917. The Germans had moved away from using Zeppelins, which were becoming increasingly vulnerable to British air defences, to the twin engine, three man Gotha bomber, which carried up to 500 kg of bombs. The risks of night time navigation and pilotage were much higher for fixed wing aircraft, so the Gotha raids (Operation Türkenkreuz) frequently took place in the day time; on 7 July a mass formation of twenty-two enemy aircraft were seen from Chelmsford on their way to London.

Previously the special constables worked in shifts overnight, but were now required during the day. The Chelmsford force was organised into five picquets:

German Gotha bombers flying over Essex 7 July 1917. [Reproduced by courtesy of the Essex Record Office ERO D/Z 137/1]

Picquet	Location	Constable in charge
1	Police Station	Inspector Creasy
2	Baddow Road Corner	Willars
3	St John's Church, Moulsham	Sgt Fox
4	Trinity Road corner	F Ward
5	Broomfield Road corner	P Ward

Additionally watching posts were set up: Post 1 in the Cathedral tower (Sgt Bernard), and Post 2 on Beehive Lane (A S Duffield). There were three objectives for the picquet posts:

1. Accessibility to and general control over every part of the town.
2. As far as possible, the assignation of Special Constables to that particular group which is nearest his residence.
3. The fact that the presence of the Special Constables in their allotted stations will tend to reassure the public and foster a spirit of confidence.

Special Constable Gripper was assigned to Post 3, with instructions to report to his post at once on hearing the warning. In the event of bombs falling he was to use his initiative, but avoid unnecessary risks. He was to provide assistance to the fire brigade and the first aiders of the Voluntary Aid Detachment, prevent the public from crowding around and obstructing operations and, as a section leader, to send his men to assist other posts, without depleting his own resources. This order, from Superintendent Wykeham Chancellor, also noted that 'the public cannot be compelled to go indoors, and special constables are to use tact and discretion in advising them to do so'.

The effect of air raids on schools was considered by the Council's Education Committee at various times. In June 1917 the Town Clerk published a notice that in the event of raid during school hours the children would be retained in school under the care and control of their teachers, but parents or guardians could call at the school to collect their children at their own risk. Under no circumstances would children be sent home alone. The History of the Chelmsford County High School records one air raid:

Air raid picquet locations.

On one occasion in 1917, after the siren and the Head's whistle, [the girls] were each in their appointed shelters in the requisite 40 seconds beneath the concrete floor and as far as possible from the windows and outer walls. There was heavy gunfire, but the lessons went on as usual, with the Sixth Form carrying on with their set text, Arnold's Palladium: 'Backwards and forward roll'd the waves of fight round Troy, but whilst this stood Troy could not fall.'

The young Richard Godfrey recalled huddling beside an old copper in the scullery 'which would have given good protection if the house fell down'. At one point the Council asked if the local VAD could send members to each school on hearing the air raid warning, but nothing came of this.

As the system for air raid precautions developed, the need for public air raid shelters was much discussed. In the early part of the war shopkeepers were asked to permit customers to use their cellars and basements for shelter. In October 1917 the Chelmsford branch of the Society of Amalgamated Toolmakers wrote to the Council, requesting that shelters should be erected for the female population of the town in the event of hostile air raids. The Toolmakers represented the munitions workers of the town, and the Clerk subsequently reported that Crompton's and Marconi's had trenches near their factories for use during air raids. He was of the opinion that 'no ordinary building would be bomb-proof in the event of a direct hit' and he pointed out that the Home Secretary himself had stated that it was 'most undesirable' that persons already under cover should then seek out shelters, and also that common shelters were likely to pose a serious risk to public health. In Chelmsford, unlike other towns, this remained the prevailing view, with the Special Purposes Committee of the Council in March 1918 reporting that, in their view:

No useful purpose would be served by constructing air raid shelters in the borough; that all persons should, as far as possible, be induced to remain in their own houses during air raids; and that in the event of air raids taking place during the daytime, persons who are in the town... should be allowed by the shopkeepers and others to take shelter in their premises.

As late as May 1918 the Germans were claiming air raid successes; on 24 May a message was passed on from the Dutch authorities about a German report of a heavy air raid launched on Sunday night 'in the City, between the Admiralty and the West India Docks. Other aeroplanes attacked Dover, Chelmsford, Chatham and Southend with the same good results.' The Fire Brigade Committee reported one single air raid alert in May. No further raids were recorded.

By October 1918 the council approached the police and military authorities for permission to relax the lighting regulations as there seemed to be a much lower risk of air raids than before. They agreed. Lights were illuminated at:

London Road	junction with	Friars Place
"	"	Anchor Street
Moulsham Street	"	Hall Street
"	"	Queen Street
Baddow Road	"	Road to Moulsham Mill
New Street	"	Hoffmann's Corner
Broomfield Road	"	Rectory Lane
"	"	Swiss Avenue
Rainsford Road	"	Rainsford Lane
"	"	Primrose Hill
Tindal Street	"	Crown Passage
Springfield Road	"	Navigation Road
"	"	Trinity Road
"	"	Arbour Lane
Station footpath	at bend in path behind garage	

Two more lamps were allowed on the High Street and on Springfield Road near the Horse Pond. The lights were coming back on.

CHAPTER 3

Billets

*I passed by the Corn Exchange, filled up as a sort of centre for the
military, where they can write letters and amuse themselves.'
Special Correspondent, Essex Chronicle, 1914*

The biggest impact on Chelmsford at the start of the war was not so
much the local Territorials and Reservists heading off to join their ships
and regiments, but instead the arrival of some six thousand or so men
of the South Midland Division. These men needed accommodation for
themselves and stabling for their horses. All of this was organised by
the local police force.

English Common Law has long held the principle that 'an
Englishman's home is his castle' and the restriction on billeting soldiers
on the civilian population goes back to Cromwell's time. Soldiers were
housed in barracks or in camps under canvas, but never in private
homes, and although the Army Act 1882 did not specifically prohibit
lodging on civilians the right was never exercised. Accommodation
could be lawfully demanded from inns, hostels, livery stables and retail
wine shops, collectively known as 'victualling houses' and this was
undertaken by the production of a document known as a 'route'. The
military authority (on behalf of the Secretary of State) was required to
specify the route to be taken by a column of soldiers on the march from
their barracks to, for example, their annual camp. The 'route' was then
given to the local chief of police, who would then be responsible for
identifying and notifying all victualling houses within a mile or less of
the intended line of march. These establishments were then issued with
a billet, or note, recording the number of men and horses who could

A column of troops marching through Chelmsford. [Spalding, author's collection]

stay (the term 'billet' subsequently came to mean the accommodation itself). Although the landlord had no say in the matter, he was entitled to compensation at rates set out in the annual Army Act. Under the provisions of the Act, the police were required to maintain a list of victualling houses and make it available for public inspection. It also set out the system for handling grievances and complaints, which had to be made to the local justice of the peace. This system worked, and was regularly used in the years before the war, before military motor transport became common.

The original billeting system was meant to be a temporary state of affairs for troops on the move and even the legislation itself, and the Manual of Military Law, suggests that stays of over seven nights were unusual; there is nothing, for example, about changing bedding. This all changed in August 1914. As mentioned, the requirement to provide accommodation in private houses existed but had not been used before. Using their powers under section 108A the police managed the task with tact and diplomacy; under the Act it was not permitted to order billets in excess of the number required, so the starting point was to find out how many soldiers required accommodation and to approach the larger houses first. As these were filled enquiries could be made in the neighbourhood to find out which households were willing to take soldiers in. In the absence of the detailed registers held of victualling houses, the police officer simply marked the number of billets in chalk on the wall of the house. Technically it was an offence to refuse to provide a billet but the good citizens seemed to have welcomed the opportunity to help the war effort in this way and cases of refusal came in future years, usually coloured by bad experiences with unclean or unruly soldiers.

There were no standards set for the housing but the sanitary officers of the military medical services were expected to inspect their men's rooms at an early stage; there are several reports of poor hygiene, for which both the Army and the Council took responsibility. The Borough's Medical Officer of Health, Dr Henry Newton, made an early report to the Council in September 1914 in which he raised concerns about the adequacy of the water supply and sewers, and the health risks of overcrowding in billets. He was satisfied with the work undertaken by the local authority in these matters, noting that two houses taken over by the military were unsatisfactory and unhygienic but had since been remedied.

One incentive for householders to take on soldiers was financial. Army Order 289 of 1914, published on 4 August 1914, set out the rates to be paid for billeting:

1. Pursuant to section 108A(3) of the Army Act, the prices to be paid to an occupier other than the keeper of a victualling house for billets requisitioned in accordance with the provisions of section 108A have been fixed at the rates shown in the subjoined schedule:

Accommodation to be provided	Price to be paid to an occupier other than the keeper of a victualling house
Lodging and attendance for soldiers where meals are furnished	9 d Night
Breakfast as specified in Part I of the Second Schedule to the Army Act	7 ½ d Each
Dinner as so specified	1s 7 ½ d Each

Supper as so specified	4 ½ d Each
Where no meals furnished, lodging and attendance, and candles, vinegar, salt, and the use of fire, and the necessary utensils for dressing and eating his meat	9d Day
Stable room and ten pounds of oats, twelve pounds of hay, and eight pounds of straw for each horse	2s 7 ½ d per day
Stable room without forage	9 d per day
Lodging and attendance for officer	3s 0 per night
Note: an officer must pay for his own food.	

2. The following special rates have been fixed for troops accommodated in buildings (other than dwelling houses) where bed and attendance are not provided, and for horses where proper stabling is not provided:

For each officer or soldier	3d Night
For each horse	3d Night

3. A revised form (A.B. 123M) for payment of billets is now being issued to all units in lieu of A.B.123.

The rates for victualling houses were lower.

Accommodation to be provided	Price to be paid to the keeper of a victualling house
Lodging and attendance for soldiers where meals are furnished	6 d Night
Breakfast as specified in Part I of the Second Schedule to the Army Act	5 d Each
Dinner as so specified	1s 1 d Each
Supper as so specified	3 d Each
Where no meals furnished, lodging and attendance, and candles, vinegar, salt, and the use of fire, and the necessary	6 d Day

utensils for dressing and eating his meat	
Stable room and ten pounds of oats,	1s 9 d per day
twelve pounds of hay, and eight pounds	
of straw for each horse	
Stable room without forage	6 d per day
Lodging and attendance for officer	2s 0 per night
Note: an officer must pay for his own food.	

Where men were to be supplied with a hot meal, it was to consist of 1 ¼ lb of meat, weighed before cooking, 1 lb of bread, 1lb of potatoes or other vegetables, 2 pints of small beer, vinegar, salt, pepper. The money, and the generous ration, would have been a welcome addition to most households at the time.

By 1917 the *Essex Newsman* columnist Reflex was commenting on an Army Order concerning the meals to be provided by the 'billeting wife':

For Breakfast: five ounces of bread, one pint of tea with milk and sugar, four ounces of bacon.

For hot Dinner: twelve ounces of meat, previous to being dressed, four ounces of bread, eight ounces of potatoes or other vegetables.

For Supper: five ounces of bread, one pint of cocoa with milk and sugar, two ounces of cheese.

There were some problems with billeting arrangements. On 14th August 1914 William Young, landlord of the Woolpack Inn on Mildmay Road, was charged with refusing accommodation for soldiers under the Army Act 1881. Inspector Barrow provided evidence that, on Saturday 8 August, he had issued a billeting notice for four men of the 1st East Anglian Field Ambulance to go to the Woolpack. Later that evening he visited the public house and found that Mrs Young was refusing to accommodate them, claiming she had no room. The policeman sent the soldiers to the Army & Navy Inn on Baddow Road. He stated that since 1906 he had sent forty men and forty horses to be billeted at the Woolpack Inn, and only four men and four horses had ever been taken in. The inspector described the situation that afternoon, when he had received telegrams instructing him to find billets for 270 men. The unfortunate Mr Young did not find out about the soldiers until after his wife had made the refusal, and found himself charged with the offence. The bench found him guilty, but gave him the minimum fine of £2, with 4s costs, the chairman stating 'We hope licensed victuallers will understand that they must take in these men or find suitable accommodation. It is most necessary that everybody should show loyalty at the present time, and we hope that this case will act as a warning.' Barney Hoggard, of the Queen's Head, Anchor Street, was also in court that day, facing the same charge, having refused to take in two RAMC men, but he then arranged for them to stay elsewhere. The specific wording of the offence was 'refusing and neglecting'; the magistrates felt that he had indeed refused to take in the men, but had not neglected them, and so he was acquitted on the technicality.

Rainsford End: many soldiers were billeted in this area. [Spalding, reproduced by courtesy of the Essex Record Office ERO SCN 35]

Soldiers in billets followed an unusual life: away from their own homes they had to live in a stranger's home. Day began with the bugle call at New Street or Moulsham Street to rouse the troops, usually at about 6 am, as recorded by the *Chronicle*'s special correspondent in September 1914: 'Early in the morning I am awakened by the strident bugle calls all around the town.' The men were required to parade at their units at 7.30, but not all Army units had messing facilities so some soldiers were required to return to their billets for breakfast, then return to camp for training and other duties, go home for lunch, and then return for more military work in the afternoon – a routine very similar to their civilian lives, especially if they had worked in industry. The men were issued with rations to take back to the billets for cooking. Richard Godfrey remembers that they had two brothers named Miller from the Ox & Bucks Light Infantry billeted on them, and they had to go to Trinity Road School each morning to collect their food, which Richard's mother cooked. Evenings were generally free, and Chelmsford was unusually fortunate with its off-duty soldiers – there were very few problems with drunkenness and the magistrates decided not to impose restrictions on licencing hours that were common elsewhere in the county. Even when the Chief Constable wrote asking for a review of the policy under the Intoxicating Liquor (Temporary Restrictions) Act in August 1915 the justices were minded only to bring the closing time forward from 11 pm to 10 pm on weekdays and they noted that this 'does not mean that the premises are closed, but only that the sale of intoxicating liquor must cease at the earlier hour'. There were little mishaps as these soldiers, used to family routines of their own, had to fit in with their billet families, and as late as 1917 Reflex was complaining about soldiers forgetting to leave their boots at the back door.

Close friendships were formed between the soldiers and their surrogate families. Richard Godfrey also remembers his men made him a little wooden rifle and got him, aged 6, to march with them from the house to the school, with the sergeant telling him the orders to shout out: 'squad quick march', 'squad halt' and 'left-right, left-right, pick 'em up there! They also bought him some lead soldiers and they would fight battles on the kitchen table. The relationship with the South Midlands Division was such that after they moved away the *Chronicle* and *Newsman* printed their promotions, awards and casualty lists alongside those of the Essex and local regiments. Mr J Southam of Hill Road was able to read about the Military Cross awarded to his billet, Company Sergeant Major Albert Sirett of the Ox & Bucks Light Infantry, whilst Alderman Thompson learned of the wounding in action of Lieutenant Bernard Green also of the Ox & Bucks, who had been billeted at his home. Herbert Gripper, the special constable, would have been saddened to read of the tragic death of Lieutenant Poulton Palmer, 4th Royal Berks Regiment and England's former rugby captain, who stayed with him in 1915.

Men such as those involved in staffing the detention centre at the prison, manning the various Army Service Corps depots or the men of the Royal Defence Corps on guard duties around the town, were able to send for their wives and families and set up home in rented accommodation. Reflex warned of the trouble in store should a soldier suggest to his landlady that his wife share his billet for a few days. And at the end of the war one councillor opposed a proposal for one thousand new homes to be built to alleviate the pressure on the housing market, as there were 'considerable number of soldiers' wives and families living in Chelmsford, who did not do so before the war, and when their husbands were demobilised many of them would be going back to their own towns and villages'.

Billeting on schools was not widely practised in Chelmsford. The Finance & General Purposes (F&GP) subcommittee of the Council's Education committee was responsible for any requests for the use of school property. In February 1915 they gave permission to Lieutenant Kerr, the medical officer of the Royal Engineers, to use a classroom at Springfield School for lectures on 'First Aid to the Injured', between 6 and 7 pm on Mondays, Wednesdays and Thursdays. Later that year they agreed that the military could use Trinity Road, Friars' and St John's schools for billeting troops on 11th and 13th October. This was probably to provide overnight accommodation for troops on the move through the district. In December 1915 the officer commanding the 2/1st Oxfordshire & Buckinghamshire (Ox & Bucks) Light Infantry obtained permission to use the lower central hall of Trinity Road School for five evenings a week for regimental boxing. This must have been exciting stuff for the troops, because there was a subsequent invoice for £21 15s 3d sent to the military authorities in respect of damages! In April 1916 five schools were taken over during the Easter holidays, and this time the Army were charged 3d per man per night and there were at least 400 soldiers in residence. The biggest impact on the schools was in the winter of 1916, when large numbers of troops were in the area. The military authorities wanted to provide centralised messing facilities and it was agreed that Trinity Road and the Friars schools would be closed, and the Education committee made arrangements for the pupils to share classrooms at the other schools and buildings in the borough. The schools were finally returned to the authority on 15th April 1917.

As camps like those at Widford and Rainsford End developed and became more established, with proper hutted accommodation, the demand for billeting in the town decreased; and as more messing facilities were provided the requirement for a full billet with meals also diminished. In its place came the 'sleeping only' arrangement which many felt was less friendly, as 'their' soldiers only turned up late at night and disappeared at reveille the next morning. Reflex also heard of some 'hard stony-hearted billeting ladies' who went the other way, and only allowed their soldiers in last thing at night!

The National Service Volunteer scheme in early 1917 was intended to encourage people to take up work of national importance by offering their skills and experience to munitions firms and the like, in order to free up men for military service. Chelmsford, of course, already had a large work force engaged in the munitions work being carried out by the large firms, and it was hoped that the National Service Volunteers, who would receive both pay and travel allowances, would move to the town to provide badly needed additional manpower. The immediate problem was the lack of housing, about which Marconi's and Hoffmann's had previously complained to the Council. The government introduced the Billeting of Civilians Act on 24 May 1917 which was designed to fit in around the existing military billeting system but was entirely voluntary. A local Billeting Committee was of course formed on behalf of the Central Billeting Board, chaired by Alderman Thompson and with Mrs Rose of Hoffmann's as vice chair, but nothing further is known of its activities, particularly as most of the National Service Volunteers who came to Essex went into agricultural work.

The billeted troops were kept off the streets by many diversions and activities. Concerts were regularly held in the Corn Exchange, and the

The Corn Exchange. [Spalding, author's collection]

YMCA was in such heavy use that in December 1916 they opened a new hut for soldiers at the corner of Market Road and Duke Street. One objective was to relieve them of their money – for charitable purposes – and there was a constant round of dramatic and choral recitals, whist drives, smoking concerts, raffles and cake sales, and the soldiers returned the favour by providing entertainment for the town.

The troops also availed themselves of the Public Library. In 1915 the librarian, John Howarth, recorded that 422 men had registered and were making good use of the reference library and the reading room. However, when the 1st South Midland Division moved out in early 1915, he found seventy-nine books missing. He reported his subsequent actions to the Council in his annual report: 'the collection of these [missing books] from the respective billets (and in many cases the billets had been changed two or three times without notice being given) has entailed considerable tramping about on my part, and correspondence with officers at the Front. I am pleased to report that

Chelmsford Museum and Library (ground floor) and the School of Science and Art. [Hartmann; author's collection]

seventy volumes have been collected; the remaining nine I cannot trace; their approximate value, new, is about 25s.' One can only imagine the reaction of those 'officers at the Front' on receiving Mr Howarth's letter! He was obliged to repeat the exercise the following year on the departure of the 2nd South Midland Division; this time sixteen books were taken and he was able to locate fourteen. He confidently reported that '[I] am in correspondence with the Commanding Officers with respect to the two books outstanding'. These were *War of the Worlds*, by HG Wells, and *Barrack Room Ballads* by Kipling.

Soldiers appeared to have advanced literary tastes and electrical, engineering and technical subjects were popular. Following a drop in student numbers at the outbreak of war, the Chelmsford School of Science and Art offered free courses to soldiers stationed in the area. The mechanical and electrical engineering courses and lectures were well attended.

The Red Triangle of the YMCA was a welcome sight to the soldiers and offered recreational facilities as well as more intellectually stimulating activities such as debates and lectures. The rooms at 26 High Street were crowded and a hundred foot long YMCA hut was opened in Writtle in 1915. In December 1916 a 'magnificent YMCA building' was opened on Market Road, courtesy of the Prudential Assurance Company.

Chelmsford was able to boast a skating rink, on New London Road, but this was taken over as barrack accommodation very early in the war. Personal hygiene has always been important to the soldier and those billeted in and around the town were able to keep themselves clean using the public baths and swimming pool which had been built in 1907. Located in a field at the bottom of Waterloo Lane, it was a large and popular open air pool and provided personal washing facilities. From the start of the war the Army used the baths, generally parading at 6 am, in companies. The Public Baths Committee had previously visited Colchester and returned to the Council with a proposal to install slipper baths, at a cost of £620. The new baths proved very popular with the soldiers, and the military authorities were charged 3d per man, with towel. In November 1914 the Council was able to report that there were more three hundred slipper baths a week, but with six thousand men in the area bathing appears not to have been a frequent activity. At the same time Mr Stonebanks and Mr Dadswell formed a committee to organise baths for soldiers 'at the houses of residents willing to grant this facility'.

In an unfortunate incident in March 1915, a number of men of the 2/8th Battalion of the Royal Scots were queuing to use the new slipper baths; Private Frederick Samuel decided to take a plunge in the main pool. The water temperature was around 40°F (4°C) and in moments he was in great difficulties. Despite the valiant efforts of Sergeant Thomas, the man disappeared under the water and drowned. It took some time to recover his body and they had to resort to dragging; at that time the water in the pool was supplied from the river and was murky. Samuel, a gardener from Dalkeith, was given a full military

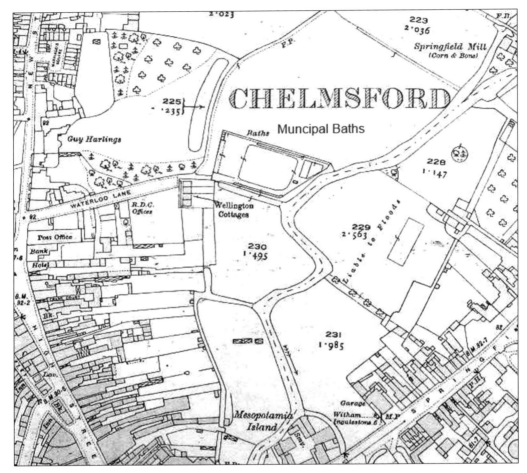

Chelmsford Municipal Baths.

funeral at Writtle Road Cemetery where his headstone can be seen today.

A number of different military formations came through Chelmsford during the war; between August 1914 and March 1915 it was home to the 1st (later renumbered 48th) South Midland Division and when they left for France they were replaced by the 2nd (61st) South Midland Division, who stayed until March 1916. The 2nd (65th)

Lowland Division then took over, until the arrival of the 73rd Division in January 1917, which remained until it was disbanded in April 1918. The Essex Regiment Museum has a wealth of information about the exploits of these formations.

Richard Godfrey paints a poignant scene of the departure of the billeted soldiers:

> When the soldiers left for France, Mother took all of us to the Recreation Ground where with many others we waved goodbye as the train went over the viaducts. That was the last we saw of them.

CHAPTER 4

The Specials

On anyone approaching a post after dark, one sentry
is to challenge <u>loudly</u> 'Halt, who comes there,' and make
the person challenged halt. Then to order 'Hands up –
advance one for my inspection.'
Instructions to Sergeants and Corporals by
Captain Ffinch, Chief Staff Officer, 14 September 1914

For many young men military service was an exciting, if not patriotic, duty and from August 1914 those who were not already in the Territorials queued up at the Drill Hall on Market Road to volunteer for the Army. Other young men, for various reasons, were not so keen to go, but did want to be seen to 'do their bit'. And there were many older men, and those whose health and fitness were not up to military standards, who wanted to contribute to the war effort.

The office of Special Constable has a long history and began to evolve into its modern form in 1820, following a number of civil disturbances across England. Magistrates, as justices of the peace, were able to appoint special constables to keep the peace. Subsequent legislation granted these volunteers the rights to the same powers of arrest as regular police, as well as to uniforms and equipment, but generally in the context of the exigencies of civil disorder. In the emergency legislation of August 1914, the Special Constables Act allowed the appointment of Special Constables in the absence of 'a tumult, riot, or felony', for the duration of the present war.

A meeting of the Essex Standing Joint Committee on 2 September 1914 discussed the role of the special constables and it was decided to enrol them to 'aid the county police in the preservation of good order'. Although regulated by the Home Office and subject to the Police Act, they were volunteers and would form themselves into units and appoint their own sergeants, who would be responsible for organising the section. It was proposed that they would serve four hours a day, in their own towns or parishes, and with as little disruption to their normal occupations as possible. They were to be issued with an armband, a truncheon and a whistle. Although conscription was a few years off, the men were to be over military age (40) and physically fit. In response to several questions, Captain Showers expressed a strong objection to the recruitment of women as special constables.

At one ceremony in September presided over by the Mayor, Alderman George Taylor, Frederick Chancellor, and Mr J Christy Smith, thirty-seven special constables were sworn in, including the Reverend W King Ormsby and the Town Clerk, Mr Melvin. Mr Magor was elected sergeant and Mr Lionel Creasy, the butcher, was selected as corporal. About fifty of the new specials met for their first drill night at the Friars Council School, during which a stone was thrown over the wall, striking Councillor Cowell on the head and leaving a bruise. During the evening the men were given their truncheons and armlets.

Recruitment continued in the town. On 2 October a group of ten 'well-dressed young men' appeared at Chelmsford court to be sworn in as special constables. The chair of the bench, Dr AE Lyster JP and father of three sons already in the Forces, objected to the proceedings

Special Constable's armband – this example belonged to Dr Salter and has the badges showing his rank as chief superintendent. [courtesy Essex Police Museum]

and expressed the view that they were all of military age and would be better off volunteering for the Army. Both the Deputy Chief Constable and the military representative, Mr Magor, had to make strong representations to convince the magistrates to proceed, claiming that they needed 200 more volunteers. The men themselves protested that they were on Government work (in fact employed at Hoffmann's on munitions work), some were married, and they simply wanted to do their bit. It was with some reluctance that the chairman finally agreed to swear them in. The men subsequently wrote an open letter to Dr Lyster demanding an apology. The matter ended up with the Lord Chancellor, who was very supportive of the men. Clearly a man of principle, Dr Lyster subsequently obtained a short-term commission in the Royal Army Medical Corps and served in France.

The special constables of Chelmsford soon fell under the jaundiced eye of Reflex. On 3 October he queried the motivations of those who volunteered to be special constables in the first place, and then reported that several of them had been heard 'grousing' about their duties, such as patrolling the Long Stomps reservoir. Apparently a squad of six specials were detailed to the reservoir each night from 6pm to 6am, two men on each watch of four hours each, and the realities of the job away from the public eye were rapidly cooling their patriotic ardour.

By December 1914 there were many complaints about the 'useless patrolling' undertaken by special constables, only 75 per cent of whom had received their armlets and truncheons. The Standing Joint Committee, which was responsible for the oversight of the system, heard from Captain Showers that there were 4,900 special constables in Essex at that time. The matter of the age of the applicants continued to cause heated discussion, with strong views expressed that the younger men should be volunteering for military service.

In June of 1915 the role of the special constable underwent a further evolution, this time in response to the demands of the War Emergency Committees. The duties of the Special Constable were divided into two: Occasional Duties, which meant 'assisting the regular police in the numerous and onerous duties necessitated by war'; and Emergency Duties, in which they supplemented the police force and undertook to carry out the scheme formulated for the 'removal of all inhabitants of the County of Essex for their own personal safety and for military purposes, and the collection or destruction of everything that might be

Extract from Instructions to Sergeants and Corporals
by CAPT. FFINCH,
Chief Staff Officer.

Dated 14th September, 1914.

SENTRY DUTIES.

All Sentries are to be posted as Double Sentries.   Sergeants
of groups are to keep a Sentry Roster, so that each man is fairly
treated as regards "nights in bed."   Sergeants are to arrange the
various reliefs of Sentries in the most convenient way to suit the
men, i.e., as regards distance from their dwellings.   I should
suggest that each term of "sentry go" should be for two hours, and
that there should be three reliefs for each post; thus two men
(forming one double sentry post) would be on sentry go for two hours
and off for four hours, when they would again come on duty for
sentry go.

FORM OF CHALLENGING.

On any one approaching a post after dark, one Sentry is to
challenge loudly "Halt, who comes there," and make the person
challenged halt.   Then to order "Hands up - advance one for my
inspection."   If there is no cause to detain the person challenged,
then to allow him to pass: but if there is cause to suspect the
challenged person, then to detain him until the Relief arrives, when
the suspected person is to be marched to the nearest Police Station
or Police Constable for further examination.   If a detained person
becomes violent he is to be roped securely.   I should recommend
that lanterns or electric torches which can be closed or left un-
lighted until wanted should be taken to every sentry post for night
duty.   Sentries should particularly remember that it is in dark,
foggy or stormy nights that nefarious attempts are most likely to
be tried.

There is no reason why dogs should not accompany their masters
on sentry duty.

*Sentry duties for the special constables [Reproduced by courtesy. of the
Essex Record Office ERO D/Z 137/1]*

Herbert Gripper's warrant card. [ERO D/Z 137/1, courtesy Essex Police Museum]

of use to a hostile force landing in the County', in other words they would have the responsibility for the execution of the evacuation plans.

It would appear that such an essential role failed to impact the routine duties of the specials. Herbert Gripper, the second son of Joseph Gripper the ironmonger, became Special Constable SC413 on 7 September 1914, with a warrant card, armlet and truncheon. He lived at Redcot, 54 New London Road, and was in charge of a section of four men: Mr Freeland, Mr Luckin the accountant, Mr B Smith and Mr C Smith. In his logbook he recorded that they had an emergency station at the corner of New London Road and Writtle Road, and they patrolled Writtle Road, Southborough Road, Elm Road, Rothesay Avenue and the top of Wood Street, 'with their dogs if they wished'. They were required to maintain contact with the group patrolling Moulsham Street and the town. One of their routine duties was to ensure that the lighting restrictions were followed.

Coastal and estuary towns had lighting controls from very early on in the war, to ensure that no lights were visible from seawards, but inland street and building lighting was permitted as long as it was 'dull and subdued', with covers over the top of street lamps to prevent aircraft from seeing definite road patterns. But in the event of an air raid alert all external lights were to be extinguished and windows were to be covered. Gripper managed to bring a number of offenders to court – in December 1915 he reported Arthur Layton of Danbury, for not having a rear red light on his car (fined 20s); and he achieved a certain notoriety for bringing a local magistrate and near neighbour, Mr F H Crittall JP, up in front of his own bench at the Chelmsford Petty Session for 'not immediately obeying a certain order, given by or under the order of the Chief Officer of the Police, to extinguish the lights in his dwelling house… a case of sudden emergency having arisen'. The errant beak lived at the White House on London Road (now Southborough House). Late on the evening of the 1st of April Superintendent Mules, Chief of Police in Chelmsford, gave an order that 'all outside lights and all lights visible from the inside of dwellings or buildings should be at once extinguished', using his powers under the Defence of the Realm regulations. This verbal instruction was given to Cpl Barnard, who relayed it to the special police group leaders. Subsequently Gripper noted lights in Crittall's downstairs and upstairs rooms, visible from outside on London Road, despite the blinds being drawn. The case rested on Crittall's failure to put out the lights immediately when ordered, it having taken him ten minutes and two visits from Gripper to take action. The court found him guilty, at which point it was revealed that the gentleman had a previous conviction for an unscreened light, and his colleagues now fined him £10 and awarded the costs of 5s to the constable. The emergency to which Superintendent Mules was responding was the raid on the east coast in which five airships attacked a number of ports and coastal towns, and Zeppelin L15 was brought down by artillery fire and ditched off the Kent coast, having overflown Essex on its way to London.

Special Constable Herbert Gripper.

As the number of special constables increased, Wykeham Chancellor, son of Frederick Chancellor, was appointed as superintendent, whose task was to visit the various stations and patrols during the night. One such post was at the Railway Station, in the office

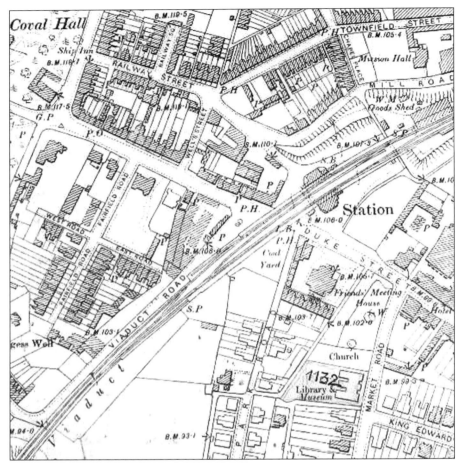

The railway station and the viaduct.

at the corner of Duke Street and Park Road, from where Viaduct Road was patrolled throughout the war (the Army guarded the railway itself). The log book for the period 1 January to 31 March 1917 has survived. The men checked the security of the various sheds, stores and shops under the railway arches from the subway to Mill Road, including Ketley's fruit and vegetable store (where the produce from the Chelmsford and District Branch of the Vegetable Products Committee was stored before the weekly distribution to the Navy), the Wells & Perry coal shed off Duke Street, and across the road down to number 45. They dutifully reported missing keys, missing whistles, and a bright light shining from the direction of the National Steam Car works. Six men were on duty each night, working two two hour shifts with a four hour break in between, when they could sleep. Seventy-seven men are recorded as carrying guard duty over this period, including Mr Melvin (the Town Clerk), Henry Marriage, Leonard Christy, and many other well-known figures in the Chelmsford business community. Richard Godfrey's father was one of these men, and he recalled that 'he had to do nightly patrols around the railway bridges, looking out for any suspicious persons about in the night'.

The night of Tuesday 27 June 1916, was very quiet. While on patrol Gripper heard a distant rumbling sound, and wrote in his diary: 'Guns in Flanders seen and felt.' This was the enormous artillery barrage that preceded the Battle of the Somme. Herbert Gripper kept some statistics of his service. During the course of the war he carried out 152 patrols, attended 54 drill nights and walked 740 miles. He reported lights at 752 houses.

The Specials continued their work throughout the war. They were officially released from service at 12 noon on Monday 14 July, 1919. Gripper's log book ends with the following:

> *Now it's all over*
> *We do not want medals or OBEs*
> *We thank the Almighty while standing at ease*
> *And having received our final dismiss*
> *Just go back to our home and family – bliss.*

Special constable 413

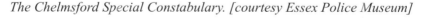

The Chelmsford Special Constabulary. [courtesy Essex Police Museum]

CHAPTER 5

The Volunteers

*'We recognise that should the Germans ever land in England
or on any part of our coasts it would be largely on the
Volunteers that we would have to depend to repel them.'*
The Duke of Connaught, speech, 1917

There had been a long tradition of part time voluntary military service in the Volunteer Force in Essex. The reforms of 1908 saw it absorbed into the new Territorial Force for the defence of the country at home. At the start of the First World War it became apparent that the British forces were already overstretched and that the Territorial units, intended for home service only, were clearly going to be sent overseas. Many men above the military age limit of forty wanted to serve under arms in the event of invasion and initially a number of *ad hoc* private groups were formed, loosely collected as a volunteer defence corps under the control of the London-based Central Association of Volunteer Training Corps. Meetings were held in Brentwood and East London. In June of 1915 there was a meeting of the deputy lieutenants in Essex to consider merging these groups into one regiment and the Essex Volunteer Regiment of the Volunteer Training Corps was born. The intention was to recruit men above military age, or in government employment (an expression used to describe munitions work), and others who for genuine reasons could not enlist into the Regular or Territorial Forces, and were aged between 17 and 60. The men also had to be physically fit. On 11 June a notice was published in the *Essex Chronicle*:

Essex Volunteer Regiment
Public Meeting to be held at the Drill Hall for the Chelmsford
Company of the Essex Volunteer Regiment
Chairman: the Mayor of Chelmsford
Speakers: Lt. Gen. Sir A R Martin; the Lord Bishop of Chelmsford;
Collingwood Hope Esq; and Lt Col Colvin.
7.30 pm. Ladies are invited

The meeting was very well stage managed, with the Grammar School Cadets marching through the town following the band of the Buckinghamshire Territorials. The meeting was to the point, concentrating on making the case for men to join. It was suggested that one objective would be that 'in case of invasion the Volunteer Training Corps could put up a *bit of a fight* until the military authority could concentrate in force' [author's emphasis]. One of the speakers neatly summarised the options facing the men at the meeting:

1. Join the Army or Navy;
2. Join the Volunteer Training Corps;
3. Join the Red Cross (VAD) or become a Special Constable; or
4. Do nothing.

Mr JE Seager served as the officer commanding of the fledgling Chelmsford company, which already had seventy men in the ranks. An efficiency badge was awarded to those men who attended at least forty drills and had passed as second class shots; at this time over thirty-five had already qualified. The problem was that they had no official recognition and had to pay for their own equipment, the members having spent around £300 from their own pockets for uniforms and rifles (indeed they were the only company in Essex to all have their own weapons), and fundraising was a recurrent theme for the next year or so. At Walthamstow they could put together a uniform for 21s each, but at Braintree the cost, including a rifle, was put at £4 10s. In 1915 the uniform was to be distinguishable from that worn by the regular and territorial forces and so a range of colours was used, from Lovat green to light grey, and sometimes a jacket of one colour and trousers of another. Chelmsford wore a grey-green rainproof drill tunic with cord breeches and matching military cap, puttees and belt.

The Motor Volunteers. [Reproduced by courtesy of the Essex Record Office ERO D/DU 787/4]

All volunteers wore a red felt armband bearing the letters 'GR' which officially stood for *Georgius Rex*, but informally stood for 'Genuine Relics', 'Good Runners', and other, less polite, terms. The importance of the armband is significant – regardless of the uniform or lack thereof, in the event of an invasion it would differentiate them as genuine combatants rather than as a guerrilla force. A very grumpy letter appeared in the *Essex Newsman* in May 1915, from 'An Old Soldier', complaining that he had seen several Chelmsfordians garbed in a costume closely resembling the uniform of an officer in the British Army, and that the ordinary Tommy took them for the real thing, saluting in the manner laid down by the regulations. It is very likely that 'Old Soldier' was taking exception over a group of 'George's Wrecks'.

Owners of motor cars and lorries were able to volunteer themselves and their vehicles under the Motor Volunteer Corps scheme, and the Automobile Association and the Royal Automobile Club provided many such members.

From the outset of the war such men had offered their services in transporting people and supplies in support of the war effort, and in particular in the transfer of the wounded from the railway station to the various hospitals in the borough. Mr Austin, who owned the County Motor Works on New London Road and Duke Street (opposite the station), had something of a reputation for the conversion of motor cars into ambulances, with the addition of stretcher racks. Their vehicles were not otherwise fitted for military service, but while on military duties the driver was entitled to free petrol coupons and general servicing and repairs were undertaken at public expense. Uniforms were not issued until 1918. The MVC was part of but separate to the Volunteer Corps and was organised at the county level; drivers of the Essex MVC provided the transport for Lord French on his inspection visit in February 1918. At a dinner held for the men of No 2 Company, Essex Motor Volunteers, in March 1918, their commanding officer, Lieutenant Colonel Harry Wrightson, claimed that the Essex Motor Volunteer Corps was the third largest in England. At the Volunteers camp in Colchester in May 1918 they were able to field fifty officers and 375 men, with a range of motor cars, motor cycles, heavy lorries and motor ambulances. They spent the week on road reconnaissance and map reading exercises.

The Chelmsford Volunteers spent Sunday 8 August 1915 on exercise. Under their platoon commanders, Barrett and Slipper, they marched from the Drill Hall to the railway station and journeyed by train for six miles (Ingatestone) and marched another five miles and met up with the Brentwood Company. They spent the day on earth works and barbed wire entanglements. A dozen men of the company spent a week at Rottingdean army camp under strict Army conditions and so impressed the drill staff that for one day 'Chelmsford' was set as the password.

An inspection in September 1915 found the Volunteers on the Grammar School playing field, carrying out drill, guard mounting, outpost work and signalling, which very much impressed Lieutenant General Sir Alfred Martin. As a professional soldier he felt it necessary to explain to them the importance of their feet, recommending strong, light shooting boots 'well dubbined'. The matter of boots was brought home to the diarist, Dr Salter. He was a member of his local unit in Tolleshunt D'Arcy but found himself one day in Chelmsford in uniform, where he was dressed down by a passing officer for wearing shoes rather than boots. Martin did much work in support of the Volunteers, and was critical of the lack of support shown by Chelmsford Council. They, as with many others, were sceptical of the possibility of invasion, and therefore saw little point in working with an organisation that would never be needed.

Trench digging was a regular feature of the Volunteer's life. [Reproduced by courtesy of the Essex Record Office ERO D/DU 787/4]

With the introduction of the Group or Derby Scheme in October 1915, many young men attested in preparation for subsequent enlistment in the forces and in many cases then informally joined the Volunteers in preparation for military life. A number of them participated in a night march exercise held on Saturday 18 December, with the Chelmsford company marching out from the Drill Hall at 8 pm to Danbury, Little Baddow, and Boreham, covering about 16 miles and returning at 2 am. On another exercise in January 1916 they engaged in field operations in Terling. Sergeant Stutfield took a detachment of twenty-five cyclists and set up an ambush. The remaining forty-five men followed on foot and attacked. This was the first occasion that blank ammunition was used.

Official recognition was achieved in March 1916. This was around the time of the introduction the Military Service Act and conscription. It was immediately suggested to, and accepted by, the Chelmsford Local Military Tribunal that service in the Volunteers should be a condition of a grant of exemption from military service. There was a rapid increase in numbers and in the same month the social aspect of volunteering was celebrated with the Company's second annual dinner at the Shire Hall. Sergeant Major Bolingbroke presided over a convivial event at which their officers were the guests, along with the men of the Detention Centre Staff at Chelmsford Prison, led by Sergeant Major Lees, who also acted as an instructor to the Volunteers. The speeches made much of the long-awaited recognition, and they emphasised their soldierly qualities, which included the ability to carry out twenty mile route marches. And not for the first time attention was drawn to Private Stuart Trotter of Broomfield Lodge, a man of wealth and substantial social standing, now aged 64, who was later described as doing 'his little bit, as best he could'.

Their new status brought about significant changes. An earlier approach to the Chief of Police to offer the Volunteers to assist the police in the event of air raids had been politely dismissed. Now a scheme of assistance was drawn up, and the Company had a definite rôle to play in the event of an invasion. The invasion theme was used for another recruitment notice which appeared on 12 May 1916:

MEN OF CHELMSFORD

What do you propose to do in the event of any invasion? By joining the Essex Volunteer Regiment you will become a member of His Majesty's Forces and entitled to assist in the defence of your country. Full particulars at the Drill Hall, any evening between 7 and 10, excepting Sundays.

This, combined with the output of the Local Tribunals, resulted in a swift increase in numbers, almost doubling them to 200 men. Later the same month they lost Lieutenant General Martin, who retired due to ill-health, and he was replaced by Colonel R Beale Colvin. Things changed rapidly; the Lord Lieutenant, Lord Warwick, wrote a letter to the Editor of the *Essex Chronicle* on 7 July 1916 in which he sought to reassure the Volunteers, and the public, that the War Office genuinely supported them and believed that they had a crucial role to play. At the same time he attended a fundraising concert at the Empire Theatre in Chelmsford which raised about £150 for regimental funds. The constant requirement for fundraising must have made the men question their real value to the government, especially as Lord Warwick then

Viscount French on the Recreation Ground [Reproduced by courtesy of the Essex Record Office ERO D/DU 787/4]

asked them to give up three days a week for training, plus Sundays, for trench digging.

Viscount French, as Commander-in-Chief of Home Forces, visited Chelmsford on Sunday 22 October 1916 to inspect the Volunteers of Essex. 131 officers and 4,912 men paraded on the Recreation Ground, with detachments from Chelmsford, Southend, Colchester, Maldon, Halstead and Braintree and with the Cadets from the Grammar School and the Chelmsford Church Lads' Brigade.

At this time the Volunteer Act 1916 was introduced, which withdrew the right of the man to resign after fourteen days, and which meant that men were effectively under military law as much as if they were in the Territorials or Regular Army. Failure to attend drills or other training could mean detention in military custody and a charge of being 'Absent With Out Leave'. Men who achieved the required level of efficiency and fitness now received a Government grant and the Lord Lieutenant set up a county fund to assist those not otherwise eligible. By December 1916 there was much greater clarity about the rôle of the Volunteers: notwithstanding their crucial function in home defence in the event of invasion, they were able to relieve regular troops for service overseas by undertaking tasks such as guarding vulnerable points, lines of communication, airfields, and constructing defence works.

February 1917 saw a renewed surge in recruitment. The King had sent a letter to all the Lord Lieutenants in the country in which he recognised that the men of the Territorial Forces, originally intended for home defence, were now fighting overseas and that 'we must now organise and equip a force to take their place as defenders of these shores in case of invasion. Men, who for reasons of health and age are unable to stand the strain of war overseas, have volunteered for this duty.' He announced the appointment of a new Colonel-in-Chief, the Duke of Connaught. In a bold gesture of support, the Mayor of Chelmsford, John Ockelford Thompson, subsequently joined the Volunteers and 'has assumed the rank, pay and emoluments of a private soldier', and with his taste for poor poetry, Reflex suggested that 'with his gun upon his shoulder, shure no man could be bolder'. At a meeting at the Empire on 18 February, amidst excited discussion of 'the new Army for Home Defence' he was joined by Councillors Bradridge and Adams on the spot. And as if they weren't doing enough already, it was announced that magistrates and special constables could also serve in the Volunteers. A further major inspection followed in April 1917 by the Duke of Connaught himself, with all the Essex battalions, now 7,000 strong, gathered onto a 'wonderful parade ground extending over several miles, and facing a road along which they were afterwards to pass in a seemingly endless column of route'. This was probably at Widford Camp, along the edge of Hylands Park (now the A414 Greenbury Way). The Duke assured the men that they would now be

The Duke of Connaught's inspection. [Reproduced by courtesy of the Essex Record Office ERO D/DU 787/4]

taken seriously: 'our great object in having a Volunteer Force is to release others who are younger and more capable of handling the hard work of active campaigning.'

Despite such assurances, funding remained a problem. Even with the Mayor and two councillors in service, the Town Council refused a request to make a grant to the Volunteers, despite the fact that other councils had done so: Maldon had voted £100, Colchester £250, and West Ham the enormous sum of £500. The opposition was led by the Deputy Mayor, who argued that there were many voluntary organisations in the borough worthy of support but who received nothing by way of grant. If a case was to be made for the Volunteers then the others should be considered at the same time. It was also suggested that funding should come from taxes, as was done with the Territorials, rather than from local rates. The voting went sixteen to seven against making the grant. In June the Mayor published an appeal for £400, which would help the Volunteers obtain a government grant, provided debts were cleared and a working balance available (in modern terms, they were looking for 'sustainability'). By the time the Mayor closed the appeal in October 1917, they had raised £561 18s.

The Volunteers went from strength to strength and steadily developed their military skills. Khaki uniforms were issued, along with the regulation 'GR' armband or brassard, and the units were given formal regimental designations: the Chelmsford group were officially C (Chelmsford) Company of the 1/2 Essex Volunteer Regiment. Captain Seager, the original officer commanding, was conscripted and joined the Artists Rifles (County of London), and he was replaced by Lieutenant Cleale. At Whitsun 1917 they held an annual camp at Jordan's Farm, Mountnessing, with 270 men from the Chelmsford, Harlow & Epping, and Maldon companies. This proved to be a convivial event, with a large marquee provided by the YMCA for music

The Volunteers march past the Duke of Connaught (probably near Widford Camp, looking towards Hylands). [Reproduced by courtesy of the Essex Record Office ERO D/DU 787/4]

and recreation, and during the Saturday evening sing-song it was announced that Lieutenant Cleale had received his promotion to captain. The next morning they held a Church Parade at St. Giles Church, Mountnessing, and marched back to Chelmsford.

In June 1917 the Company began posting its weekly orders in the *Essex Chronicle*:

'C' (Chelmsford) Company 1/2nd Battalion Essex Volunteer Regiment
Drill Hall, Chelmsford

Company Orders for the week ending Sunday June 17th, 1917

Orderly Officer for the week: Capt. A G Cleale (Ardyne, Market Road)
Next for duty: Lt G F Barrett (Faircross, Springfield)
Orderly Corporal for the week: Cpl G Christy
Monday June 11th: Meeting of Officers and NCOs at 6.15 pm
Tuesday June 12th: Bayonet fighting, 8 to 9 pm
Wednesday June 13th: Drill, 6.15 am; 7.15 am; Bombing lecture, 8.15 pm.
Thursday June 14th: Musketry, 6 to 9 pm; Squad drill, 9 to 10 pm.
Friday 15th June: Squad drill, 8 to 9 pm; Special courses of musketry for 10 NCOs, 8.15 to 9.30 pm (continuation of)
Saturday 16th June: Miniature rifle range, 7 to 9 pm.
Sunday 17th June: Bombing, 9.15 am to 12.15 pm.
                                    Arthur J Cleale, OC 'C' Company

This routine is repeated, more or less the same, for the next thirteen months, with the addition of topics such as Entrenching and Field Training, Care of Arms and Fitting Equipment, Company Drill, Gassing, Machine Gun, First Aid and Stretcher Bearing, along with all manner of inspections and parades. Church parades at various locations around the district were taken as an opportunity for both inspection, as the men were appearing in public, and for a route march, which, if they were lucky, was in skeleton order: webbing straps, light haversack, water bottle and rifle, and rations to be carried. 'Full marching order',

The digging didn't stop. [Reproduced by courtesy of the Essex Record Office ERO D/DU 787/4]

if ordered, involved backpacks (containing greatcoats, spare socks, and wash kit), and if en route to camp might involve carrying ammunition pouches, specialist weapons, entrenching tools and stretchers. In May 1918 the men would have been delighted to read that for the Whitsun camp at Wivenhoe they were to travel by train.

The church parade at Sandon in July 1917 seems fairly typical. The villagers arrived at St Andrew's Church early and decked the war shrine at the entrance with flowers. Over the sound of the church bells was heard the tramping of the boots of some 140 men marching down the lane. The service was given by one of their own, as the Reverend John Best was a Volunteer. A collection was made for the Essex Regiment Prisoner of War Fund, raising £7 1s 6d. Following an inspection by Major General Johnson, the men carried out military work in a field at Potash, off the Maldon Road, to the approval of the inspecting officer. At their next inspection they were able to show off their newly-issued machine gun to General Egerton, the Inspector of Infantry. By September's annual camp at the Old Rodney, Little Baddow, they were able to impress the supervising officer of the Volunteer Force, the twice wounded Colonel Clive of the Grenadier Guards, with their military skills and fitness, culminating in a football match in which the married men played the single men, winning 8-0.

Field Marshal Viscount French visited Chelmsford again at the end of January 1918 to inspect the Volunteers from Essex, Middlesex and Suffolk. Most travelled down on special trains and many of them spent the night before the parade in hastily arranged accommodation in Trinity Road and Friars Schools. The parade took place in Admiral's Park and, as the *Chronicle* described it, the three brigades comprised 'many hardy veterans, grey-haired, alert, and also many youngsters… too youthful for the regular forces'. Regimental bands played throughout, and the VAD men of Essex 3 were in attendance, to render aid to those who fell out from the ranks. Following the imposition of military law on this volunteer force at the end of 1916, French announced a relaxation of the rules for men who were unable to attend drill nights regularly, recognising that 'they had other things to do, their living to make'. There was also to be a review of the fitness rules: men who were in the lowest Army Category D were to be discharged (Lord French actually described them rather cruelly as 'useless men'); the Volunteers were to be fit and healthy fighting men.

The demand for men for active service was unrelenting and the unexpectedly successful German spring offensives of 1918 and Field Marshal Sir Douglas Haig's famous 'backs to the wall' message put an additional pressure on available manpower. In May 1918 the military authorities looked again at the Reservists who had been serving in the United Kingdom on various garrison, supply, transport and guard duties, with a view to sending them overseas. The gap they left would be filled by Volunteers. A notice appeared in the *Chronicle* on 31 May:

Official Notice: to the Volunteers of the Essex Regiment

Having yesterday attended a Conference in London of all the County Commandants of the United Kingdom, at which a very important announcement was made by the Secretary of State, I make the following appeal to the Essex Infantry Volunteers:

In order to temporarily set free for service overseas Men of the Regular Army, it is desired to enrol Volunteers for special service in Special Service Companies at once.

The Deputy Secretary of State has emphasised the fact that the need is great and urgent. Compulsion is not possible, as it would entail legislation, and there is not time for the delay inseparable from legislation. The Special Service Companies required must therefore be obtained upon a Voluntary Basis, and upon the following conditions:

1. Sections Eligible
Efficient men of Sections A, B, and D are eligible. Any D men taken would be clothed and equipped. Any physically developed lad of Section C who may volunteer would probably be taken.
2. Medical Qualification
No man of Grade 1 (Army Category) is eligible. They are required for the Army. Men of Grade 2 (Army Category), and possibly Grade 3 (Army Category), are eligible.
3. Pay
Officers, NCOs, and men who may join the Special Service Companies will be required to sign Agreements on A. F. V. 4012 and V. 4013. They will, while employed on this Army duty, draw the pay and allowances of their rank, including Separation Allowance for married NCOs and men.
4. Period
The period for which the service is required is a minimum of two months.
5. Exemption from Army Service
Men enrolled in these Special Service Companies will be exempt from being called up for Army Service during the period of employment in a Volunteer Special Service Company.
6. Locality of Employment
As far as possible Essex men who may enrol will be employed within the County of Essex or an adjoining County.
7. Strength of Companies
The strength of each Company required will be 114 all ranks, including probably 4 officers.

I appeal to all officers and men of the Essex Volunteers to whom it may be possible, even at great inconvenience, to comply with the above conditions, to come forward now and volunteer for this important duty. I appeal at the same time to the Employers of the County to make, where possible, the required sacrifice and temporarily set free from employment men who may desire to take up the duty.

If all make the necessary sacrifice each Infantry Battalion should be able to produce a Special Service Company, or at least half a Company. In the latter event a Company would be formed from each two Battalions.

Essex has never been behindhand in facing an emergency and I am confident that Essex Volunteer Infantry Battalions will not fail now.

F F Johnson, Major-General, County Commandant

The Special Service Companies were assigned to coastal defences; sufficient regulars were released and rushed to France to assist in halting the Germans and then push them back. Within five months the war was over. On 18 December 1918 nearly 200 men of 'C' (Chelmsford) Company of the 2nd Volunteer Battalion, Essex Regiment, gathered together at the Shire Hall for a dinner. The Food Control Committee had agreed to allow an extra 50lb of beef, for which each man had to contribute a ration coupon, but the evening was very much a farewell, as the orders for the Volunteers to stand down had been received earlier in the month. They were officially disbanded in January 1920.

CHAPTER 6

Joining Up

Englishmen generally like fair play,
and if the shirkers do not line up, I shouldn't wonder
if our countrymen's sense of fair play will say to the
Government – 'Recruit voluntarily if you can, but recruit.'

So let's be up and doing
And ere the day appear
Find everyman in England
A gallant Volunteer
Reflexions by Reflex, 1915

The Army and Royal Navy played a large part in British life before the First World War, both physically in terms of men, ships, and materiel, but also morally, in conveying the sense of power that allowed a small island nation to control the largest empire the world had ever seen. Recent wars in South Africa had swept away any complacency about the role of the Army in the modern world and, against a backdrop of a real or perceived threat of a European war, thorough reforms had taken place throughout the armed forces. The regular army was small, given its potential range of operations, but highly professional and Britain, unlike its continental neighbours, did not have a conscript army or any form of national service, but it did possess a new, reasonably effective territorial force of volunteers, and a large body of reservists – men who had already served in the forces but who would be recalled if required. The Army Reserve was arranged in three sections: section A men had recently served in the regular army and had to undergo periodic training

A 1914 recruiting poster.

while in this category. The man would then move into Section B for a further three to five years, finally transferring to section D for four final years. B and D men could only be called up on a general mobilisation. The National Reserve was comprised of former soldiers, sailors and marines who had completed their regular, territorial or reserve service and who were willing to remain on a register. They were also in three classes: Class I, the General Reserve were men below forty-two years of age and fit to serve overseas, if required. Class II were under fifty and fit to serve in home defence. Class III were unable to serve, for various reasons. Chelmsford National Reservists were quite active and had a particularly skilful shooting team, winning the county cup at Colchester and performing well at the national event at Bisley as late as July 1914. The Special Reserve was more like the territorial force, in which a man undertook an initial six months of regular training but then served as a part-time soldier, with around a month of training a year.

The Chelmsford Drill Hall.

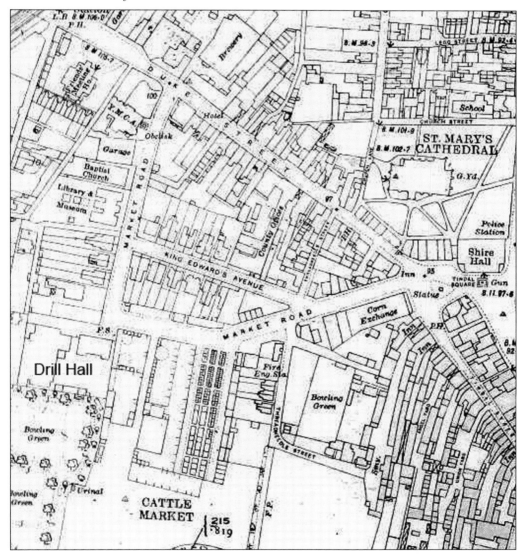

The Territorial Force itself – the 'Saturday night soldiers' – was an evolution of the previous volunteer militia, and had the same function of providing home defence. Unlike the reserves they were not obliged to serve overseas. They were recruited locally and men undertook an evening of drill each week, a weekend of training each month, and one or two weeks' annual camp. In the event of mobilisation they became full time soldiers.

Although Chelmsford had a long history of involvement with the regular army and the militia, the part of town known as Barrack Square was by 1914 a grubby commercial area, the home of a number of small light industrial concerns and the Chelmsford Star Co-operative Society. The regular army was based in Colchester. The newly constructed Drill Hall on Market Road, opened by Earl Roberts in 1903, was the home of the Territorial Force Association of the County of Essex, which comprised the following units, located in various parts of the district:

Essex Yeomanry Royal Horse Artillery	4th Battalion, Essex Regiment (Ilford)
Mounted Brigade	5th Battalion, Essex Regiment (Chelmsford)
Headquarters, Royal Field Artillery	6th Battalion, Essex Regiment (West Ham)
1st Essex Battery, Royal Field Artillery	7th Battalion, Essex Regiment (Walthamstow)
2nd Essex Battery, RFA Regiment	8th (Cyclist) Battalion, Essex (Colchester)
3rd Essex Battery, RFA	Eastern Mounted Brigade Transport and Supply Column, Army Service Corps
2nd East Anglian Ammunition Column, RFA	East Anglian Divisional Transport and Supply Column Headquarters, ASC

East Anglian (Essex) Heavy Battery, Royal Garrison Artillery	Headquarters Company, ASC
No 1 Company Essex & Suffolk, RGA	Essex Infantry Brigade Company ASC
No 2 Company Essex & Suffolk, RGA	3rd East Anglian Field Ambulance Royal Army Medical Corps
No 3 Company Essex & Suffolk, RGA	Army Veterinary Corps
Royal Engineers (Essex Fortress)	

Of these, the 5th Essex was considered the Chelmsford battalion, and 'A' Company in particular was identified with the town. The Drill Hall was also the designated depot for the Essex (Fortress) Royal Engineers and the Eastern Mounted Brigade Transport and Supply Column, Army Service Corps.

The annual Territorial parade held on Sunday 19 July 1914 gives some insight into the martial spirit of the town: Major Taylor led 102 men of the 5th Essex, Captain Neville commanded thirty-three men of the Royal Engineers, fourteen men of the Essex Yeomanry followed behind Captain Tufnell, Captain Dawson had forty-five Army Service Corps men, and Colonel Greville was at the head of no fewer than ninety National Reservists. There were also contingents of the King Edward's Grammar School Cadets and the women of the Voluntary Aid Detachments. Neither the sermon, delivered in the Cathedral by the Reverend Canon Lake, nor the subsequent address by the Lord Lieutenant, the Earl of Warwick, carried any hint of the storm clouds gathering over Europe, with war only a matter of days away.

As international tension increased, the secretary of the Essex County Territorial Force Association issued a mobilisation statement on the morning of 30 July. Orders were issued calling up the Special

Service Section of the Essex (Fortress) Royal Engineers. This unit was tasked with the operation of searchlights at naval establishments and, on assembly at the Drill Hall, they were despatched to the forts at Landguard, in Harwich, with forty men leaving by train from Chelmsford at 9 am and a further eleven men at 3 pm. During the day the Special Service Sections of the Essex Yeomanry were called up, along with the 8th (Cyclist) Battalion.

In the last few days of peace the naval reserves were called up, on 2nd August; those from Essex typically serving on the minesweepers and destroyers operating from the east coast ports. Men such as Seaman Gunner HF Elliott, of 23 New London Road, and 1st Class Stoker W Hubbard were sent to Harwich to join the crew on the cruiser HMS *Cressy*. At the same time the men of the 5th Essex were under orders at what had been the annual camp at Clacton. Each man was issued with twenty rounds of live ammunition and the commanding officer, Lieutenant Colonel Welch, led them to Dovercourt in Harwich on anti-invasion duties. One of his soldiers was Corporal Arthur Baker, of 32 Seymour Street, also known as Councillor Baker of Chelmsford Council.

With general mobilisation, the Territorials and reservists were called up. The general principle was that a Territorial soldier served with his existing unit but reservists would be assigned to fill vacancies in any unit. In July the Essex Territorials were under strength but the response from the reservists was sufficient in most cases to make up the numbers; in Essex alone there were around 7,000 of them. A very large proportion of the men volunteered for Class I overseas service. The impact on the town was substantial: seventy men from Marconi's were called up, along with two hundred or so from Hoffmann's, another one hundred from the Arc Works, and Clarkson's National Steam Car Company lost about forty. Harold Stevens, of 35 Rainsford Road, working 'on the confectionery side' of the Star Co-operative Society bakery in Wells Street, was called up and joined the 1st Battalion Hertfordshire Regiment, and his colleague, Private Samuel D Pilgrim, joined the Essex Regiment. Bertram Hazell, of 4 Quarry View, Beehive Lane, a postman, joined the 4th Battalion Middlesex Regiment. Despite the potential labour problems, employers were very supportive and, recognising that the pay of a full time soldier was likely to be much less than in normal employment, the management of Marconi's announced that 'Every man in the company's employ who is called to service in His Majesty's Navy or Army will have his position in the Company reserved for him, and during such service his salary will be dealt with as he may direct.' In support of the latter point most Chelmsford firms made up the difference between the service pay and the man's original wages or offered half pay.

And then came the volunteers. Even before Lord Kitchener, the Secretary of State for War, launched his iconic campaign to raise 100,000 men aged between 19 and 30 for his new army on 11 August, young men were queuing outside the Drill Hall and into Market Road to sign up. The Drill Hall was open from 9 am to 10 pm, seven days a week, and in the first few days there were thirty applications for commissions whilst the Royal Flying Corps had to suspend recruitment, having been overwhelmed with applicants. Some employers were very blunt in their patriotism: the management of the Great Eastern Railway declared that they 'expect every single man of serviceable age to make application for enlistment in the Army'.

Men were not always placed in a local regiment. Chelmsford was in the 44th Recruiting Area (Southend, Chelmsford, Colchester, Grays, Ilford, Romford, Harwich, Shoebury, Brentwood), within the 9th District (Essex, Suffolk, Norfolk, Northamptonshire and Bedfordshire) and the local regiments formed part of the Eastern Division which comprised the following:

Norfolk Regiment
Suffolk Regiment
Essex Regiment
Princess Charlotte of Wales (Royal Berkshires) Regiment
Royal Fusiliers (City of London) Regiment
Royal Sussex Regiment
Duke of Cambridge's Own (Middlesex) Regiment
Queen's (Royal West Surrey) Regiment
Buffs (East Kent) Regiment
East Surrey Regiment
Queen's Own (Royal West Kent) Regiment

Men who were originally Territorials could also volunteer to transfer to the regular army under Kitchener's scheme, which left gaps in the

G.R.

Royal Garrison Artillery.

Men of good physique are urgently required for the
Royal Garrison Artillery.

Gunners, Drivers, Telephonists,
Shoeing Smiths and Saddlers.

Height from 5ft. 6in. up.   Chest Measurement from 36in,

Training for this Branch of the Service is undergone in Coast
Defence Batteries, but employment in this splendid force is with
Siege and Heavy Batteries in the Field.
Those desirous of joining should apply to the nearest
Recruiting Officer, or Recruiting Sergeant.

GOD SAVE THE KING.

Recruitment advertisement in the Essex Chronicle.

ranks that were either filled by reservists or by new recruits. Civilians could volunteer to join the regular army or the Territorials. Furthermore, men with specialist skills such as in electrical and mechanical engineering, as found in the big Chelmsford firms, were likely to be assigned to the Royal Engineers or Army Service Corps. And there was nothing to stop a man, swayed by the skirl of the bagpipes, from joining a Scottish or any other regiment, provided they had vacancies. Perhaps surprisingly, advertisements for specific regiments appeared in the press throughout the war. A man could sign up in the Drill Hall in Chelmsford, undergo a medical examination, and then pick up a travel warrant to the Essex Regiment Depot at Warley Barracks in Brentwood, or to the Eastern Division centre at Shorncliffe in Kent, or to the regimental headquarters of his preferred unit.

By drawing on Classes I and II of the National Reserves, by the end of August the local Territorial units were reported as fully up to strength, and an additional unit, the 9th (Service) Battalion of the Essex Regiment was formed, followed by the 10th, 11th, and 13th Battalions. The response to Kitchener's appeal was impressive and the *Essex Chronicle* was able to report that:

Up to last Saturday [29 August] there had been at Chelmsford 439 recruits, including 42 on the Friday and 15 on the Saturday. Since then the numbers have been: Sunday 33, Monday 34, Tuesday 132, Wednesday 114, Thursday (up to 2 o'clock) 133. This makes a grand total of 900, and with the long waiting line of men, it was hoped to complete the 1,000 by the time this paper is printed.

It was subsequently recorded that by the time the *Essex Newsman* was printed on Saturday 5 September a total of 1,060 men had enlisted at Chelmsford, of whom 609 had joined the Essex Regiment. Although under Kitchener's scheme it was announced that 'in the case of a number of friends volunteering at the same time to serve in Lord Kitchener's new Army, the utmost endeavour will be made to enlist them in the same battalion so that they may be able to serve together', there were no Chelmsford or Essex 'Pal's Battalions', as were seen mainly in the northern cities.

Not everyone was as keen to go off to war. A seaman, John Sleet, had been reported absent from HMS *Lowestoft* in Chatham since 3 August. PC Parrott found the man when he called at his house in Anchor Street and he was brought to the Police Court, where he was detained to await a naval escort.

Men continued to volunteer for military service over the next few months but by mid-1915 it was apparent that more men were needed. Britain was still committed to voluntary service but the Government lacked the important statistical information about the availability of manpower in the nation. On 13th August 1915 the *Chronicle* gave due warning to the citizens of Chelmsford about the forthcoming national register:

Borough of Chelmsford
National Registration Act 1915
Notice is hereby given that it is the duty of every person between the age of 15 and 65 (not being members of His Majesty's Naval Forces or of His Majesty's Regular or Territorial Forces, and certain other exceptions) to FILL UP and SIGN a FORM OF REGISTRATION stating his or her name, place of residence, age and other particulars.

It went on to explain that a Form of Registration would be left at every home in the borough by Sunday 5 August. The *Chronicle* of the following week provided further information about the form and the nine questions it contained. These were:

1. Age last birthday
2. If born abroad and not British, state nationality
3. State whether single, married, widow or widower
4. How many children are dependent on you? Under fifteen years? Over fifteen years?
5. How many other persons are dependent on you, excluding employees? Wholly dependent? Partially dependent?
6. Profession or occupation. State fully the particular kind of work done and the material worked or dealt in (if any)
7. Name, business, and business address of employer
8. Are you employed for or under any Government department? Say 'Yes', or 'No', or 'Do Not Know'
9. Are you skilled in any work other than that upon which you are at present employed, and, if so, what? Are you able and willing to undertake such work?

A comprehensive set of explanations and commentary on the questions accompanied the notice, and there was a meeting organised at the Shire Hall to help answer any questions. The whole country sat down with pen and paper on the evening of Sunday 15 August, the men filling in blue forms and the women white. The whole process of distributing and collecting the forms was done by a massive team of volunteers, in

War Service Badges: the triangular badge was for women workers. [author's collection]

Chelmsford it was the responsibility of the Town Clerk, Mr Melvin and his staff. The returns were compiled using blue index cards for the men, and again white for the women, and there was also a green index card for those who had reported a secondary occupation (question 9). The chief interest for many was the pink cards on which were recorded the details of all men between 18 and 41 years of age, the so-called 'pink list'.

NATIONAL REGISTRATION ACT, 1915.

Another outcome of the register would be the formal recognition of those whose employment or occupation was in work in the national interest. Those working at Marconi's or Hoffmann's, for example, were engaged on Government munitions work (answering 'Yes' to question 8) and were entitled to wear an official War Service Badge

The National Registration Card. [author's collection]

(issued from December 1914 by the Admiralty and Ministry of Munitions), but others, particularly in private firms, could be engaged in equally important work, often of a national importance. Once identified, these were then marked with an asterisk in the Register, and they were described as 'starred' occupations. Such occupations included agricultural labourers and dairymen, but farmers were initially excluded (this later evolved into the reserved occupations system; and the list of reserved or certified occupations was regularly reviewed throughout the war). From September everyone was issued with a National Registration certificate, which carried their name, occupation and address, and which was essentially an identity card.

One of the early outcomes of this age and skills census of the nation was the realisation that many eligible men were still in civilian life. The recruitment officers had their pink lists to work on but it would require a big effort to encourage these men to join.

At the Quarter Session at Chelmsford on 20 October 1915 the Lord Lieutenant broke with ceremony and read a telegram he had received from the King two days previously:

To the Lord-Lieutenant of Essex, Easton Lodge, Dunmow
A recruiting campaign is being organised by the Parliamentary Recruiting Committee, acting in conjunction with the Joint

Labour Committee. I would ask you kindly to give this campaign all the valuable assistance which in your position you can exercise.
George R

Perhaps with the understated language of the telegram the message was lost on the Chelmsford newspapers; in any event they did not publish the King's appeal to the country, which was announced on 23 October 1915:

The King's Appeal
More Men Wanted
Come Forward Voluntarily
Buckingham Palace
To My People

At this grave moment in the struggle between my people and a highly organised enemy who has transgressed the Laws of Nations and change the ordinance that binds civilized Europe together, I appeal to you.

I rejoice in my Empire's efforts, and I feel pride in the voluntary response from my Subjects all over the world who have sacrificed home, fortune, and life itself, in order that another may not inherit the free Empire which their ancestors and mine have built.

I ask you to make good those sacrifices.

The end is not in sight. More men and yet more men are wanted to keep my Armies in the Field, and through them to secure Victory and enduring Peace.

In ancient days the darkest moment has ever produced in men of our race the sternest resolve.

I ask you, men of all classes, to come forward voluntarily and take your share in the fight.

In freely responding to my appeal, you will be giving your support to our brothers, who, for long months, have nobly upheld Britain's past traditions, and the glory of her Arms.
George R I

This was to be the last attempt to encourage voluntary service. Following the King's appeal a new policy was introduced by Lord Derby, known as the Derby or Group Scheme, in which men voluntarily attested for military service. The concept of 'attestation' is that of taking the oath of allegiance to the Sovereign and on doing so the man actually joined Class B of the Army Reserve, with a fine khaki armlet to prove it, although he then went about his normal work and family life. These men were to be formed into groups by age and by marital status. A single man aged 18 was in Group 1, aged 19 in Group 2 and so on up to Group 23, which contained single men aged 40. Married men of the same ages were put in later groups, so a 20 year old married man would be in group 26. The intention was that the groups would be called up in numerical order, beginning with the young single men and only calling on the married men once this category had been exhausted.

On 9 November 1915 the Council formed a Local Recruiting Committee, with the Mayor and Deputy Mayor, Alderman Chancellor and Councillors Thompson and Dixon, and with the District Recruitment Officer, Captain Douglas Smith, as the military adviser. It was in fact a tribunal and its task was to consider appeals from men who wished to postpone their call up date, or employers who wished to retain their men should they be called up under the scheme. Another rôle for the new committee was to apply itself to the 'pink list', and the *Essex Newsman* published a letter from the Mayor in which he urgently required 'the assistance of a large number of voluntary canvassers over military age to call upon men eligible to serve in H. M. Forces. The help of ladies is also cordially invited'.

Reflex was sceptical of the Council's commitment to the recruitment drive. The job of 'assistant overseer and rate collector' was advertised and the Town Clerk had received fifty applications for the post. Four candidates were selected, all married men of military age, and the man appointed was 27 years old. At the last Council meeting of the year it was reported that all of the Council's men of military age had been attested or rejected, and it was decided that 'in the event of the Council's chief officers being called upon an appeal be made to the Local Tribunal', the chairman of which was of course the Mayor. The Town Clerk, the Borough Engineer, and the Accountant had all put themselves forward for the Derby scheme.

Both Lord Derby and the Prime Minister, Mr Asquith, had promised that married men would never be called up until all the single men had gone, but by December it was apparent that the single men were not attesting in anywhere near the same numbers as the married men. This was particularly apparent at Chelmsford, where a big response had required the staff to work from 9 am to midnight, with all the doctors of the town assisting with the medical examinations (one candidate presented himself at ten minutes to midnight on a Sunday but was still processed). Starred and badged men were encouraged to attest so that they could be assigned to the proper groups and granted their

The Group System.

exemptions. It was reported that not only were a large number of Chelmsford men married, but also that many of them were in starred occupations.

Alderman Frederick Spalding had two sons, both employed in his photography business which, at the time, was engaged in government work. The eldest, Fred junior, was the shop manager. His brother, Ernest, decided to join up. He attested on 11 December 1915, at the age of 22 years and 11 months, which put him in Group 5. He then went back to the shop to await his call-up notice.

The silver war badge, for men discharged from military service. [author's collection]

In a society in which badges and armbands were proliferating it was decided to issue the khaki Derby armbands to men who had been rejected on medical grounds, on condition that they submit to a further re-examination. There were two possible outcomes, that they would be certified as medically unfit on the ground of organic disease, or that they had poor eyesight or some slight physical defect. Both would be placed in the Army Reserve and issued with an armband, but the second group were liable to be called up if the military authorities decided to amend the medical standards for certain trades. Obviously an armlet was not necessary for men who were clearly unfit, such as the blind or limbless, and armlets were not issued after January 15 1916 (a silver war badge, worn on the right lapel, was issued to officers and men who had been discharged from Forces for medical reasons).

On 19 December 1915 a proclamation was issued to call up the first groups for service: groups 2, 3, 4 and 5 (group 1 men were technically too young for military service). This was a first warning, the actual official notification was a poster which was put up in public places around Chelmsford the next day. It was intended that the call up would begin on 20 January 1916 and, to enable a smooth flow of recruits, they would attend in batches at two hour intervals over several days. Individual notices were sent to the man's registered address and his call-up date was to be fourteen days later, to allow him time to settle his affairs. However, under the Army Act the official poster was deemed sufficient legal notification even if a letter had not been received. Starred or badged men were exempt, provided they were still in the same employment. Men wishing to appeal for postponement, on 'grounds personal to himself, or (with the consent of the man) by his employer on the grounds that a man is indispensable to his civil employment', were to apply in writing to the local tribunal by 30 December. At the start of January 1916 Lord Derby issued a booklet of 'Guiding Principles' for members of tribunals (and in particular the military representatives), in which he set out the slogan of 'Men, Munitions, Money', emphasising the importance of men in munitions work and that tribunals should recognise that these men were indispensable to the prosecution of the war and should not be called up. The first Recruitment Tribunal at Chelmsford was held on 25 January 1916 at the Municipal Offices. Forty one appeals were considered, twenty four for simple postponement and seventeen for starring or exemption. It took seven hours to work through the list and the deliberations of the panel are not recorded, but only five claims were dismissed.

As the first men went about handing in their notices and otherwise preparing themselves for the big day, a second proclamation was published on 8 January, notifying the men of Groups 6, 7, 8 and 9 of their call up date on or about 22 January. Ernest Spalding was called up on 19 January and he joined the 15th Battalion London Regiment (the Prince of Wales' Own Civil Service Rifles). On 20 January about 60 young men presented themselves at the Drill Hall and were sent off to the Essex Regiment Depot at Warley for medical examinations and were issued with uniforms in exchange for their armlets. Under the Derby Scheme the recruits had less choice about their regimental destination and by this time the Household Cavalry and the Royal Army Medical Corps had very few vacancies. There was some resentment expressed by existing soldiers to the 'Derbyites', as they were known. The units formed from earlier recruitment campaigns had trained together and developed a sense of camaraderie that seemingly made it difficult to assimilate new men. Reflex's Scottish soldier-poet, Company Sergeant Major MacNaught, of the King's Own Scottish Borderers at Widford Camp, complained:

I thocht when I enlisted, 'twas a Scottish corps I joined,
But since the Derbyites hae landed, I hae quickly changed my mind.

For we've got the queerest mixture, that ever carried a gun,
For I think they've gathered frae every tribe, that's underneath
the sun.

But he looked on the bright side:

But still they seem gey willin', an' try tae dae their bit
An' in a month or twa I reckon, I will make them smart an' fit
An' if I canna make them Scotchmen, I'll sweer, before I've
dune, them intae sodgers, that's a credit tae their King.

It was almost immediately apparent that the Derby Scheme would fail.
Even as the first proclamation notices were being posted, a Military
Service Bill was being drafted, to introduce conscription. The week
after the first groups were called up, on 27 January 1916, the Bill

Army Service Corps recruitment advertisement in the Essex Chronicle.

The following SKILLED MEN are REQUIRED for the

MECHANICAL TRANSPORT SECTION

OF THE

ARMY SERVICE CORPS:

MOTOR DRIVERS,
STEAM WAGON DRIVERS,
MOTOR FITTERS,
TURNERS,
MOTOR CYCLE FITTERS,
PEDAL CYCLE FITTERS,
MOTOR SMITHS,
MOTOR ELECTRICIANS,
SHEET METAL WORKERS,
PANEL BEATERS,
MOTOR SPARE PART STOREKEEPERS,
TECHNICAL DRAUGHTSMEN (used to Engine Work).
Also Learner Fitters, Turners, Smiths, etc.

A MECHANICAL TRANSPORT OFFICER will INTERVIEW RECRUITS,
who should bring references at
DRILL HALL, CHELMSFORD, on TUESDAY, OCT. 3rd, 1916,
at 10.30 a.m.

became law. On midnight of 1 March all single men between 18 and 41 who had not already joined up or attested were automatically reckoned as enlisted in His Majesty's Forces for the duration of the war (on 25 May this was extended to all men of military age). The remaining Derby groups were called up over the next few months, with groups 14 to 23 called up on 2 March after which the scheme was suspended. Men now waited to receive the letter from Captain Smith ordering them to attend the Drill Hall for conscription into His Majesty's Forces.

Even with the introduction of conscription it was still possible for a man to present himself voluntarily and throughout the war the newspapers carried advertisements for vacancies, especially in the technical branches, such as the Army Service Corps.

On 1 April 1916 Harry English, a 25-year-old threshing attendant from West Hanningfield, was brought before Chelmsford magistrates and charged under section 15 of the Reserve Forces Act 1882, in that he failed to appear at the Drill Hall on 11 March when called up for military service, the first such prosecution in Chelmsford. The man does not appear to have been particularly bright: his excuse was that he did not want to go. He claimed to have been unwell, but had no medical certificate and had not informed the Army. As the Mayor, as chairman of the bench, put it 'you are English by name, but not by nature', and he fined him an exemplary £3, to be deducted from his Army pay, and he was handed over to the military.

The tribunal system had barely been tested in Chelmsford when on 10 February 1916 the Council considered the requirement for a new Local Military Tribunal (in Chelmsford this was invariably known only as the Local Tribunal), 'for the purpose of dealing with all applications for certificates for exemption from military service under the Military Service Act'. Councillor Dixon reported that a strong criticism had been made of the existing tribunal, which was made up of two architects (Chancellor and Whitmore), two newspaper proprietors (Thompson and Taylor) and himself, and was not in the least representative of the employers or the workers, but after discussion it was decided that the membership would be the same for the new tribunal. On Friday 18 February a notice was published in the *Chronicle* announcing the details of the Military Service Act and inviting applications for Certificates of Exemption from Military

Service to be submitted to the Town Clerk before 2 March. Applications for exemption could be made by or in respect of any man:

(a) On the ground that it is expedient in the national interests that he should, instead of being employed in military service, be engaged in other work in which he is habitually engaged, or in which he wishes to be engaged, or, if he is being educated or trained for any work, that he should continue to be so educated or trained; or

(b) On the ground that serious hardship would ensue if the man were called up for Army Service, owing to his exceptional financial or business obligations or domestic position; or

(c) On the ground of ill-health or infirmity; or

(d) On the ground of a conscientious objection to the undertaking of military service; or

(e) On the ground that he is engaged in a certified occupation, a list of which may be inspected at [the Town Clerk's] office.

If a man has previously been starred he must still make an application if he wishes to claim exemption, unless he already has a certificate in connection with an official war badge.

Exemptions were usually conditional, the conditions either being an additional period of time granted to put a man's affairs in order, or to carry out some form of voluntary service. In August 1916 Henry Pigg, the landlord of the Red Lion Inn, Anchor Street, was on the borderline for medical fitness but the tribunal granted a conditional exemption that he join the Special Police or the VAD. In December 1916, Mr Rowe, who ran his own fish and chip shop on Springfield Road, appealed that his one man business was in the national interest, to the surprise of Captain Smith, the military representative. He was given a month to sell up.

The number of appeals heard over the next couple of years runs into the hundreds, and most of them have a brief note in the columns of the *Chronicle*, offering a glimpse into what often must have been emotional and distressing circumstances, with a man or his employer having just a few minutes to set out their reasons for exemption. And in some cases the man simply did not wish to join up at all. There is one case that neatly captures the spirit of the times: Ronald Young.

At the start of the First World War the Corporation of Chelmsford ran seven elementary schools in the borough and had plans for two more. With the outbreak of war the first teacher to enlist was Mr W Woodfield, an uncertificated teacher at Victoria Boys School, who joined the Royal Engineers in August 1914. Mr AG Suckling, a certificated teacher working at the same school, also volunteered. On 9 February 1915 the Finance & General Purposes (F&GP) Sub-committee of the Council's Education Committee gave permission for him to enlist, and notified him that his position would be kept open and he would receive an allowance to bring his Army pay up to his teacher's salary. He decided not to go at the time and joined the Volunteer Corps instead. With the introduction of the Derby scheme on 8 November 1915 the F&GP sub-committee wrote to the twelve male teachers of military age in the borough and notified them that they were permitted to enlist under the Derby scheme and that, should they do so and subsequently go away on active service, their jobs would be held open and they would be entitled to the usual allowances. It was further noted that the Council reserved the right to appeal if it felt that the individual was of too great a value to the school and not replaceable. Mr Archibald Whitehead, a trained certificated teacher at St. John's, formally requested and was granted leave of absence to enlist in the 14th Battalion London Regiment.

The F&GP sub-committee at its meeting on the 14 December 1915 noted that out of the twelve eligible teachers in the borough, one was already serving and ten had enrolled under the Derby scheme. Seven had been accepted and three were rejected as medically unfit. All of these men were subject to the Military Service Act, and Suckling, of Broomfield, and his colleague William Petchey, of 9 Hill Road, previously put back from Group 7 to 17, were called up. The Victoria School managers appealed on their behalf but were unsuccessful.

But one teacher had not responded to the F&GP committee's letter. Ronald James Young was a 24-year-old, unmarried, certificated teacher, also working at the Victoria Boys' School. Originally from Sandown on the Isle of Wight, he lived at 100 Mildmay Road. He appeared at the Local Tribunal on Monday 6 March 1916 at the same hearing as his fellow teachers. He was the first conscientious objector in Chelmsford.

As was reported at the time, the Tribunal was remarkably gentle with him:

> Ronald James Young, 24, unmarried, teacher in the Victoria Boys' School, applied for exemption on conscientious grounds. He said he declined at any cost to take part in the prosecution or continuance of the war.
>
> The Mayor: How long have you had these feelings?
> Young: For many years. Young also said he was a member of the Church of England.
> The Town Clerk: Would you help in non-combatant service?
> Young: I would help in nothing that would in any way aid towards the war; nor would I have anything to do with it at all.
> Mayor: Would you help forward the cause of peace?
> Young: Yes, all I could.
> Mayor: Do you think we are going to obtain peace by sitting at home?
> Young: I don't think we should get it by slaughtering men on the battlefield.
> Mayor: How are you going to get it then?
> Young: By negotiating. My feelings tell me that to kill men is something which God would not have you do, and I would rather lose my life than take a life of another. I am prepared to bring about a speedy peace in a moral way.
>
> Applicant was passed for non-combatant service, and said he should appeal.

Young next appeared before the Essex Appeal Tribunal on 12 April 1916. The chair was Mr Collingwood Hope, KC JP, who was concerned that they had over thirty conscientious objection appeals to deal with that day.

> 'A Son of God' scorned at Chelmsford
>
> Ronald James Young, certificated teacher, Chelmsford, unattested, said he could not be incriminated in the military machine which

existed for the prosecution of the war. He believed that warfare was contrary to the life and teaching of Christ and the higher instincts of man, and he must refuse to aid in any way the prosecution of the war. He made conscience the sole basis of his objection. The Local Tribunal had exempted Young from combatant service. Mr. Young now stated that the Local Tribunal did not question him on the fact of his being a Pacifist.

This time Young was given rough treatment and the Tribunal challenged him robustly on his definitions of pacifism, on his Christianity, his attitude to war and those fighting it, and his contribution to the national effort through teaching. The appeal was dismissed.

> Young: I should like to say I still intend to carry out my views.
> Chairman: That is a matter we have no jurisdiction over.

On 8 May Young was arrested in New Street by Inspector Jacob, as an absentee under the Military Service Act. The next day he was taken before Chelmsford magistrates. When searched he was found in possession of the exemption from combatant service issued on 6 March. He claimed that he had received letters to report for duty but had sent them back. Captain Smith, the recruiting officer, showed a letter from Young stating 'I have no intention of obeying that call or any subsequent order of the military authorities,' and adding that he would keep the captain informed of his movements during and after the summer holidays, which he would spend at his home in Sandown, Isle of Wight. He told the court that he was intending to appeal to the Central Tribunal, having discovered that under Section 3 of the Act he could ask for the case to be reviewed, especially where there were any new facts. These were that he had learned that the Pelham Committee (the Committee on Work of National Importance) had decided that teaching was a work of national importance; and also he would like to show his card in which he explains his reasons for being a sincere objector. He had filled in the appeal application form but since his arrest had been unable to submit it to the Town Clerk.

Captain Smith objected to the application as there were no grounds for his case. Young warned 'what is the use of having a man like me in the Army when I don't intend to carry out any order? I should benefit the country more by being in school than in the Army.'

The bench decided to put the case back to the Petty Session on Friday, and requested that Captain Smith clarify the point about the teaching profession being work of national importance. Young was released on £10 bail. On 12 May it was clear that Young had done some homework and he claimed that he should be discharged under Clause 3, Section 1 of the Military Service Act, under which a person's certificate may be reviewed by the Local Tribunal, the person not to be called to the Colours until the application is disposed of (this was not strictly correct, as the Act said nothing about the man remaining in civilian life while his case is reviewed).

Captain Smith submitted that the circumstances had not in any way materially changed since the case was before the Tribunal. He had taken instructions from the War Office and they reminded him of the Army Council Instructions – teachers (or indeed any man) would not be accepted unless they were certified by a Medical Board as fit for general service. If Young was fit for general service he would be taken and if he was not he would probably be returned to his teaching. The 'defendant was an absentee pure and simple'.

Young argued that teaching had been included in the list of works which in certain circumstances were of national importance, and he went on to explain that the Ventnor (Isle of Wight) Tribunal, instead of simply exempting a unattested single man from combatant service, they exempted him from military service provided he undertook one of the works of national importance. Young's point was that he was already doing such work, and that the tribunal could exempt him on that basis. The bench were unable to agree, and they fined him £2 and handed him over to the military authorities.

Somehow Young's application for a variation of his certificate ended up back at the Local Tribunal on 15 May 1916 but he did not attend. The matter of his work being of national importance had been referred to the Local Government Board, but the tribunal heard that he was now in the hands of the military and had gone to Warley. By the following Monday the tribunal had heard from the Local Government Board, who simply reiterated that it was lawful for a man to request a review of his certificate and the Local Tribunal could accept or reject it. The Pelham Committee had sent a list of occupations of national importance, but regretted that they were unable to advise on cases involving conscientious objection. Despite this advice, the tribunal invited Young to send in a further application. On 29 May they received another letter, from Warley Barracks, in which he set out the grounds for his appeal:

1. That since my hearing education has been officially recognised by the Board of Trade Committee as a work of national importance, and this, I contend, strengthens my case for absolute exemption.
2. I realised, and stated publicly, that I should cause trouble to Army officials because of my principles. This has resulted, and the officers here will only be pleased to be relieved of the duty of having to endeavour to persuade genuine pacifists to adopt a course of action against the dictates of their consciences.
3. Although I realise by my present course of action I am helping to forward the cause of peace, yet it is a matter of regret to me that I have been forcibly prevented from following a profession which I believe is rendering a valuable service to humanity.
4. My sincerity as an objector was recognised and stated in writing by the Local Tribunal, and yet my sincerity in asking for absolute exemption, the only relief I can conscientiously accept was denied. This seems to me illogical. I am now awaiting trial by court-martial, and am prepared to accept the consequences if you refuse to grant the application. In event of your refusing I should like to appear in person and argue my case.'

The Clerk said that the Local Government Board stated that a Local Tribunal could consider an application such as the present one if 'further and better grounds' were advanced for it. The Tribunal decided that there were no such grounds and finally dismissed the application. It is difficult to suggest that the Local Tribunal sympathised with Ronald Young, but his case is not marked by the hostility and ridicule which marks so many of the other conscientious objection hearings of the time. Young was an 'absolutist', and a certificate of exemption from combatant service was not sufficient – he wanted a full certificate of exemption from any service, non-combatant or otherwise, without conditions. The matter did not end immediately, however, in July he wrote again asking for a review and the tribunal, incredibly, allowed him three days to state his case in writing. His address was given as the Royal Fusiliers Depot, at Happy Valley in Shoreham. The letter from the tribunal was returned, marked 'Gone to France'.

His Army records show that following his brief sojourn at Warley he was assigned to No. 3 Eastern Company of the Non-Combatant Corps and was sent to join them as part of 16th Battalion Royal Fusiliers in Shoreham, in October 1916. No. 3 Company NCC were themselves based in France, but a letter sent concerning Young to Henriville Camp in Boulogne was returned 'as the soldier referred to is unknown in this Company of the NCC', so it may be that Young did not leave England. He was relegated to the Class B Army Reserve – effectively a discharge – on 31 October 1916, and sent a rather plaintive letter to Chelmsford Council asking to be allowed to return as an Assistant Teacher. At the Finance & General Purposes Subcommittee on 14 November they considered his request and made a terse comment to the Education Committee: 'Your subcommittee do not feel able to recommend Mr Young's reinstatement.' Young found employment at the Friends' School in Great Ayton, North Yorkshire, where he spent the rest of the war.

Conscription affected people at all levels of Chelmsford society. On 6 March 1916, at the very first session of the Local Tribunal at which Young and the other teachers appeared, Fred Spalding appealed on behalf of his son, Fred Spalding junior, 25 and single, who was the manager at their photography shop at 4-5 High Street. At the Derby Scheme tribunal in January he had been put back ten groups 'on account of his photographic work for the Government and Government-controlled firms'. Spalding senior was of course an alderman, and the tribunal was made up of Alderman Taylor, Alderman Thompson, Alderman Chancellor, and Councillor Dixon. The tribunal retired for 'an interview in private' with the father and agreed to a temporary exemption for one month. Following a further hearing at the end of March Spalding junior appealed to the County Tribunal in Romford, which in July agreed to give a conditional exemption on the grounds of financial hardship and national service. The military successfully appealed his exemption in December 1916, and he joined the Artists' Rifles and was later commissioned in the Royal Flying Corps.

In June 1916 Herbert Gripper, the special constable, represented his father's firm (J Gripper Iron Merchants) at an appeal on behalf of

William Edwards, 7 Bradford Street, who delivered goods to blacksmiths, wheelwrights and builders in the county. Gripper had already lost seven men and Edwards was the only one left, and irreplaceable. Captain Smith was convinced and the tribunal agreed to a conditional exemption. Alderman Thompson sat on the tribunal in December 1916 at which his own company (Meggy, Thompson & Creasey, owners of the *Chronicle*), appealed on behalf of two of their employees, Mr Harold Cowper, who was their representative in Brentwood and South Essex and who obtained a temporary exemption with leave to appeal again, and Albert Rippingale of 10 Manor Road, store hand and head of dispatch room. Captain Smith agreed that this was a reserved occupation.

In one hearing in November 1916 the Chelmsford Star Co-operative Society appealed on behalf of forty-two of its employees. Seven were dismissed, two were over age, seven were medically rejected, two had joined the Army, and seven were to be released for service. The rest secured conditional exemptions, which led to a heated argument between Councillor Dixon and the military representative Captain Smith, in which Dixon took issue with the apparent ease with which Smith agreed to exemptions, apparently having so far agreed to over 1,500 in Chelmsford and District. In his defence Smith mentioned that there was to be a review of exemptions granted to those under thirty years of age, but Dixon had clearly showed that he was not going to be easily convinced.

By 1917 all exemptions were carefully reviewed and all men holding certificates were required to be medically examined and graded according to the military system. The classification scheme used from 1 July 1916 was as follows:

'Route March': a sketch of a soldier in Chelmsford by Edward Prust, a student at the School of Science and Art. [author's collection]

A. Able to march, see to shoot, hear well and stand active service conditions
    1. Fit for dispatching overseas, as regards physical and mental health and training
    2. As 1, except for training
    3. Returned Expeditionary Force men, ready except for physical condition
    4. Men under 19 who would be Grade A1 or A2 when 19

B. Free from serious organic diseases, able to stand service on the lines of communication in France, or in garrisons in the tropics
    1. Able to march five miles, see to shoot with glasses, and hear well
    2. Able to walk five miles, see and hear sufficiently for ordinary purposes
    3. Only suitable for sedentary work

C. Free from serious organic disease, able to stand service conditions in garrison at home
    1. As B1
    2. As B2
    3. As B3

D. Unfit but likely to become fit within six months
    1. Regular RA, RE, infantry in command depots
    2. Regular RA, RE, infantry in regimental depots
    3. Men in any depot or unit awaiting treatment

E. Unfit and unlikely to become fit within 6 months

The fitness classification influenced the tribunal's attitude to the appeal. The tribunal in Chelmsford in April 1917 considered twenty-eight renewals of conditional exemptions granted to men under 31 years of age and the list included:

Ropemaker's works manager, age 30, class A; butcher 22, B2; cinema manager 30, A; solicitor's clerk 26, A; clerk 23, A; confidential clerk 28, A; ironmonger's assistant 29, A; butcher's manager 27, A; grocery manager 27, A.

The military authorities put great pressure on the tribunals to make sure that exemptions were not granted unnecessarily. At the same hearing a firm of provision merchants appealed for a director, 27 A; a despatch hand, 30 C1; a provision hand, 26 B1; and a storeman, 29 A. They employed nine men over military age, and nine men under, eight of whom were class A. Captain Smith was deeply unhappy and had the matter put back for a week so that he could investigate and review all the cases of men of military age in the firm's employment.

In late April 1917 the *Chronicle* published a letter from a soldier in the Royal Marines Light Infantry, home on leave:

> I was disgusted on a recent visit to my old home at Chelmsford to see so many young men younger than I am (and I am now 36 years of age) who were clerks and shop assistants for a considerable time after war broke out, and who are now exempted. I know of several who have entered munitions factories to escape the Military Service Act. Can men become efficient mechanics in a few months? And how many men of military age have been allowed to do part-time work? If necessary I will forward you their names.

The National Service Volunteer scheme introduced in early 1917 introduced a new dimension to the work of the Local Tribunals. The military representative became the National Service Representative (NSR), with a brief not just to get men into military service but, failing that, to have them volunteer for work of National Importance. In November 1917 Frank Gowers, of 24 Cramphorn Road, aged 29 and classed as B2, had previously served in the Army but had been discharged for health reasons. The Tribunal granted him an exemption on the provision he obtained work of national importance. One difficulty at this time was that conditional exemptions had previously been granted because men were undertaking this type of work; from late 1917 a lot of the work of the tribunal was reviewing certificates previously granted and the NSR was particularly keen to 'debadge' the young men working in the reserved occupations.

As late as 30 September 1918 the Chelmsford tribunal was still at work, one of its last cases being the application for the withdrawal of the conditional exemption certificate held by Frederick Clay, a clerk in the service of Essex County Council. Fortunately there had just been another change in the list of certified occupations and Clay remained exempt. On 28 October 1918 the tribunal sat again, to discuss a proposal to amalgamate the Borough and the District Tribunals for reason of economy.

Basil Harrison turned 18 on 23 July 1918 and was summoned to the Drill Hall for a medical examination just three days later. He remembered: 'After a brief look at me the Medical Officer pronounced me A1 and fit for active service. I was "in".' He was ordered to report to the Army tent at the Westfield camp, on Broomfield Road, on Wednesday 7 August. It was late in the afternoon when he and fifteen other 'raw conscripts' were marched down Broomfield Road to the railway station, to be taken on the train to Warley Barracks in Brentwood. He did not see any active service – the war ended before he got to France, and he ended up serving in the British Army occupying the Rhine.

CHAPTER 7

Camps and Airfields

For a week or twa I wasna weel,
sae obeyed the Doctor's orders
An' left the slush at Widford Camp,
an' crossed the Scottish borders.
Company Sergeant Major MacNaught,
King's Own Scottish Borderers, Widford, 1916

The Army has had a long history in Chelmsford. In 1859 the Armoury and Depot of the West Essex Militia was established in the area off Moulsham Street known as Barrack Square, now the site of the Chelmsford Star Co-Operative Stores. The Depot moved in 1879 to the headquarters of the Essex Regiment in Warley Barracks, Brentwood, but on 4 July 1903 Earl Roberts of Kandahar opened a new Drill Hall off Market Road for the peacetime equipment and drill of volunteer units. The site is now under the Royal & Sun Alliance building at the bottom of Victoria Road South. It was described as a fine building, with a great hall one hundred feet by sixty feet. It held a recreation room, stores, an officers' room and a sergeants' room, both with lavatory facilities. The orderly room and armoury were to the left of the front entrance, and the living accommodation of the sergeant-instructor was on the right, consisting of three bedrooms and three downstairs rooms. The building was designed by the firm of Chancellors, with both Frederick Chancellor and his son Wykeham holding Territorial Force ranks.

The military authorities had powers under the Defence of the Realm Act and the Military Lands Act to acquire or requisition land and property for military purposes. The process was supervised by the military land agent, an officer with a legal background who was able to deal with all the issues associated with temporary or permanent property deals. A Colchester solicitor, Henry V MacMaster, was originally a civilian working on behalf of the War Office but was subsequently commissioned into the Army and he oversaw many of the land transactions in the Eastern region from his office at 124 London Road. He also led his own military cricket team. The government took over a number of fields and properties in and around Chelmsford, many of which are recorded in the *List of Land & Buildings in the Occupation of the War Department* and in the advertisements of the Ministry of Munitions Disposal Board in the period August 1919 to April 1921.

On 30 August 1914 there was much excitement in Chelmsford when a naval biplane 'of the Sopwith type' flew over the town at lunchtime and then landed on Baddow Meads. Later the aviator entertained the crowds with a flying display before flying away towards Danbury in the early evening. Whether this was a formal reconnaissance is not known, but within months an airstrip was set up in Springfield. The *Essex Chronicle* published a notice on the 27 November:

> We are requested by the military authorities to state that no persons are permitted to enter the field situated at the back of the police headquarters in Sandford Road, where the military aeroplanes are now located. The police are instructed to arrest any persons, military or civil, found on the field, except members of the Royal Flying Corps. To this order there is absolutely no exception.

Sandford Road formed the northern and eastern boundary, with the prison on the north east, Hill Road on the west and the river to the south. Richard Godfrey remembers the aerodrome and that the aircraft were housed in large tents along Sandford Road. They took off down the slope towards the Baddow Meads and landed in the opposite direction. Trinity Road School, then a very new building, faced over the airfield and there is an anecdote that when the wind was in the right direction the aircraft took off towards the school directly towards the classrooms of Standards III and IV, and that the children hid under their desks as the aircraft flew past their windows.

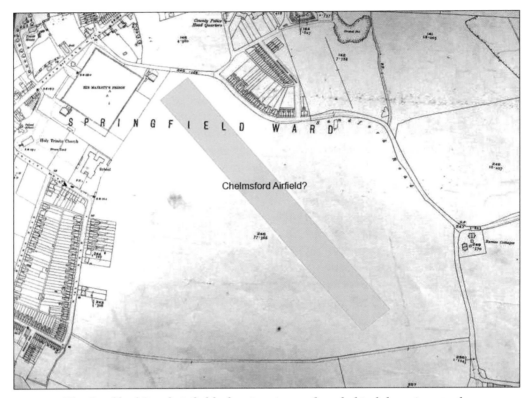

*The Sandford Road airfield: the airstrip ran from behind the prison to the
bottom right of the map*

In the *Official History of the Great War: The War in the Air* it is
recorded that two aircraft were required to be held in operational
readiness in Chelmsford. In the Zeppelin raid of 17 August 1915 in
which the two bombs were dropped on the town, both aircraft were
sent up. Flight Sub-Lieutenant CD Morrison and his observer Flight
Sub-Lieutenant HH Square managed to see the airship but then lost it.
On return to the airfield they accidentally dropped one of their own
bombs on landing, injuring the pilot.

There is documentary evidence to suggest that the Sandford Road
airfield was operated as a Royal Naval Air Station for a period in 1915.
It is more correctly described as a substation, the main flight being

initially Hendon but subsequently Chingford. A Royal Navy report recorded it as an aeroplane station, with shed, petrol store, magazine, and it had cost £2,450 to construct, in the accounts up to 1915. The shed was 70 feet long, 70 feet wide, and 16 feet high. It was used for training purposes and under the Navy's invasion and evacuation plans was graded as a List C station, which meant that it was 'of minor importance for which [defence] provision should be made on completion of defences of stations in Lists A and B'. It did not feature in the list of night landing grounds nor was it used for naval airships. A memo from the Naval Director of Air Services in January 1916 mentioned that it was probable that Chelmsford 'would be abandoned as an air station in the near future'; and it does not appear in a list of air fields operated by the 9th Wing of the Royal Flying Corps in September 1916, which listed nearby sites such as Goldhangar and Stow Maries.

There is an aerial photograph taken over Chelmsford in 1926 which seems to show a grass airstrip around 300 yards long by 50 yards wide,

Aerial photograph of Chelmsford airfield. [English Heritage EPW016554]

in the area off Sandford Road area and suggesting that it might still have been in use at that time.

The location of a military airfield within a mile of the town centre seems to have attracted little attention. In November 1914 a flying accident was recorded, when one of the biplanes struck some ploughed earth on landing, and the aircraft overturned. The propeller was smashed but there was no injury to the two man crew. In December another accident occurred, when a 200 hp Maurice Farman biplane flown by Lieutenant Murray and Captain Milne RFC, crashed from a height of forty feet. The men were taken to Chelmsford Hospital. The next month an aircraft from Chelmsford suffered engine failure and came down in a field at Rochetts in South Weald. Although the airmen managed to repair the engine they crashed on take off, wrecking the aircraft. A further incident was recalled in the *Book of Chelmsford* when another aeroplane crashed at the end of St Margaret's Road (probably where the allotments are now) in the early summer of 1916. The pilot had landed safely in the field, which was carrying a crop of wheat. A low hedge obstructed his intended take off path, so he rounded up help from among the onlookers and they broke down the foliage. His attempt to take off across the soft field ended in disaster, again with the aircraft overturning and smashing the propeller. As happened elsewhere, a broken aeroplane was seen as public property and the machine was stripped by souvenir hunters. In 1917 Captain Cotterall was reported as being in Chelmsford Hospital with a fractured jaw and other injuries caused by his aircraft falling from a height of 200 feet.

Early military aviation was still an experimental and hazardous affair. Technical and meteorological difficulties could force an aircraft down at any time, and in anticipation of such problems the authorities identified suitable sites as landing grounds. These were simply equipped with a windsock, a shed or two to store aviation fuel and oil, and perhaps a telephone. Importantly the locations were known to both the airmen and to the local Royal Flying Corps or Royal Naval Air Service detachment. Aircraft in trouble could find a safe, prepared area to land, and the ground crew would know where to find them. The Royal Naval Air Service set up a landing ground in Widford in December 1914 and closed it in September the following year. There was a fifty-four acre landing ground in the fields to the west of Lawford Lane in Writtle, operated by No. 1 Reserve Squadron between

December 1914 and November 1916. Broomfield Court was a thirty-six acre second class RFC landing ground and was operational from 1916 to 1919. This may be the same location as the airfield to the south of Broomfield Hall (now Broomfield Hospital) which went on to become the home of a civilian flying club in the period between the wars. Gilbert Torry, in *Chelmsford Through The Ages*, mentions an airfield or landing ground in the 'fields on the left-hand side of [Pump] lane going towards Broomfield'.

The other side of Sandford Road (now Kingston Crescent and Kingston Avenue) had been used as an infantry training ground and firing range long before the war. A network of trenches was constructed across the field and, as described in the *History of Chelmsford*, 'in between the trenches sacks were filled with straw, hung on wire between upright wooden posts cemented into the ground at intervals across the field to the hedge bounding the field – now part of the Police Headquarters Sports Ground. The first trench was close to the hedge by Sandford Road near a beautiful old oak tree; it has long since been cut down and the space occupied by the garden of 103 Sandford Road.'

Little record survives of specific defence installations but there are suggestions that there were anti-aircraft batteries near Writtle and in Broomfield, and there was a searchlight and 'gun park' in Fryerning Road in Ingatestone. A mobile anti-aircraft gun and searchlight sub-station was located in Chelmsford, possibly associated with the Sandford Road airfield. It comprised a number of high angle machine guns and a 1lb pom-pom. These defences were described as ineffective but the Zeppelin crews did attempt to avoid the town.

There were several military camps around the town and the term is somewhat vague. Generally speaking the camps were comprised of huts, particularly towards the end of the war. The camps had a variety of functions, from military training to storage, and may or may not have had sleeping accommodation or messing or dining facilities. Many men lived in billets off camp, and would have made their way home at the end of each day, with a small number of men remaining behind on guard duty. Certainly confirmation that these sites existed and were of a semi-permanent nature comes from the Council's Sewer and Water Supply Committee, which recorded the installation of water pipes and meters for all of the camps and buildings mentioned here. Unfortunately, as so often happens, a description such as 'Widford

Essex Territorial camp in the Recreation Ground before the war.
[Reproduced by courtesy of the Essex Record Office ERO T/Z 297/1]

Camp' would have been so well known that further details are not provided. There were temporary, tented camps set up at various times: there are photographs of a number of such camps on the Recreation Ground and Admiral's Park for occasions such as the inspection of the Volunteers by Lord French in February 1917.

The Army took over 'Brooklands', 'Martells' and 'Brownings', large houses on Broomfield Road. Marconi's had constructed a wireless station at the top of Pottery Lane, off Broomfield Road, in 1902 and this was used by the Royal Navy and later the Army. Known as the Marconi Camp, in 1916 it was defined as a 'vulnerable point' and was home to a Protection Company of the Royal Defence Corps. A military camp was erected on Westfield on Broomfield Road, adjacent to the King Edward's School and extending over what is now Westfield Avenue. There was an Army Service Corps Forage Depot across the road (on the site of the John Henry Keene Memorial Homes), which extended down to the end of Henry Road. It contained a large stable block, which caused occasional annoyance to the gardeners of the Bishop's Hall allotments when the horses broke out (although the abundant supply of horse manure was probably adequate compensation). This was on the field behind the Anglia Ruskin University. In February 1916 the Town Clerk had to write to the military authorities about damage to crops from horses straying from adjoining land.

There was a Royal Engineers unit based in the New Street Huts, now the parade of shops between Bishop Road and Marconi Road. The RE District Officer occupied the New Street Maltings, as well as the

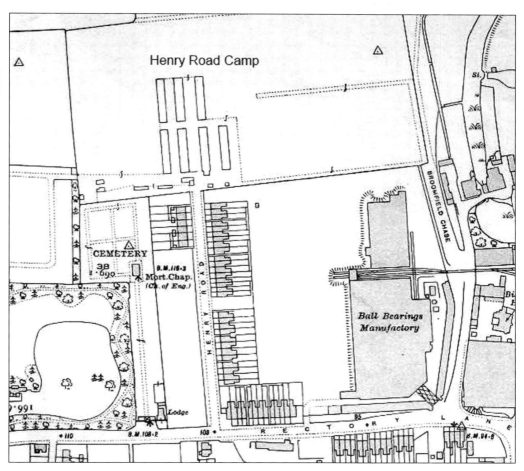

Henry Road Army Service Corps camp.

Lion & Lamb Hotel and an office at 69 Duke Street. The land at the north end of the new development of St. Fabian's Drive (now the grounds of the former St Peter's College) was used by the Army, and they also negotiated an agreement for the use of the Council's land in a field off Roxwell Road, next to the water works in Admiral's Park, at £5 per annum. This camp, now the bowling green and tennis courts, was the centre of an argument in June 1917, when it was noticed that excavations had taken place and it subsequently transpired that the men

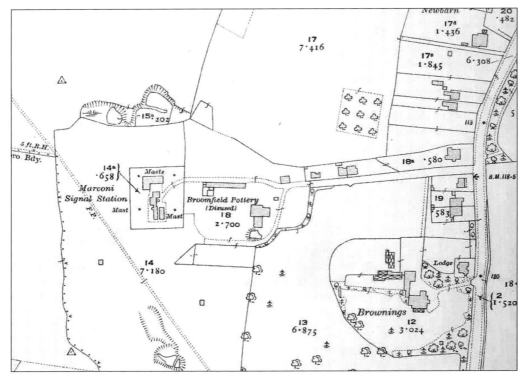

Marconi Camp, at the top of Pottery Lane.

of 220 Infantry Brigade had been removing large quantities of sand for use in sandbags at the rifle range in Boreham, urgently required for repairing damaged fire trenches. A financial settlement was reached, but this part of the park still retains a sculpted landscape. An account from King Edward's School records the presence of trenches in Rainsford End, which would fit with a large camp at this site.

There is a reference to another Army Service Corps supply depot at Anchor Street, and there was a Forage and Chaffing depot on Fairfield Road, probably in the area of the bus station. It was used by the 2/8th Battalion Royal Scots before their departure to France at the start of 1917. The ASC also requisitioned the Baddow Road Maltings as a Repair Depot, the Picture Palace on Springfield Road and the

Springfield Maltings. The men of the ASC lived in barracks at the Skating Rink at 113 London Road.

Herbert Bohannan recalled the Army in a park on Springfield Road between Navigation Road and Weight Road, which was known locally as Gripper's Park, after the family who lived in the big house on the corner of Weight Road (Special Constable Gripper's parents). There was a substantial ordnance depot at the nearby Albert Ironworks.

A camp was also set up in Widford in an area now covered by the industrial park. It must have been fairly substantial as Mr Picken not only set up a canteen for the troops there, but he also had to recruit two young saleswomen to help out. The battalion quartermaster was based in the Widford Parish Hall. Company Sergeant Major George McNaught, of the King's Own Scottish Borderers, was a regular contributor of fairly dire poetry written in the Scottish brogue to the columnist behind 'Reflexions by Reflex' in the *Essex Newsman*, and in one case he bemoans the fact that he is still 'up here in Widford Camp, amang the slush an' mud an' damp'. The conditions did not suit him, and he was sent home on medical leave for a while:

'For a week or twa I wasna weel, sae obeyed the Doctor's orders
An' left the slush at Widford Camp, an' crossed the Scottish borders'

It is likely that this camp extended north from Widford and across the Writtle Road, as a Council minute of 27 March 1918 refers to the potential for allotments on the 'grass field on the north side of Writtle Road (recently vacated by the military authorities)'. The Army is known to have used large parts of the Hylands estate at various times.

Very early in the war, in September 1914, the Royal Artillery established what became a substantial camp at Great Baddow, in the area of Vicarage Lane and what is now Park View Crescent up to Colley Road. The camp had an additional use after the war, when it was used as a convalescent hospital for soldiers returning from various parts of the Empire suffering from malaria. The Artillery also used the grandstand of the Galleywood racecourse for accommodation and stores.

Other camps were on Arbour Lane, somewhere in the fields between the railway and the Tulip Inn; and Springfield Road, which is

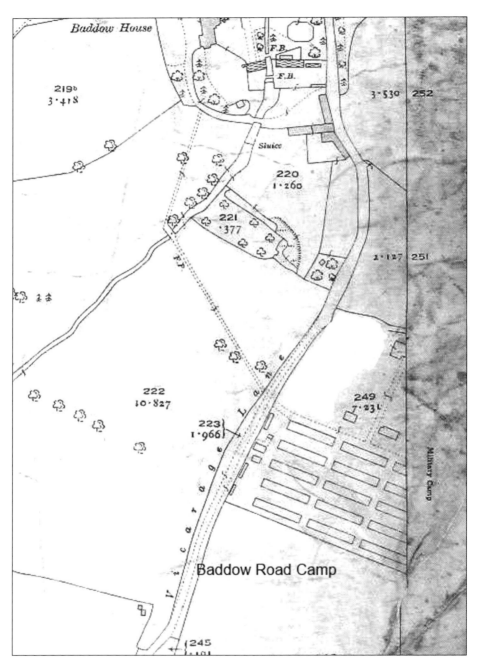

Great Baddow camp.

most likely to have been the pre-war Sandford Road range as extended during the war. The use of Oaklands House, Hylands House, Skreens Park and Kenilworth as military hospitals and convalescent homes will be discussed separately.

Boreham House was the home of the Central Quartering Committee under Colonel Sherer, which dealt with all aspects of the billeting of troops in Chelmsford and the surrounding area. When the 73rd Division arrived in Essex in 1917 they used it as their headquarters.

Within Chelmsford the military took over several buildings as offices, such as 4 King Edward Avenue and 42 London Road and most notably the Saracen's Head, which was used as the headquarters of the South Midland Division. In April 1915 Major General Heath presented the landlord and his wife, Mr & Mrs Haylock, with a handsome silver salver, George III style, with the inscription

> Presented to Mr & Mrs Haylock, of the Saracen's Head Hotel, Chelmsford, by Major General H N C Heath CB, and the officers, headquarters staff, 1st South Midland Division, as a token of their appreciation of the courtesy and civility shown by them and the patriotic manner in which the entire accommodation of the hotel was given up for the Headquarters of the Division from August 1914 to March 1915.

There were some less pleasant aspects of the military presence: in October of 1914 the Sanitary Officer of South Midland Division requested closet access for soldiers on guard duties at Railway Arches. In the words of Dr Newton, the Medical Officer of Health for the borough: 'I would also recommend that the accumulated excrement in a corner under one of those Arches should at once be removed.' The Council suggested that soldiers use public conveniences in Viaduct Road and near Railway Arches in the Recreation Grounds. They could also use the facilities of the National Steam Car Garage, also under the Arches.

As the demand for manpower in the Army grew in the first months of the war, magistrates and judges were respectfully prevailed upon to avoid giving custodial sentences to otherwise fit and healthy young men and, with many of the 'criminal classes' joining up voluntarily, in a short space of time the prison population began to shrink. Chelmsford

Gaol, built in 1830 to serve the county, and with a capacity of 300, had a population of between twenty and eighty by the middle of 1915. It was decided to hand over the accommodation to the military authorities and the last inmates were removed on 3 July 1915, transferring to Pentonville, Ipswich and Cambridge, and a number of the prison staff being similarly dispersed for the duration. The Army was to use it as a detention centre for British soldiers under punishment and also for prisoners of war convicted of military offences. The Governor, Mr FWH Blake, became the Military Commandant and the War Office confirmed on him his previous military rank of major. The prison was the setting for an audacious escape. On Whit Sunday, 27 May 1917, Leutnant Otto Thelen, who had previously escaped from two other camps, and Leutnant Emil Lehmann, were reported missing. This caused immense excitement in Chelmsford and the district, with military, regular and special police, and even boy scouts forming search parties. Richard Godfrey's father was a special constable and he remembers him being called out to hunt for the escaped Germans and returning home late that night, 'with his thick boots worn right through with the tramping around the district'. The two men were recaptured by a party of Army Cyclist Corps near Billericay around 5 am the following morning. Chelmsford Prison continued to be used by the War Office until 1919 and was eventually reopened as a civilian prison in 1930.

CHAPTER 8

Trade and Industry

I am glad to note that the girls, God bless 'em, have taken
to munition making like the young ducks, as they are, to water.
I hear that in many cases young shop ladies are even on the job,
and, instead of measuring tape and calico and selling the
last word in Parisian fashions, they are measuring up and
fixing munition material like experts. And, between us, they
can help the Tommies, who they love so well, a lot in that way.
More power to 'em.
Reflexions by Reflex, 1916

According to MR Davies and JB Lane, in *A Survey of Industrial Development in Chelmsford*, there is no economic reason to explain why Chelmsford was the home of so many large industrial concerns. The first of these was perhaps the Broomfield Road Ironworks, set up in the 1860s and later acquired by James Norris. Fell Christy owned a house and land on the same road and began building wind and water mills and in 1883 his son Frank Christy started a firm which manufactured electrical power installations – generators, lighting, and electrical grinding. A Blue Plaque now marks the site of the works on Broomfield Road. The firms merged into Christy & Norris in the late 1880s but they never achieved the pre-eminence of their Chelmsford rivals at Crompton's Arc Works.

In the south of the borough the firm of THP Dennis began manufacturing mills and engineering equipment, and in the mid-1870s a retired army officer, Colonel R E Crompton joined the firm. A

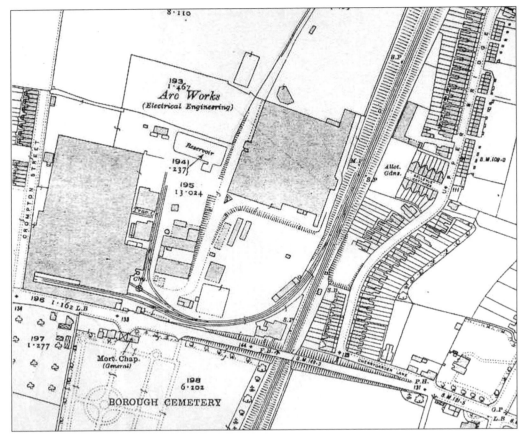

Crompton's Arc Works.

visionary engineer, he believed in the potential of electric lighting and set about improving the technology used at the time. In 1878 he bought out the Dennis interest to form Crompton & Co. His first factory was in Anchor Street (also now commemorated with a Blue Plaque), and he and his firm pioneered arc and incandescent light bulbs, and a range of dynamos, electrical motors and other electrical equipment. After a disastrous fire on 23 November 1895 the Arc Works moved to new premises on the Waterhouse Farm estate on Writtle Road, complete with its own railway siding.

The War Office was interested in the company's research into searchlights and in 1912 they held a demonstration of their latest product in front of military officials:

> The new [searchlight] units for field service comprise wagons, one carrying the engine, dynamo and switchboard, another carrying the projector, cable and accessories, and others supplying two collapsible towers. These towers are unique... when erected they have a height of over 40 feet.

Crompton dined the War Office representatives at the Chelmsford Club on New London Road while his men erected the equipment in the yard. He had obtained the services of the Essex Fortress Engineers (Territorials) who set themselves up in Admiral's Park and the men were easily viewed from the top floor of the club almost a mile away. The searchlights were then played around the night sky, and it was reported that the beams were distinctly seen as far away as Ingatestone.

The Hoffmann Manufacturing Company was established in New Street in 1898 and manufactured ball and roller bearings to an astonishing accuracy (1/10,000 of an inch), which were a vital component of all forms of machinery. Again, the reason why a firm so heavily dependent on steel and coal should establish itself in Chelmsford is not clear. Even with ready access to the railway – they had their own light railway and marshalling yards (now in the waste ground off Brook Street) – transport of raw materials and of finished product to and from the industrial heartlands of the north of England was expensive. At the outbreak of war they employed around 1,800 workers.

Guglielmo Marconi came to Chelmsford in 1898, apparently under the impression that the flat land of Essex would allow his radio waves to travel further. He set up a factory in an old silk mill on Hall Street, with a 180 foot mast. The Marconi Wireless Telegraph Company was both a manufacturer of wireless equipment but at the same time a laboratory, working at the leading edge of radio research. After a brush with bankruptcy, the firm's fortunes changed with the appointment of Godfrey Isaacs as the chairman. With a near monopoly on maritime wireless, the demand forced Marconi's to look for a new site, and they built a factory on New Street in 1912, including a pair of 450 foot masts

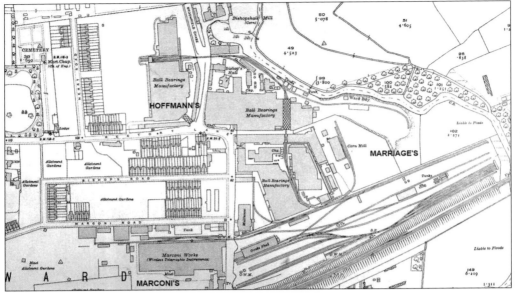

The great factories of Hoffmann's and Marconi's on New Street

Marconi's factory and signal station on Hall Street

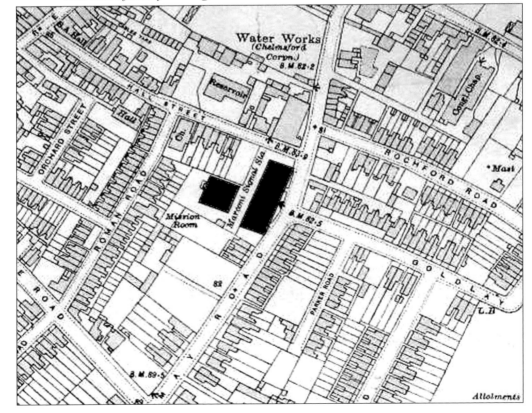

Early photograph of Hoffmann's Works. [Author's collection]

which were a very visible feature of the town. With the technology of the time, one mast was used for transmitting signals and the other for receiving, and they reported wireless contact with their remote station situated at Poldhu, in Cornwall, some 275 miles away, which subsequently became the base for transatlantic communications, and to Clifden, in Galway. They also tested devices for wireless telephony, broadcasting speech from Chelmsford to Bournemouth. The firm built an experimental wireless station at the top of Pottery Lane, off Broomfield Road, now under the area of 57 Sunrise Avenue, with four 110' masts and a staff of fifty wireless engineers.

Thomas Clarkson was an engineer who believed passionately in the future of steam driven vehicles: cars, buses and lorries. From the outset it is important to put away the stereotype of the steam traction engine, seen at county shows and steam fairs today. In appearance a Clarkson omnibus was no different to its petrol engined equivalent, and was considerably quieter (a steam bus can be seen today carrying holiday makers in the town of Whitby). Clarkson used two methods of generating steam, one involving a kerosene fired burner, and the other, after a lot of development, granulated coke.

Marconi's on New Street, with the 450' masts. Note the railway trucks in the foreground. [Kingsway, author's collection]

Although Clarkson achieved good publicity when he drove Field Marshal Lord Roberts from the opening ceremony of the Drill Hall in 1903 to the railway station – the soldier learning that this would be 'a rapid and most comfortable means of conveying wounded soldiers from the battlefield' – the steam car never really took hold of the public's interest, as the internal combustion engine was capable of higher speeds. Clarkson instead focussed on motor transport, of people and goods, in which, in an era of poor roads where a top speed of fourteen mph was considered almost reckless, economy and efficiency were the key factors. He calculated that petrol, at 1s 4d per gallon, would give 3.1 ton miles to the penny, and with graded coke at 16s a ton, he could get 11.6 ton miles to the penny. The running costs for the petrol vehicle would be £193/year, and his steam lorry would be £52/year. After several years of investment and development, 1914 promised to be a good year for the company and Clarkson attracted a lot of interest from the motoring press. He provided steam buses to the London bus companies, ran his own routes and he provided bus services in Chelmsford – in fact at his annual shareholders' meetings there was constant criticism that they could not decide if they were in the business of providing passenger services or if they were an engineering concern.

Another major engineering concern was the Crown Works on New London Road (now Greenwood House), owned by HM Budgett. which was involved in the manufacture of generators and instrumentation.

As a market town Chelmsford had a wide range of small retailers and businesses; some of which, such Marriage's, Gepp & Sons Solicitors and Lucking's Funeral Directors, are still in existence today. The Munnion Brothers, at 11 Springfield Road, were one of several motor body and carriage builders in the town.

The Chelmsford Star Co-operative Society, founded in 1867, was one of the largest suppliers of food and goods in the town and, although not taken into Government control, its operations were as much affected by the war as any of the industrial concerns. By the summer of 1914 it had its central stores in Moulsham Street (still there), with No 1 Branch Store in Wells Street, No 2 Branch Store in Springfield Road, an Outfitting Department on Baddow Road, a Machine Bakery at Railway Street, and a Coal Depot on New Street. It had 124

Munnion's motor works. [courtesy Robin Tippler]

Marriage's flour mill. [courtesy Robin Tippler]

employees, 3,680 members, and the annual turnover was £22,006. At the start of the war a number of employees were called up and, as with most employers, a grant was paid to the families of these men, amounting to around £77 by the time the scheme was withdrawn when conscription started in 1916. It was only at this time that the Co-op started taking on women workers, initially with a handful of shop assistants but by 1918 there were fifty-five women, working in every department. By the end of the war it had increased membership to 4,350, with 138 employees, and had forty-nine men in the Forces. Throughout the war the Society struggled to manage its supply chain; it was ethically committed to charging reasonable prices for its members and so was very resistant to cost increases, which meant that suppliers would often sell their goods to other retailers who were more prepared to pass on price rises to their customers. The Co-operative recognised the problems in ensuring equitable distribution of supplies to members and had introduced a form of rationing in its stores some time before the official scheme commenced in 1918 and continued to exercise food control by implementing a card system for non-rationed but scarce foodstuffs such as cheese, lard, and jam.

The Great Eastern Railway was central to the big industrial firms and to the daily life of many in Chelmsford. Then, as now, hundreds of clerks, writers, and accountants made the daily commute into the City of London, and the Essex County Council and the Essex Territorial Association regularly met at River Plate House, in Finsbury Circus, just outside Liverpool Street station. Slightly north of Chelmsford station there were extensive marshalling yards, which were accessed by a track descending from the main line. The yards were accessed from New Street (now the Brook Street area), and contained numerous sidings, sheds and cattle pens. There were also two ramps just beyond the station which led down to street level. Both can still be seen: the one at the end of Platform 1 (the up line, towards London) runs down to New Street behind Victoria Road (this was blocked off during the war when a platform extension was built); and the other at the end of Platform 2, across to Mill Road; it is likely that this is the ramp known as the 'milk cart ramp', later used for unloading casualties from the hospital trains coming from London onto the waiting motor transport.

At the outbreak of war the railways were immediately taken into government control under existing legislation (section 16 of the

Extension to Chelmsford Station Platform 1. [Edwin A Pratt, British Railways and the Great War, 1921]

Regulation of the Forces Act 1871), and as a result of some extremely sophisticated pre-war planning the massive troop movements around the country in August were very smoothly executed. The railways were seen as vulnerable points and were guarded and patrolled by men of the Class II National Reserve. The Great Eastern Railway maintained a normal timetable as well as providing additional freight and passenger services. In 1916 the GER reported that it was running 230 extra trains a week, or thirty-two per day, exclusively for military purposes and, in a widely quoted interview published in an American journal, the management claimed that 278 trains, carrying around 75,000 passengers, arrived at Liverpool Street station between 6 am and 9.30 am each morning. According to NetworkRail, the number of passengers today is the same!

All four of the Chelmsford industrial concerns were taken over by the military authorities in the first week of August under the provisions of the Defence of the Realm Act (1914). The first version of the legislation was rather vague and simply enabled the Government to 'issue regulations… for securing the public safety and the defence of the realm', which in simple terms meant ordering firms to direct their output to the government. Firms engaged in such business were often described as being in 'government work'; more commonly known as munitions. This latter term often causes some confusion: according to the definition used by the Ministry of Munitions Act 1915:

> 7. (1) In this Act the expression 'munitions of war' and the expression 'munitions' mean anything required to be provided for war purposes, and include arms, ammunition, war-like stores or material, and anything required for equipment or transport purposes for or in connection with the production of munitions.

This would therefore cover the switching equipment, dynamos, generators, vacuum tubes, instrumentation, carburettors, valves, ball bearings and so on produced by the local firms. Apart from a brief period, probably in late 1915 following the Shell Shortage Scandal, when Herbert Bohannan recalled Marconi's producing percussion caps for artillery shells, Chelmsford companies were not involved in the manufacture of armaments as such.

Marconi's contribution to the war effort began even before war broke out. The array of enormous radio masts at New Street, Hall Street and Broomfield Road allowed the reception of wireless signals, both from their own transmissions in England and Ireland and also from any other wireless equipment, including that of the German Navy across the other side of the North Sea. Just two days before the outbreak of war one of Marconi's engineers, Maurice Wright, was working on a new receiving circuit at Hall Street when he intercepted what transpired to be German naval wireless signals – in these early days messages were broadcast in the clear, without any coding. In a fascinating story, related in *Marconi's New Street Works*, Wright took the batch of messages to the Works Manager, Andrew Gray, who happened to be a personal friend of Captain Reggie Hall, head of Naval Intelligence. So important was the news that Wright travelled to Liverpool Street station on the footplate of a specially chartered locomotive. Hall 'realised the bonanza in his hands and put Wright to work building a chain of wireless intercept stations for the Admiralty'.

Marconi's New Street works. [Spalding, author's collection]

The Marconi Wireless Telegraph Company Ltd was taken over by the Admiralty immediately the war broke out. The value of wireless communications was already recognised by the War Office and both the Army and Navy were using Marconi equipment of various forms, from portable field units for infantry and cavalry use to larger higher power stations on board ships and in naval installations. Additionally, Marconi was a major provider of trained wireless operators and had established a school 'in Broomfield' prior to the war – this was the Broomfield Road facility. In August 1914 the Chief of the school was seconded to the War Office to set up a large scale wireless training operation at the Crystal Palace. Morse code operators and wireless technicians were also trained at King's College and at Birkbeck College in London.

Marconi's also had a Field Station department, which experimented with air-to-ground wireless, which may explain the rationale for the Royal Naval Air Station at Sandford. The Hall Street site was retained as an experimental works and in wartime it was used as a monitoring station, able to listen in to German wireless transmissions. For a short period in 1914-15 the *Times* and other newspapers carried regular Marconi intercept news reports. Maurice Wright continued working on the development of equipment for the long range eavesdropping of enemy transmissions. During the war they established a number of

Admiralty wireless stations around Britain, including at Aberdeen, York, Flamborough Head and Lowestoft, and an early form of radio direction finding was developed, in which wireless transmissions from Zeppelins were used to track their courses across the North Sea.

Herbert Bohannan lived at 9 Navigation Road and worked at Marconi's from 1911. He started out as a switchboard operator in Hall Street. The term 'munitions work' tends to conjure up images of steam and smoke and factories, but he mentions that among the reserved occupations were men such as French polishers – Marconi wireless sets were mounted in teak cases and for Admiralty work these were highly lacquered. Other equipment was silver plated and the assembly of vacuum tubes and valves was a very delicate operation involving highly skilled technicians.

The Marconi works expanded during the war and in 1916 they had a level crossing built across New Street to connect to the marshalling yards and the railway. With both the Marconi and Hoffmann's works at the end of New Street the transport problems and congestion were a cause of concern throughout the war, in particular the erosion of the road surfaces on New Street and Duke Street (Reflex complained about New Street as 'that... terribly dusty thoroughfare'). At that time the Marconi/Hoffmann site was at the very northern edge of town and the only road access was New Street or Rectory Lane.

Hoffmann's output of ball and roller bearings was seen as so significant for the war effort that in September 1917 the firm was nationalised and, for the remainder of the war, was known as the 'National Ball Bearing Factory'. The workers at Hoffmann's would have identified with the Second World War song by Gracie Fields, making their 'thing-ummy-bobs' by the thousand and with no idea what they would ultimately be used for. The factory expanded across what are now Hoffmann's Way and Bishop Hall Lane (now Anglia Ruskin University), the Bishop Hall itself being used as a mess hall. A Ministry of Munitions Record of Property in 1918 states that the railway sidings were extensively used:

Hoffmann's: [rail]	200 trucks/week in	12 out
traffic capacity	20 lorries in	20 out
Track capacity	27 trucks, leaving siding clear	

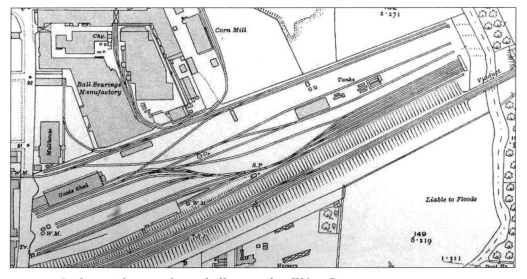

Railway sidings and marshalling yards off New Street.

The 200 trucks per week inbound reflect the large amount of fuel brought in as well as the raw materials.

In December 1914 the *Financial Times* reported that the War Office had purchased thirty of the National Steam Bus Company's omnibus chassis at a 'fair and reasonable price', and that they were manufacturing the Crawley-Boevey 'non-skid device, used extensively by motor vehicles at the front, which allows them to operate on soft ground'. An adaption of snow chains for mud invented by an army transport officer, Clarkson had secured the sole manufacturing rights; but it is not known what became of this contraption. In 1916 JR Anderson designed military bath caravans for troops in France, based around the Clarkson boiler and burner, which at the time was the 'most powerful apparatus for its weight and size for the rapid production of water'. It could fill sixty baths an hour and in fourteen hours of operation provide baths for 800 men (compare this with Chelmsford's slipper baths in 1914 offering 300 baths a week!). It certainly impressed the King and Queen, who saw it demonstrated at Buckingham Palace in December 1916.

One of Clarkson's pet projects was the development of the metal wheel – up to this time cars and lorries tended to have wooden spoked wheels which were rather unreliable. By 1917 he had come up with a casting method for producing wheels for his buses and transport vehicles and in the Anchor Street works he installed an electric steel furnace and foundry for smelting scrap metal. The *Chronicle* was clearly proud to report that Chelmsford steel was being sent to Sheffield (although this was short-lived and contributed to Clarkson's financial problems immediately after the war). Petrol prices rose steeply throughout the war and the economy of the coke fuelled steam engine became more compelling. Again in 1917 the decision was taken to convert the 127-strong fleet of National steam buses in London from kerosene to coke, supported by the claim that two small buckets of coke were sufficient for a twelve mile journey.

Clarkson ran the omnibus service in Chelmsford between 1913 and 1919, and he was one of the first to employ women to take over men's work. Bus conductors were replaced with conductresses in July 1915. They wore the same long white coats and hats as the men and 'the change has hardly been noticed, except by the passengers'. For Miss

A Clarkson Steam Bus, outside Oaklands. [courtesy Robin Tippler]

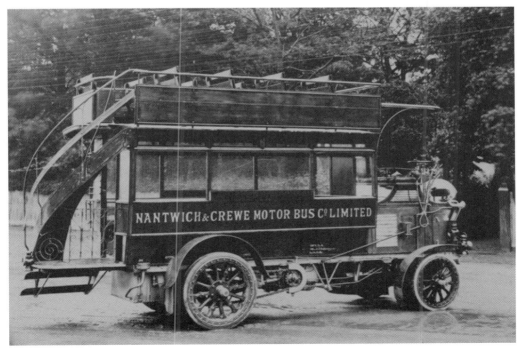

Winifred Trotter (daughter of Mr Stuart Trotter of Broomfield Lodge, and Girl Guide leader) the main reason she wanted to work on the buses was to release men to go to munitions work.

Clarkson operated the following routes in central Essex:

Great Baddow (Blue Lion)	Cherry Tree	Broomfield Lodge	Arbour Lane	St John's Church	Cross Keys, Roxwell	Little Waltham
Danbury (The Bell)	Writtle (Rose and Crown)	Broomfield Green	Stumps Lane	Rising Sun	Fountain, Good Easter	Chatham Green
Danbury (The Griffin)	**Oxney Green (Chequers)**	Little Waltham Corner	Springfield Post Office	Galleywood	**King William IV, Leaden Roding**	St Anne's Castle
Oak Corner	Writtle (Rose and Crown)	**Great Waltham**	**Boreham Cock**	Stock	Fountain, Good Easter	Green Dragon
Maldon (The Swan)	Cherry Tree	Little Waltham Corner	Springfield Post Office	**Billericay**	Cross Keys, Roxwell	**Braintree**
Oak Corner		Broomfield Green	Stumps Lane	Stock		Green Dragon
Danbury (The Griffin)		Broomfield Lodge	Arbour Lane	Galleywood		St Anne's Castle
Danbury (The Bell)				Rising Sun		Chatham Green
Great Baddow (Blue Lion)				St John's Church		Little Waltham
			Chelmsford Railway Station			
1hr 12 mins	51 mins	1hr 8 mins	1hr 2 mins	1 hr	2hrs	2hrs 35 mins

In 1918 the Council agreed to a new fare system proposed by Mr Banks, the traffic manager at Clarkson's, in which travel within the borough was capped at a flat rate of 1d and on the following routes:

Galleywood, Writtle and Widford Route: railway station, Shire Hall, Essex Weekly News office, Springfield Road, Baddow Road, Grove Road, St John's Church, Elm Road, Rising Sun

Broomfield Route: railway station, Broomfield Road corner, Cedar Avenue, Rectory Lane, High School for Girls, Compasses

Boreham Route: railway station, Shire Hall, Essex Weekly News office, Springfield Road, Rosebery Temperance Hotel, Navigation Road, Three Cups Inn, Arbour Lane, Bishop's Court

Baddow Route: railway station, Shire Hall, Essex Weekly News office, Springfield Road, Baddow Road, Van Diemens Road, Beehive Lane.
(The *Essex Weekly News* office was at 26 High Street)

Both before and after the war Hoffmann's printed sales catalogues to promote their products but for security reasons these did not appear during the war. Hoffmann's and Marconi's produced annual financial reports but because of the sensitive nature of their operations the usual discussion of the management's activities and plans was very much curtailed. As commercial operations these firms were guaranteed a market for their products and the government paid sensible prices for them. However, as any business person knows, the certainty of future sales is a useful negotiating tool with suppliers, who might be encouraged to discount their own prices and so increase the profit margin. The government was clearly sensitive to this and in 1915 introduced the Excess Profits Duty in the Finance (No 2) Act. Taking the average of two out of three financial years prior to 1914 as the base, any increase in profit over £200 was subject to the new tax at 50 per cent. For example a firm which calculated its historic profit as £1,000 and now earned £1,300, would have to pay £50 in Excess Profit Duty, as well as any corporation tax due. Introduced in late 1916 it was backdated to the start of the war, which meant that firms had to make substantial provisions to cover what could be large tax liabilities. The base year was reset each year and caused much vexation to the accountants as the tax computations were performed after the financial year end, with the result that annual reports and the directors' meetings with shareholders offered only broad descriptions of the profitability of the company. In 1916 the directors of Crompton's reported a profit of £37,950 after allowing for deductions and charges, but because of the uncertainty over the excess profit tax they did 'not deem it prudent

The Arc Works. [author's collection]

to recommend a dividend on the ordinary shares'. The Star Co-operative Society ended up with an excess profits tax of £391 for the two years to November 1916, and Clarkson declared a 10 per cent dividend at his annual general meeting in January 1917 but also stated that he was 'in negotiations with the Government Departments concerned' in assessing his liability to the excess profits duty.

With the onset of conscription in 1916 there was a constant attrition of skilled manpower away from civilian employment into military service, and even work of a national importance might not prevent a man of military age in good health from having his exemption appealed by Captain Smith at the local military tribunal. To address the continual need for skilled workers and to encourage people to consider work of which they may not previously have been aware, a Government campaign was launched in early 1917 for National Service Volunteers. This appealed to all men up to the age of 61, and to women of any age, to volunteer 'for agriculture, munitions factories, ship-building, government offices, and especially to replace fit men of military age'.

The idea was primarily that of substitution – for example where perhaps a 45-year-old grocer's assistant with eight years of experience of keeping a couple of pigs on his allotment might be better off employed on a farm, which would release a younger, starred man for military service. A National Service Department was created, and Chelmsford fell into G District, with AS Duffield as the honorary secretary. National Service Volunteers would put themselves at the disposal of the Director General for the period of the war 'for allocation to such employment as may be considered necessary by him, every care being taken that a volunteer will be engaged upon work for which he is best suited'. It is not clear if the results of the National Register question relating to secondary employment were used for this, but officials of the Employment Exchanges, local political agents and even teachers were recruited to help canvass for volunteers. A pamphlet was issued, in February 1917, which set out the terms and conditions of service:

> The Volunteer agrees to ... undertake wholetime work of National Importance in the employment of any Government department or other employer named by the Director General of National Service, and to remain in such employment during the War.
>
> i. The rate of wages... will be the current rate of the job or 25s/week, whichever rate is higher.
> ii. Allowances ... a sufficient allowance for travelling expenses (daily); or a free railway warrant to travel to take up employment, and free return when the work is completed, plus a subsistence allowance not exceeding 2s 6d a week, 7 days a week.

It was apparent that National Service Volunteers were not expected to stay in their own communities, unlike the VADs and other volunteer groups. A National Service Week was held in the week commencing Saturday 24 March 1917 with a big parade through the town on 25 March. It is not clear that Chelmsford, with its large factories already given over to munitions work, was particularly concerned about this additional form of service, although Mr H Ostler, of the Star Co-operative Society, is recorded as having left the firm to take up a place at a munitions firm; and Miss Hampshire, a clerk at the Great Eastern Railway goods office, took up an appointment with Hoffmann's.

For those engaged in work of national importance, whether in munitions, agriculture or government work, wages were fixed centrally and were good. Although industrial disputes were rife in the mining and shipbuilding sectors, Chelmsford workers seem to have been reasonably contented. The big factories were heavily unionised and the local Trades' and Labour Council was primarily concerned with opposing profiteering and ensuring worker representation on the many committees that dominated civil life, such as the War Relief Fund, Food Control and War Pensions. This was not always accepted and as late as October 1917 the secretary, Mr JW Austin, had to write a letter to the *Chronicle* explaining what the Trades' Council was, and that it represented some 2,000 members in Chelmsford alone. They demonstrated their solidarity with the agricultural workers in a big demonstration held in Chelmsford in June 1918, but the event was actually organised by the National Union of Railwaymen. By the end of the war the workers were putting in a forty seven hour week: the Arc Works and Hoffmann's started at 7.30 in the morning and finished at 5 pm, with an hour for lunch. Marconi's worked from 7.45 am to 5.15 pm and it is likely that these timings were arranged to avoid the congestion of the New Street area that would occur if both factories clocked on and off at the same time. All the works shut at midday on Saturdays.

As the war ended, the big problem was the management of the demobilisation of the Forces and the return of these men to the work force.

CHAPTER 9

Home Life

*You won't be offended, will you dear?' said the old lady
who was calling on the young and inexperienced mother,
'but I have brought you a little book I picked up in a shop for
sixpence today. I am sure it will help you bring up baby properly.'
'Oh, how good of you. What is it called?'
'Infantry training, 1914'*

One of Reflex's odd little anecdotes provides an insight into the way in which the war permeated all aspects of society. From the early days of offering ways to help our boys at the front by sending clothes to the Red Cross Depot on Duke Street, or to Mrs Selkirk Wells' Boot and Sock Fund, or by contributing to the *Chronicle's* War Tobacco Fund, a gradual change took place in which the individual's contribution became much more indirect and involved personal sacrifice in ways that must have seemed very remote from the war itself. This increase in regulation and control of everyday life was in the hands of the many committees of the Town Council and of the

Alderman Frederick Chancellor.

charities and voluntary groups that flourished during the war years and beyond.

Chelmsford Town Council became increasingly central to life in the town during the war years. The town was divided into three Wards: North, South and Springfield, returning twenty-six councillors. There was also a small group of influential aldermen, including the great architect Frederick Chancellor, who had been the first Mayor of Chelmsford and served in the office seven times; John Ockelford Thompson, who was the proprietor of the *Essex Chronicle* and *Essex Newsman*; and newspaper proprietor George Taylor; Frederick Spalding, the photographer; and Frank Whitmore, another architect. Taylor served as Mayor until 1916, followed by Thompson for the civic year 1916-17, Councillor Jesse Gowers for 1917-18, and Councillor Walter Cowell at the end of the war. The law was changed at the outbreak of war to allow councillors to volunteer for active service without becoming disqualified, and Councillors Baker and Smith went to serve with the Colours. There were no elections during the war years and the casual vacancies (including one from the death in action of Councillor Baker in August 1918) were met by an application process. The local Member of Parliament was the Rt. Hon. Ernest George Pretyman. He was very much a career politician, serving on the Board of Trade, in the Admiralty, and as a Privy Counsellor; and although he regularly appeared amongst the great and good at public events in the borough, his interests clearly lay at Westminster.

Alderman Frederick Spalding

The Council ran its business through a number of committees and by late 1917 there were eighteen of them:

Finance	Fire Brigade
Gas Works	Education
Lighting	Market
Public Baths	Public Library
Museum and Science & Art School	Recreation Ground
Road	Sanitary
Sewer and Water Supply	Special Purposes
Town Planning	Hackney Carriages &c Licences
Joint Sewerage	Housing of Working Classes, Small Holding and Allotments

Various other committees, such as the Food
Control Committee, Recruiting Committee and
the Local Military Tribunal, were formed as
required, whilst many committees had outside
representation, such as the War Pensions
Committee.

In November each year the outgoing Lady
Mayoress planted an oak tree in the Recreation
Ground. The location of specific trees cannot be
identified but there is a description of the trees
forming an avenue and there are now two lines of
oaks in our Central Park which may owe their
origins to this tradition. The Recreation Ground
committee   maintained   a   programme   of

*Alderman John Ockelford
Thompson.*

entertainment at the now demolished bandstand throughout the war, at
a cost of £50 per year, which was the source of much grievance
amongst the other committees. Regular performers were the bands
from the Industrial School, Arc Works, Salvation Army, Poplar
Training School and, later on, the regimental bands from the many units
billeted in the area. The Committee were delighted with the gift of Bell
Mead from Mr Ridley, of the Elms, in Broomfield Road, in November
1915, and at the end of the war they also acquired the fourteen acres of
Admiral's Park, for the sum of £2,350.

*The Bandstand in the Recreation Ground. [Spalding, reproduced by
courtesy of the Essex Record Office ERO SCN 52]*

The Housing of the Working Classes, etc., Committee had achieved much in the years before the war, and had recently started letting out the 144 properties in the new estate on Rainsford Road and Primrose Hill areas. There was a shortage of housing in the borough but plans for further development were put on hold when in March 1915 the Local Government Board imposed restrictions on new work except for public health or war requirements. The Medical Officer of Health brought an alarming report to the Sanitary Committee in July 1916, when it was discovered that at 7 Compasses Row (off Broomfield Road, now the car park behind the Compasses Public House), a property with two living rooms and two bedrooms, there were eleven occupants. Under the orders of Dr Newton, Willie and Emily Smith were allowed only the five children under 13 years of age. What happened to the elder children is not known; Chelmsford Union workhouse (which later became St John's Hospital and is now a housing project) might have been an option. It was run by the Overseers of the Poor of the Parish of Chelmsford: Leonard Fell Christy, Charles Hawkes, George Mason, and Josiah Rankin, who met every other Tuesday to consider the fate of the less fortunate members of society.

One project that was put on indefinite hold was the wood block paving scheme for the High Street, Moulsham Street, and Springfield Road. The town's roads at this time were made up of crushed Channel Island granite – basically railway ballast. Herbert Bohannan recalled that the Council workmen applied 'tan' which was wood bark from the tannery off Baddow Road (now the trendy wine bar between the Odeon cinema and the Meadows car park). The tan was to keep the dust down. Away from the town centre roads were often covered in cinders from the gas works. In 1914 the residents of the grand new houses in Braemar Road petitioned for road resurfacing; but the Council only agreed to pavements.

Although there was no new building the developments from before the war were coming to fruition, and in March 1915 the Road Committee adopted Lionmead Road (now gone, in Springfield), Cramphorn Road (now the garage access road off Wheatfield Way), Admiral Road and Nelson Road (both off Cramphorn Road), Rothesay Avenue and St Fabian's Drive, and in 1916 Braemar Avenue and Marconi Road were also taken over.

There was immense pressure for additional housing for munitions

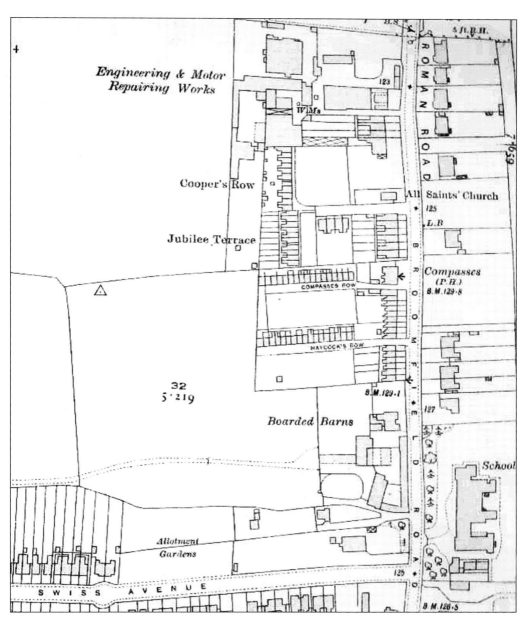

*The Compasses Public House on Broomfield Road (next to Christy &
Norris)*

Crushed granite road surface on the High Street. [Reproduced by courtesy of the Essex Record Office ERO T/Z 297/1]

workers in particular. Prompted by an appeal from Mr T Clarkson of the National Steam Car Company, Mr T Britton of Cromptons, Mr C Mitchell of Marconi's and Mr A Haskins of Hoffmann's, in 1917 the Town Council and the Local Government Board put pressure on the Ministry of Munitions, warning that the output of munitions was being affected and the Borough Engineer made a direct representation to Whitehall, but the official view was that there appeared to be a considerable amount of available lodging in the town and therefore they would not assist in any new housing scheme.

The Road Committee was also vexed by the problem faced by workers from Springfield who had to travel to the factories in New Street. Victoria Road at that time ran from New Street to Regina Road. There was a path down to the river, with a ford for wheeled traffic and a footbridge for pedestrians by the Mill, with a path up to Springfield Road. Councillor Bradridge owned Springfield Mill and he offered land between Springfield Road and Victoria Road to the Council for £3,000, which they politely declined. The preferred plan was to drive a road from Arbour Lane to Rectory Lane.

The war brought a vast increase in the amount of wheeled traffic in the town. The main London-Colchester road came up Moulsham Street to the High Street and then into Springfield Road. The north-south axis

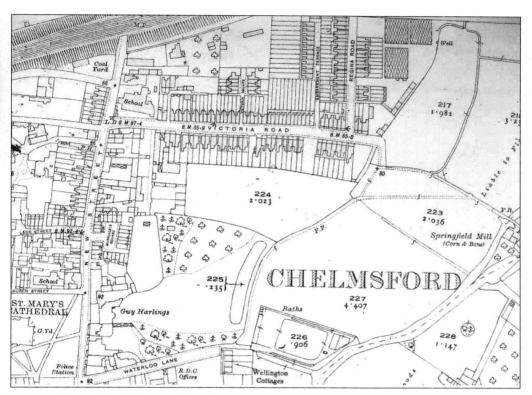

The original Victoria Road.

was from New London Road or Moulsham Street, up the High Street
and Duke Street to Broomfield Road. The east-west route was Baddow
Road, up the High Street and Duke Street and out on Rainsford Road.
Congestion was an inconvenience, but the mixture of horse and motor
traffic was the main problem and the Road Committee came up with a
plan for a 10 mph speed restriction in the town centre. There was strong
opposition from the Automobile Association and others, but in 1917,
after two years' of negotiation, it was agreed that the limit would apply
to Moulsham Street from the junction of New Writtle Street to High
Street; all of the High Street, Tindal Street and Tindal Square; and on
Duke Street from the junction with Tindal Square to the junction with
Wells Street; and on Springfield Road from the junction with High
Street to the junction with Navigation Road.

New London Road junction with Queen Street. [Spalding, reproduced by courtesy of the Essex Record Office ERO SCN 3102]

The Education Committee did most of its work through its Finance & General Purposes Committee, which in turn oversaw the boards of managers which ran the elementary and secondary schools in the borough. The children would have been disappointed in late August 1914 that, after all the marching bands and the columns of troops and the flow of horses, gun carriages and motor vehicles, all of the borough's elementary schools, except Springfield Green, were to re-open on Monday 7 September. At this time there were seven elementary schools in the town:

No 1a Trinity Road (still in use), which had boys, girls and a separate infants school (still standing);
No 1 Friars (since demolished, at the corner of Friars Walk and Parkway), an infants' school;
No 2 Roman Catholic School (original building demolished, now Our Lady Immaculate Catholic Primary School on New London Road), mixed boys and girls;

No 3 St John's (on Moulsham Street, building still standing and used for offices), for boys, girls, and infants;
No 4 Victoria: girls and infants (since demolished, now Victoria Court), boys, (Church Street, still there, not used);
No 4a St Peter's (demolished, now 73-95 Rainsford Road), an infants' school;
No 5 Springfield (demolished, at the site of Old School Field road), mixed boys and girls, and infants.

Because of the recent housing developments on Rainsford Road and east of Moulsham Street and the consequent increase in population, there were plans in 1914 to build new schools at South Primrose Hill and Lady Lane the Council had actually acquired the land in the former area (now Nelson Grove) but the Local Government Board restriction on funding for such projects brought them to a halt.

The school leaving age was thirteen. Parents could pay the fees for their children to attend King Edward VI's Grammar School or the Chelmsford County High School for Girls, both in a rural setting on Broomfield Road. These were endowed grammar schools, which meant that they received a grant from the Council but other than a councillor or two on the school governing body they were otherwise free of local authority control and received most of their income from fees. Pupils were drawn from the ranks of the lower middle classes, such as Basil Harrison, the grocer's son, and local children could win scholarships. Most school leavers went into employment, clutching their new School Leaver's Certificates. In those years the job market for youngsters was good: Hoffmann's, Crompton's, Clarkson's and Marconi's were regularly listed as work destinations in the annual report of the School Attendance Sub-committee, along with work as shop assistants and domestic service.

The health of the children was another matter. The Medical Officer of Health for the Borough was Dr Henry Newton and he also served as the School Medical Officer. It was not an easy job, particularly as the Council seemed not to value his professional opinion. In his 'Seventh Annual Report of the School Medical Officer for the year ending 31 December 1914' he complained: 'I would, at the outset, say that, as in the past six years, none of the recommendations I made in my last report have been adopted.' In particular he had performed many medical inspections but there was no follow up with any medical treatment. He inspected children at two points in their school career, when they were admitted to the school and once more at age twelve (although from 1916 he inspected them at age eight as well); his annual report was therefore based on a proportion of the overall school population but, even so, the results are alarming. In this Seventh Report he found:

Defective sight	75 cases
Defective speech	4
Defective nutrition	117
Defective hearing	7
Defective teeth	117
Defective clothing	2
Dirty body	47
Pulmonary tuberculosis	4
Enlarged tonsils and adenoids	56
Infantile paralysis	8
Mentally dull	25
Eczema	5
Ringworm	2
Otitis media	9
Cardiac disease	6
Bronchitis	2
Epilepsy	3
Unspecified	5

In all he found 494 defects out of 1,163 children examined. By December 1916 Newton's repeated complaints led the Council to ask the Sanitary Committee and Education Committee to look at the problem, and they came up with a proposal to appoint a Health Visitor and School Nurse at £100 per annum, with a uniform and bicycle. As this was a public health matter, the Local Government Board agreed to pay a grant equivalent to one half of the salary. The post was duly advertised and after receiving twenty-three applications and interviewing three, the Council appointed Miss Louisa Annie Briscoe, a school nurse from Hereford, to take up her post in December 1917, with a new Child Welfare Centre and School Clinic in the Girl's Club in New London Road.

The reduction in street lighting as an air raid precaution affected the school day. In June 1916 the military authorities requested the Council to change the afternoon school hours from 2 to 4.15, to 1.30 to 3.45. A further request came from the Chelmsford Trades Council in September 1917, when both pedestrian and road and rail traffic congestion from the factories and marshalling yards in New Street at lunchtime made it unsafe for the Victoria Road children and they were permitted to leave school at 11.50 am. A couple of months later the same adjustment was made concerning St John's School pupils because of the rush from Clarkson's National Steam Car works in Anchor Street and Moulsham Street.

Chelmsford Council adopted the general policy of refusing to allow the use of school buildings for billeting or other purposes, but the large number of troops stationed in and around Chelmsford in late 1916 resulted in the military authorities requesting the use of schools to provide accommodation and a centralised messing or canteen facility. The Finance and General Purposes (F&GP) Subcommittee of the Education Committee managed to put together a scheme in November that lasted until the following April. Trinity Road School was taken over by the Army and the younger boys went to Victoria Boys for a half day session (as remembered by Richard Godfrey), whilst the senior boys had classes arranged at Holy Trinity Church Hall and Springfield Church Hall. The Trinity Girls went to the Chelmsford Institute on New London Road (still standing) and the Friends' Meeting House on Duke Street. The infants spent half days at the Victoria infants' school, and the Friars School children spent the mornings at St John's.

The boys of Victoria and Trinity Road schools saw some of their teachers go off to war: Mr Suckling, Mr Petchey, Mr Doole and Mr Smith from Victoria, and Mr Dixon, Mr Barker and Mr Goodwin from Trinity. Sadly Dixon and Barker were killed in the German offensive of spring 1918 and Mr Smith was wounded at the same time; he was invalided out of the Army and resumed his teaching duties in September 1918. The girls' and infants' schools were staffed by women and a number of the vacancies amongst the junior staff were met by young ladies from the County High School.

As the competing demands of military service and munitions work put immense pressure on the working population it was natural that some should think about the contribution the children could make. In

February 1916 the F&GP subcommittee received a peremptory letter from secretary of East Anglian Institute of Agriculture, stating that the War Agricultural Committee of the County Council, owing to the shortage of labour, had passed a resolution 'that boys over 12 years of age should be allowed to work for farmers from Lady Day to Michaelmas' [25 March to 29 September]. The proposal was not accepted.

The Food Control Committee had much better results. Children were very keen to join in with collecting kitchen waste, newspaper and rags, and in October 1917 the Borough's schools collected nearly six tons of horse chestnuts (apparently used in the production of acetone, which was used to manufacture explosives). In the autumn of the following year the boys at Victoria Road collected 16½ cwt of blackberries.

Outside of school the children could attend the Boy Scouts. There were three troops, the 1st Springfield, the 2nd Chelmsford College (a private school in Arbour Lane, Springfield) and the 3rd Chelmsford. Boys could also join the 2nd Battalion, Chelmsford Regiment, Church Lads' Brigade. The girls could join the 1st Chelmsford or 2nd Chelmsford Girl Guides. Miss Winifred Trotter was the leading spirit of the Guides and in June 1916 Miss Baden-Powell, Chief of the Girl Guides, visited Broomfield Lodge and was very impressed with the girls' turnout and achievements. Both Scouts and Guides played an important but understated role in the town. From the outset of the war the boys in particular acted as runners for the military and civilian authorities. They regularly appeared at the many parades, fêtes and functions in the town, and they were particularly willing to help with the many charitable causes that sprang up. One of the first wartime charities to be formed was the Prince of Wales' National Relief Fund in August 1914. The Mayor, George Taylor, set up the Chelmsford branch on 31 August, setting the objects as being 'obtaining donations towards the National Relief Fund… for the relief of distress, occasioned by the war, and also towards the funds of the Red Cross Society'. At the very first meeting he was able to announce that £1,144 14s 9d had been contributed already, as the premium agents of the Prudential Assurance Company had undertaken to act as authorised collectors and the scheme had been widely promoted in the local press. The duties of the Committee were also defined:

a. To watch the local labour markets and to report to the County Committee all alterations in employment due to war;

b. To distribute (when necessary) relief in ease of distress to the war, other than soldiers or sailors who should be referred to SSFA and to the Territorial Association;

c. To keep the prescribed register of cases dealt with.

The Mayor also had a letter from Mr Barratt, the managing director of Hoffmann's, undertaking to support families of employees who had gone to war but advising that he would not be able to assist in the event of death. Surprisingly perhaps, this was not a busy committee, which was probably just as well as it had twenty-eight members! The minute book records eight meetings during the whole of the war. The first application came from Mr Williamson at 1 Brown's Cottages, Moulsham Street, who was unemployed; but by the time the committee came to consider his case he had been taken on at Hoffmann's. By 1915 they were granting small weekly allowances to five or so deserving cases, including Mrs Sarah Jane Button of 74 Rainsford Road, whose husband, Herbert, had been killed in action in November 1914 (his name appears on the Menin Gate). The Fund made regular contributions to the local Red Cross throughout the war, but its most notable donation was the £10 given to Mr Harry Childs, of 7 Glebe Road, to 'replace his furniture damaged by the dropping of a bomb from a hostile aircraft'. The War Relief Fund was wound up in 1923.

War Bonds were used by the government to raise short term funding from the population. Not to be confused with the modern Premium Bonds and potential prize money, these were a simple investment in which a bond was purchased and held over a fixed period, during which time it earned a regular interest payment every six months. At the end of the period it was cashed in, or redeemed, for its face value. Although the first bonds were issued in November 1914 and with an interest rate of 3.5 per cent they did not appeal to the general public, as the minimum subscription was £100 and multiples thereof, payable through the Bank of England. Known initially as War Loan Stock and then as Exchequer Bonds they attracted the wealthier classes and financial services firms. The government was keen to encourage 'the small capitalist and the working man' and, in July 1915 in what was described as the 'greatest financial operation ever undertaken by the

British Treasury', the second issue carried a 4.5 per cent interest rate, and bonds of £5 and £25 were offered, which could be purchased from the post office.

The National Savings Committee was formed in March 1916 and, in a major step for the lower paid, they introduced war savings certificates, for a minimum sum of one of His Majesty's pounds and free of income tax. The idea that the war loan was actually an altruistic personal savings scheme took hold, and war savings associations were formed which were particularly popular and effective amongst trades unions, friendly societies, and in factories; in January 1917 the Chelmsford Co-operative Society stated that in the previous quarter it had invested £2,500 in the War Loan. In the same month the third loan scheme was put in place, offering 5 per cent interest (although it is worth noting that inflation was rising at a higher rate). As with the other schemes this was discounted so that a £1 savings certificate would cost 15s 6d; or £5 of loan stock could be purchased for £4 15s; the interest would be paid every six months, through the post or into a post office savings bank account. The loans would be redeemed in 1923, 1925 or 1928, and the certificates at any time.

The Chelmsford Local Committee for War Savings, with John Stutfield as the honorary secretary, was set up in the County Offices in Duke Street. War savings rapidly became a patriotic duty – on 9 February 1917 a *Chronicle* advert asked 'Have you helped the big push that has started by putting all the money you possibly can behind it? If not – buy a War Loan today: the more you lend, the sooner the War will end'. The Crompton's, Hoffmann's and Marconi's Charity Sports Fête on 25 August 1917 offered savings certificates in the prize draw. One of the certificates went unclaimed, so at a public auction at the Regent Theatre Police Constable Hubbard purchased it for £2 and promptly handed it back for resale, when it was bought by Sergeant Ebenezer Jupp, of the Baddow Road Hutments, for £2 8s.

In February 1918 Captain Unett, the honorary secretary of Chelmsford No. 34 War Savings Association, presented his first annual report in which he announced that the ninety four members had saved £537. No. 33 (Queen's Road, Hill Road and Trinity Road) collected £464 19s. The Hoffmann Association saved £840 18s 6d in the same period. Bolingbroke & Sons, the ladies' and childrens' outfitters at 74-75 High Street, became agents for the sale of government securities and certificates, and in March 1918 made the claim that 'Chelmsford leads the county in war savings', with the average being approximately £5 per person. In April there was a joint meeting of the Chelmsford War Savings Association, the Council and the Traders' Association at which they decided to hold an 'Aeroplane Week' in the week commencing Saturday 4 May. The objective was to raise £50,000 in National War Bonds and War Savings Certificates to secure twenty aeroplanes for the Royal Air Force at £2,500; the slogan was to be 'Bomb the Huns with your Money'. Publicity was boosted by parking the SE5a 'Happy Days' flown by fighter ace Major Bishop VC outside Shire Hall, and there was a grand effort from the many voluntary organisations in the town. At the conclusion the Mayor was able to announce that the grand total for the week was £87,018 18s; the Bank of England inflation calculator returns this as equivalent to £4,314,606. The success of this event led to what was to be a final effort, a 'Guns Week' in the week of 11 November 1918. With the slogan this time of 'Feeding the Guns', it was suggested that a £5 bond would provide two rounds of 18 pounder shrapnel, and a 15s 6d certificate would purchase 14lbs of high explosive. Notwithstanding the momentous events of Monday 11 November, the campaign went ahead because 'your country still needs money – LEND IT'. With a slight change in terminology War Loans became Victory Loans, and the 'Feed the Guns' week raised £72,602 5s (approximately £3,599,818 today).

Advertisement for the Aeroplane Week in the Essex Newsman.

Charities in support of the war effort proliferated. In 1914 the Mayoress set up a War Garment Depot at 80 Duke Street, collecting blankets, socks and belts. There was the Essex Regiments' Prisoners of War Fund and the Essex Regiments' Comfort Fund. Chelmsford RSPCA collected for the Wounded British Horses Fund. The County High School performed dramatic recitations on behalf of the Romanian Relief Fund and the YMCA Hut Fund. In September 1916 there was a major fête at the Recreation Ground in aid of the Russian Wounded. The Rt Hon Winston Churchill attended, and to a cheering crowd he gave a banal but uplifting speech.

The Freemasons were active and popular with visiting servicemen; there were two Lodges in Chelmsford, No 276 Lodge of Good Fellowship, and Springfield 3183 (both still in existence). The Provincial Grand Lodge of Essex met in the County Room of the Shire Hall; the Deputy Provincial Master was the diarist Dr JH Salter. Reports of the proceedings of the major meetings of the Freemasons were regularly published in the local press and with nearly 4,000 members across Essex by 1917 they contributed much to charitable

Essex Chronicle *tobacco offer.*

work in the county and, in particular, to the Chelmsford Hospital. Conspiracy theorists will be disappointed to see that the membership was rather aged and, with the occasional death and funeral announcements in the *Chronicle* and *Newsman*, few of the political, business or community leaders appear in the lists of Masonic mourners.

One cause that might not win so much support today was the *Essex Chronicle* campaign for 'Tobacco for our Soldiers at the Front'.

With a Government ration of 2 oz of tobacco a week, the newspaper clearly felt that more was needed. For a contribution of 6d each soldier would get:

1 cake dark tobacco
1 cake light tobacco
10 cigarettes

For £5 they would send 200 packets to a particular regiment 'without delay'. The Comrades of the Great War association was formed in 1917 for men discharged from the Army, with the Chelmsford Branch run by Mr Hayes, of 33 Cramphorn Road.

The 'Flag Day' was a popular fundraising activity. In return for a copper or two a small flag was pinned to the donor's lapel. Twenty-six flag days were recorded in the four years of the war, in support of causes such as for the people of Belgium, Russia and Serbia, the YMCA and the RNLI; the Essex Regiment Comfort Fund; the Farmers' Red Cross; Railway Benevolent Fund; and for Wounded Horses.

The Chelmsford War Work Depot was affiliated to the British Red Cross Society and the Order of St John. Set up in 1917, it took rooms at 8 Crane Court and the women volunteers who worked there produced swabs, bandages and dressings, splints and other appliances for the local and county Red Cross hospitals and convalescent homes. And then the Red Cross had one of the most popular collectors in town, Brenda, the St. Bernard dog.

Brenda was a familiar sight on the streets of Chelmsford. Her owners, Mr and Mrs Nathan Smith, lived at 20 New London Road, where Mr Smith practised as a dentist. At the outbreak of war Elizabeth Smith contacted Colonel Colvin, chair of the Essex Branch of the British Red Cross, for permission to collect funds from the public on its behalf. Brenda was issued with a VAD nurse's cap and a Red Cross

M⁰ˢ NATHAN SMITH'S "BRENDA" Collects for The Red Cross. Chelmsford

Brenda, the Red Cross St Bernard. [Reproduced by courtesy of the Essex Record Office ERO D/DU 787/4]

collecting box, fastened to her collar, and the dog was regularly seen at fundraising events. In the week up to 4 September she collected £12, and in the next few weeks a further £13 12s 6d. By the middle of October her fame and success were such that the Smiths sent her portrait to Queen Alexandra, who in graciously accepting the gift replied that Brenda was 'a beautiful and patriotic dog'. In the accounts to the Annual Report of the Essex Branch of the British Red Cross Society for 1915 it was recorded that Brenda had raised £111 11s 9 ¼d; against which it might be noted that the flagship Prince of Wales Fund for the Relief of Distress, to which the leading lights of Chelmsford civic society contributed and donations to which were publicised in the *Essex Chronicle*, had raised £200. By October 1916 Brenda's contributions merited a silver medal for her collar and a silver rose bowl for the Smiths, presented with due ceremony by Colonel Colvin and the grateful committee of the Red Cross Society. The bowl bore the inscription 'In recognition of their untiring efforts, assisted by Brenda, on behalf of our wounded soldiers in the Great War.' Brenda worked tirelessly throughout the war, and following her death, aged

11, in April 1922, it was recorded that she had raised a total of £368, equivalent to around £17,700 today.

The Joint Hospital Board was a body that ran the hospitals of the borough. The civilian sick and injured of town were treated at the Chelmsford and Essex Hospital & Dispensary on New London Road, managed by the Joint Hospital Board, and cases of diphtheria and scarlet fever were taken to the Isolation Hospital off Baddow Road. There was also a smallpox hospital in Bakers Lane, West Hanningfield. The Army looked after their own sick at the military hospitals in

The Isolation Hospital off Baddow Road.

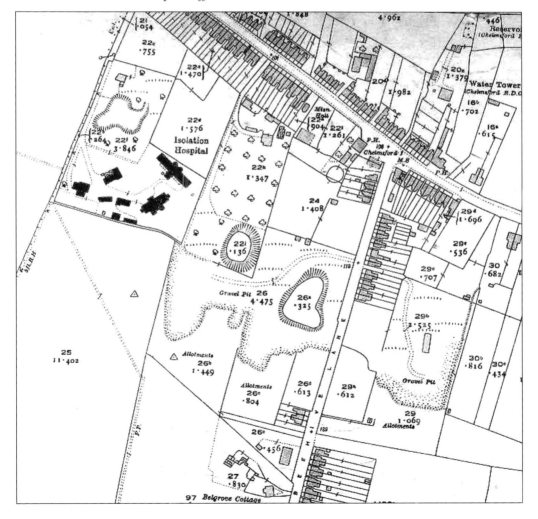

Oaklands House and in Danbury, but the civilian and military medical services came together at two occasions during the war, firstly with the cerebro-spinal fever (meningitis) outbreak in 1915 and, towards the end of the war, with the great influenza pandemic. The Spanish 'flu was described in the *Chronicle* as differing from all other kinds of influenza by 'the suddenness of its attack, rapid progress, and widespread character'. In the first wave of the disease, over the spring and summer of 1918, there were a number of cases reported, including Mr Haskins, the works manager at Hoffmanns, and the Mayor, Councillor Gowers, but there were few fatalities in the town; in September 1918 Dr Newton, the Borough Medical Officer of Health, confidently reported that the influenza epidemic had passed. Within weeks the 'flu came back, and this time with serious results, with nine deaths in November alone. Dr Newton reported that he had 'never seen an epidemic of any kind so universal, so severe, or so fatal in its character', and he blamed the strain of the war and the reduced diet; although his colleague, Dr Thresh, the County Medical Officer of Health, believed that the second outbreak seemed to be following the lines of the railway out of London and blamed overcrowding on the trains. In late October Newton closed the borough's schools for a month. In November the Council received the Public Health (Influenza) Regulations 1918 and, following advice from the Local Government Board imposed the following order:

Order
a. Public entertainment not to be carried on for more than three hours consecutively (cinematograph exhibitions not more than four hours)
b. Interval of not less than 30 minutes between any two entertainments during which the room should be effectively and thoroughly ventilated
c. Children from schools closed because of the influenza are not to be admitted to a.
d. Local authority to enforce the order.

The epidemic claimed sixty-four lives in the Chelmsford district in 1918. The worldwide pandemic claimed at least twice as many lives as were lost in military action.

CHAPTER 10

Food

*'All persons desirous of obtaining plots of land for
the growth of substantial foodstuffs such as potatoes etc.
should make application without delay to the Town Clerk.'*
January 1917

As a market town in the centre of an agricultural region, Chelmsford seemed well placed to ensure a regular supply of fresh food and meat to its inhabitants. Market day was Friday, when farmers arrived from across the county, bringing produce for sale; wheat and grain were traded at the Corn Exchange and livestock was sold in the Cattle

*Prior's Fish & Chip Shop on Moulsham Street. [Spalding, reproduced by
courtesy of the Essex Record Office ERO SCN 442]*

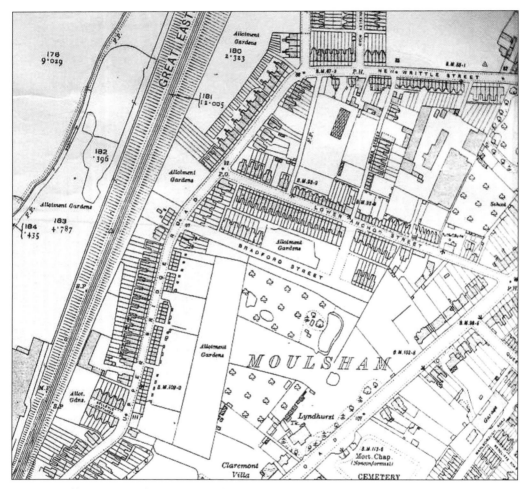

Allotments in the Upper Bridge Road area.

Market, often driven in from the farms and into town along Rainsford Road and Duke Street, as remembered by Basil Harrison. The town was amply provided with grocers, greengrocers, bakeries, butchers, pork butchers, fishmongers, and sweet shops along Duke Street and the High Street. There were dining rooms around New Street and Tindal Street for the workers at Marconi's and Hoffmann's, and public houses aplenty. There was even a fish and chip shop, Augustus Prior's, at 168 Moulsham Street ('motto: quality, civility, and cleanliness' and still there today, as Robinson's).

There were nurseries supplying fruit and vegetables on a commercial scale and a striking feature of the town was the large number of allotments and small holdings. There were allotments in Marconi Road, Bishop's Road, off Broomfield Road, behind Manor Road, Cedar Avenue, Primrose Hill, and down to the Arc Works. There were even sheep grazing on Bell Mead and on the Recreation Ground.

A campaign was launched to source fresh vegetables for the Navy in 1915; the Mayor, George Taylor, formed the Chelmsford & District branch of the Vegetable Products Committee, with the objects of 'collecting and delivering fresh fruit, vegetables, jams etc., to the crews of warships in accessible stations'. The first consignment was collected on 7 July 1915, by the good offices of Mr Ketley, who owned livery stables under the Railway Arches (the northern end) and was able to offer storage for the produce. The first effort consisted of thirty hampers and crates with 7 cwt of vegetables, packed by volunteers and despatched by train, free of charge, to the naval base at Harwich. The people of Chelmsford were invited to bring goods to the Arches between 11 am and 2 pm on Wednesdays, though it was politely pointed out that potatoes were not to be sent, as these were freely available to the Navy. By the end of August sixteen depots had been formed from twenty-one towns and parishes around the area and it was proving very popular with school children. The Mayor even arranged with Mr Austin to put up a sign at his Duke Street garage opposite the railway station (now under Marks & Spencer), directing people to the depot. It is interesting that at this stage of the war the Rev H Marshall, of High Easter, the district honorary secretary, asked members to plant up 'every spare piece of ground' simply to provide a regular weekly supply to the Navy, with no suggestion of food economy or domestic supply.

The Chelmsford allotment holders gave so freely to the Vegetable Products Committee that by January 1916 it amounted to over twenty two tons; the second highest contribution in the country. A grateful Navy awarded 'pretty brooch badges of the Royal Ensign in gilt and enamel' along with a letter of appreciation from the Central Committee to seven of the committee members, including Mr Ketley and his son. They subsequently received a certificate of thanks at the end of the war, signed by Admiral David Beatty, Commander-in-Chief of the Grand Fleet. The final meeting was held at Guy Harlings on 17 November 1919 by which time they had delivered around 300 tons of fresh produce.

In December 1916 the Vegetable Products Committee instigated a collection for 'Christmas Puddings for the Sailors'. They raised £40 16s – enough for 450 lbs of puddings! They also sent four boxes of apples, two crates of oranges and bags of nuts. Around the same time a campaign started to collect eggs for the wounded soldiers in the local Red Cross hospitals. These were to be sent to the depot at 96 High Street, the office of the Chelmsford Corn Exchange.

In November 1915 Chelmsford Council was surprised by the generous gift of Bell Mead by Mr CE Ridley, of The Elms on Broomfield Road. It was given freehold and was to be used as a public recreation ground, to provide a pleasant walk from the Market and London Road to the current Recreation Ground. At the time this was simply an urban farmland, occupied by 'horrible little pig styes and huts', with the adjoining river full of litter but, as noted elsewhere, the grazing rights continued and were negotiated each year by the Council. It was a timely gift. In late 1916 the Board of Agriculture and Fisheries

Chelmsford Railway Station, with steam bus. [Spalding, author's collection]

The river, with Bell Mead on the left. [Spalding, author's collection]

issued an Order under Regulation 2L of the Defence of the Realm Act, as the Cultivation of Lands Order 1916. This gave local authorities the rights to acquire land in the borough for the purposes of food supply where labour was available; a notice was published in the *Chronicle* on 5 January 1917:

Borough of Chelmsford

Cultivation of Lands Order, 1916

Under the above Order the Town Council of Chelmsford have power to enter into possession of unoccupied land in the Borough without payment of rent, and let the same to a society or to individual cultivators for the growth of substantial foodstuffs such as potatoes.

The Town Council invite immediate applications from any Society of Individuals who are prepared to undertake the Cultivation of Allotments provided under and in accordance with the provisions of the Order.

Forms of application may be obtained at the Municipal Offices, 16 London Road, Chelmsford.

By Order
George Melvin, Town Clerk

There was an immediate response from an enthusiastic public. Following the Council's advertisement, sixty-five applications were received. Alderman Whitmore, chair of the Recreation Ground Committee, proposed that part of the park could be used for the cultivation of potatoes and Lieutenant Cleale offered the services of the men of Chelmsford Company of the Volunteer Regiment to dig up the football field. Councillor Driver offered four plots of land on Swiss Avenue and Mr Brookhouse had four more plots on the same road. The management of the scheme was given to the Council's 'Housing of the Working Classes, Small Holdings and Allotments Committee', which of course promptly formed a sub-committee and they requested that the Borough Engineer identify any suitable unoccupied land in the borough. In the first week of operation they took possession of land in Bouverie Road, Cedar Avenue, Rectory Lane, Swiss Avenue, Tower Avenue, Upper Bridge Road and Rainsford Avenue, giving eighty plots of ten rods each. True to form the Town Council refused the use of the Recreation Ground, claiming 'sufficient other land is available in the Borough for this purpose'.

By March the Council had acquired 275 plots of land, including ninety in six acres at Bishop's Hall Farm, given by Mr Hoskin of Boarded Barns Farm. Plots ranged from sixty-seven on Writtle Road to a single plot on Mildmay Road belonging to Mr Smith. Reginald Marriage offered 1¼ acres on Hill Road. Another thirteen plots were found on Seymour Street and Bradford Street. All allotments were let at 1s per annum. Various groups took on the work: employees from Hoffmann's cultivated the land in the Waterhouse Estate (in the Crompton Road-Waterhouse Street-Waterhouse Lane area) on Writtle Road, and of course there were the members of the Chelmsford & District Branch of the Vegetable Products Committee.

Reflex commented on the problem some people had with the description 'allotment holder' and were looking for something shorter. The name 'lotter' was proposed: as he 'spends a lotter money on a lotter seeds and a lotter plants; spends a lotter time doing a lotter work, and hopes to get a lotter crops'. In November 1917 the new Mayor, Councillor Gowers, formed an Allotment Holders' Association, intending to bring together the various groups run by the factories and others, to economise on costs and to share experience and advice. Mr Tilley from Marconi's brought along eighty of his members and offered

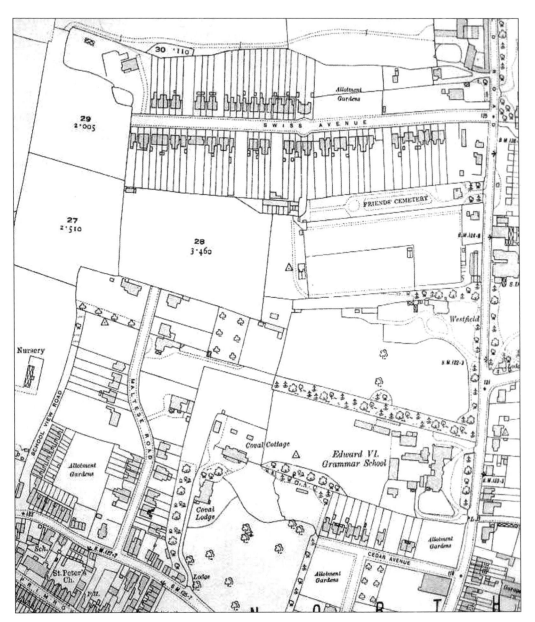

Allotments off Swiss Avenue, Cedar Avenue and Maltese Road.

the new association their full support. Ignoring Reflex's suggestion, they decided to call themselves the 'Chelmsford and District Cottage Gardeners' and Allotment Holders' Association', and its objects were:

To produce more food
To organise collection of produce
To provide local markets for all produce
To connect more closely the Producer and Consumer

The Council purchased six tons each of early and main crop seed potatoes through Mr Wilson at the East Anglian Agricultural Institute. By January 1918 they had sold a stock of 4 tons 8 cwt to the allotment holders, and the Council placed a further order for six tons of King Edwards and three tons of Arran Chief Scotch, to be sold at cost. The association prospered and by June it had a stall in Chelmsford market to sell its surplus produce.

In early 1918 the Council finally relented on the use of public land and the top part of the Bell Meadow was put into use; as was the land previously purchased as the site of the proposed South Primrose Hill School (still there). The borough was certainly being intensively used, with additional plots in a field off Roxwell Road owned by Wells & Perry, Goldlay Road and two pieces of waste land near the railway embankment at Seymour Street (also still there today).

One of the lesser-known aspects of Chelmsford Council was that it owned a farm at Brookend. The town's sewers drained by gravity down to this sewage farm, where it collected in standing ponds for treatment. The solid material was eventually used as fertilizer and the liquid effluent ran through earthenware pipes under the surrounding fields, eventually draining into the Chelmer and the canal. The farm was run as a commercial operation, by Mr Cox, the bailiff, on behalf of the Farm sub-committee of the Joint Sewage Committee of Chelmsford Urban and Rural District Councils. The food produced appears to have been sold on the local markets and the farm did not contribute to the Food for Navy scheme. In January 1915 the Council purchased Storms Farm and the combined site, now in the hands of Anglian Water, remains in use today.

The annual accounts give an insight into land use during the war. Taking 1917 as an example, the farm was growing the following:

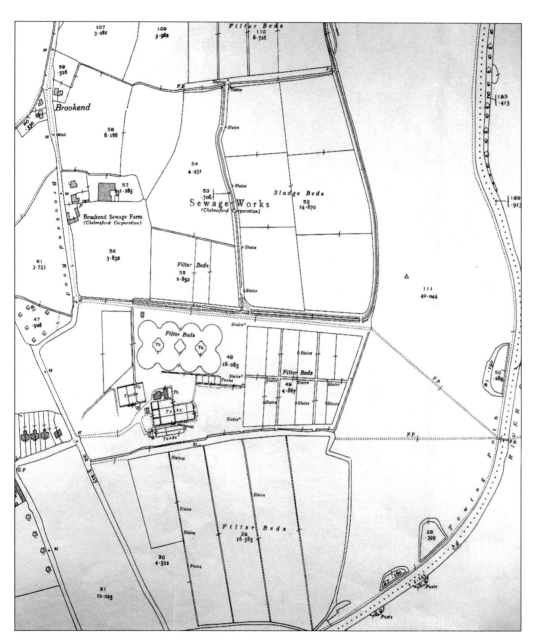

Brookend Sewage Works and Farm.

Potatoes	5 ¼ acres under cultivation
Mangold	10 acres under cultivation
Celery	4
Savoys	1 ¼
Spring Broccoli	¾
Cauliflowers	¼
Collards	½
Kohl rabi	1
Brussels sprouts	1 ¾
Spring cabbage	¼
Marrows	½
Barley	5 ½
Oats	16 ½
Wheat and wheat straw	4 ½
Hay	1
Pea and Rye grass	1
New rye grass	1

With a bean crop and pasturage, the amount under cultivation was around fifty eight acres. In essence a small market garden, a large part of the produce – mangolds, barley, oats, and the grasses – would have been for animal feed. The farm also had a small dairy herd, with thirty-two heifers and calves in 1917. There was also rental from the thatched cottages at Brookend Farm, and £8 a year from Dr Gimson for the shooting rights over the land. The profit for the year was £640 17s 2d. Hay and straw had to be sold to the military at £5/ton, with permits for those who wished to use it for cattle feed. The Government also controlled potatoes: under section 12 of the Potatoes Order in 1917, small holders were able to grow enough for domestic use but the farm was able to produce commercial quantities. The Food Controller set the price at £5 per ton for quantities over four tons and £6 per ton for less; the farm was able to sell nineteen tons to the Ministry of Food. At this time the Food Economy Committee launched a campaign to collect waste and to encourage the keeping of pigs on allotments and sewage farms. The managers of Trinity Road School had an arrangement where the boys brought in household refuse (or more properly, kitchen refuse, such as cabbage leaves and potato peelings) and stored them in a tub in the playground. The tubs were emptied as

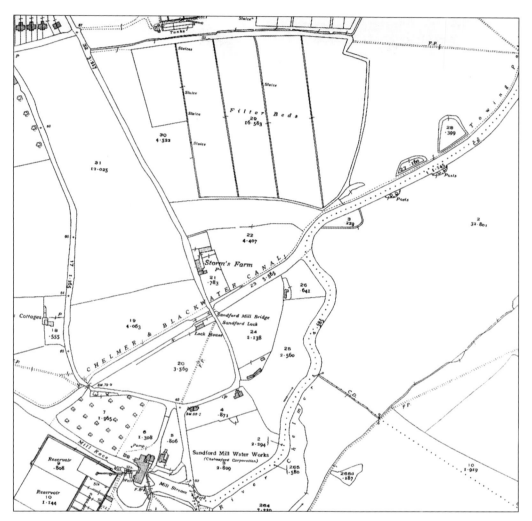

Storm's Sewage Farm. (immediately south of Brookend)

required, the contents being used as food for pigs (most household waste up to this time was collected by the council and tipped into a field at Moulsham Lodge Farm by arrangement with Mr Currie). Despite the ready supply of food from the town, the Farm Sub-committee decided against keeping swine because of the high prices and restrictions on the additional pig feed required to maintain a stock at a profitable level, and so the boys' pig swill went to the allotment holders.

The farm was under constant pressure from the military authorities to release their workers to the Army. Under the original provisions of the Military Service Act in 1916, agricultural workers were exempt, but the manpower demands were such that by 1917 firstly general labourers and later dairy workers were called up. Mr Cox was a constant visitor to the Local Military Tribunal in an effort to obtain exemptions; the Farm Sub-committee viewed all the labourers as indispensable. Captain Smith, the Chelmsford Recruiting Officer, was particularly interested in Mr Cox's sons, who also worked on the farm, and suggested that the Council transfer other Corporation men over to cover for them, but this was refused. As late as September 1918 the Cox boys had to appear at the Tribunal for yet another exemption.

The East Anglian Institute of Agriculture ran classes throughout the war and played an important role not only in encouraging women to contribute to the war effort by working on farms but by changing the attitudes of farmers to employing them – despite grave labour shortages some farmers were as keen to engage women as they were to take on conscientious objectors! The Institute, on King Edward's Avenue (now under the Chelmsford Library), ran a four week induction course for women from July 1916, alongside courses in dairy management and butter and cheese production. The principal, Mr Robert Wilson, was also the secretary of the Essex War Agricultural Committee and, through the committee, the Institute played a central role in educating and supporting the small holders and allotment keepers of Chelmsford and beyond.

The Institute had a model dairy at Britton's Farm, Chignall and they sent twenty gallons of milk daily back to the Institute for butter and cheese production. Towards the end of the war staff shortages meant the closure of some of the courses and Wilson thought it would be a better use of the milk to send it the people of Walthamstow. The Food Control Committee unanimously opposed his plan, which drew an ascerbic letter from Mr EC Seear, of Upper Walthamstow, in which he expressed astonishment at the Committee's decision to prevent the milk being sent to 'the mothers and babies' of his town and instead use it to manufacture butter and cheese for 'a few well-to-do people in the borough of Chelmsford'. He took the opportunity to remind the Committee that Walthamstow had a financial interest in the Institute and the Urban District Council had released its own labourers to assist with agricultural work in the summer. The committee was unswayed and the Institute's milk stayed in Chelmsford.

The Board of Agriculture and Fisheries invited the Council to nominate an individual interested in horticulture to liaise between the Board and the small cultivator, and Mr Wakely, a horticultural instructor at the East Anglian Agricultural Institute in Market Road, was appointed. Through the efforts of the Chelmsford and District Cottage Gardeners' and Allotment Holders' Association and hundreds of keen gardeners and 'lotters' the Town was able to continue supplying fresh vegetables for the Navy – and for itself – right up until the end of the war. But they were not able to solve all of Chelmsford's food supply problems, which was the domain of the Food Control Committee.

CHAPTER 11

Rationing

*'I am pleased to say that the streets have returned to normal
conditions, and look like old Chelmsford again (hear, hear).
There are no queues, the policemen are walking about in pairs
with nothing to do, and everybody is happy.'*
Councillor Simmons, 1st March 1918

The first two years of the war had provided good harvests,
supplemented by imports of foodstuffs from North America and the
Empire. The steep rise in prices seen immediately after the outbreak
of the war had proved to be very temporary, but in February 1915 food
prices were some 25 per cent above pre-war levels and by late 1917
prices were almost double what they had been at the start of the war,
although not all items in the shopping basket were affected the same
way. Social tensions increased as it seemed that the 'poorer classes'
were unable to afford what produce was available, and that the
wealthier classes could not only afford to pay, but were accused of
buying more at the same time. The reality was that as the war
progressed the German submarine campaign made itself increasingly
felt, with both the loss of imported foodstuffs and the reduction in
shipping to transport the goods. The 1916 harvest was not as good as
in the previous years. The Government again used the Defence of the
Realm Act to enable it 'to proceed against any person who wastes or
unnecessarily delays any article'; the solution to ensuring that there
was a regular distribution to all would be the introduction of food
tickets (rationing was not an acceptable term at this time); but this was
seen as a last measure. The Government also explored the options for

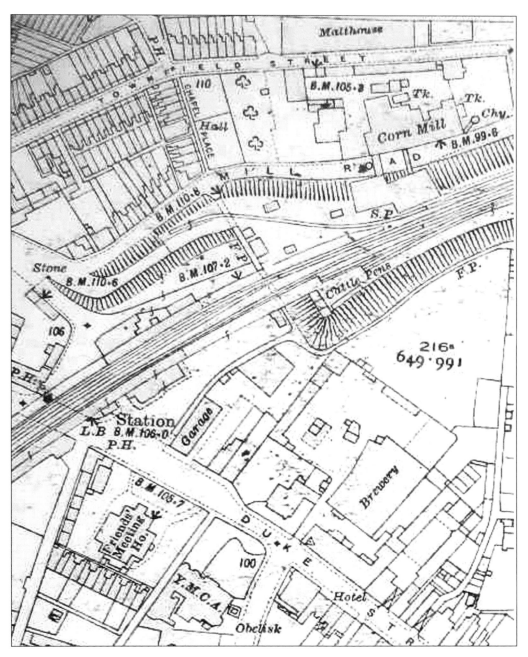

Wells & Perry Chelmsford Brewery on Duke Street.

it to fix prices, which was again an unpopular step. Interestingly, there was little understanding of the mechanisms of pricing and the actual costs of production, for example of milk, were not known. Lord Devonport was appointed as the Food Controller at the head of the new Ministry of Food, with a focus on price control and increasing food production.

In order to maintain the grain supply in 1917, the decision was taken to cut beer brewing to 70 per cent of the 1916 level, with substantial savings in barley and sugar. Chelmsford had a number of large brewers, including Ridley & Sons on Railway Street, Gray & Sons on Springfield Road and the Chelmsford Brewery (Wells & Perry) on Duke Street and out at Hartford End. The beer industry had already suffered from the restrictions in the licensing hours and this was a further blow to their business. They had little sympathy from one group: the Chelmsford Branch of the Women's Total Abstinence Union wrote to the Food Controller in January 1918 expressing disappointment 'that while the people are asked to eat less bread large quantities of corn are being used in the manufacture of intoxicating liquor'.

In February 1917 the people of Chelmsford were asked to restrict their diet to no more than 4 lbs of bread, 2½ lbs of meat, and ¾ lb of sugar per week. The following month Reflex complained about a proposal for two meatless days (Tuesdays and Fridays), two potato-less days (Wednesdays and Saturdays) and not more than five ounces of uncooked meat for each person. In May 1917 King George issued a somewhat rambling proclamation exhorting the reduction in the consumption of bread; and in his last notice Lord Devonport echoed the request:

Circular No. 67 Ministry of Food

I wish to appeal for the immediate help of every man, woman and child in my effort to reduce the consumption of bread.

We must all eat less food; especially we must all eat less bread and none of it must be wasted. The enemy is trying to take away our daily bread. He is sinking our wheat ships. If he succeeds in starving us our soldiers will have died in vain.

In the interests of our country, I call upon you all to deny yourselves, and so loyally to bridge over the anxious days between now and the harvest. Every man must deny himself, every mother, for she is the mistress of the home, must see that her family makes its own sacrifice and that not a crumb or crust is wasted.

By a strict care of our daily bread we can best help the men who are gallantly fighting on sea and land to achieve victory, and to share with them the joys of peace which will follow.

No true citizen, no patriotic man or woman will fail the country in this hour of need. I ask all the members of your household to pledge themselves to respond to the King's recent appeal for economy and frugality and to wear the purple ribbon as a token.

29th May 1917 Food Controller

People showed their commitment to the King's appeal by wearing a purple ribbon. The Food Controller believed that a voluntary approach was better than rationing but it soon became clear that a firmer policy was necessary and, as the Board of Trade reported a 98 per cent increase in the cost of food since the war began, Lord Devonport resigned. His replacement was Lord Rhondda who had an immediate impact. On 1 June 1917 the *Chronicle* carried a large notice:

Borough of Chelmsford

Defence of the Realm Regulations

Local Authorities (Food Control) Order 1917

Notice is hereby given that under the provisions of the above Order the Town Council are the Local Authority for enforcing the provision of the undermentioned Orders of the Food Controller within the Borough of Chelmsford

The Brewers' Sugar Order (Clause 2)	As to the price of Brewers' Sugar.
The Potatoes 1916 Main Crops (Prices) Order (No. 2) (as retail sales only)	Limiting the price of Potatoes of the 1916 crop sold by retail after 31st March, 1917, to 1 ¾ d per lb.

The Price of Milk Order (as to retail sales only)	Limiting price of Milk.
The Feeding of Game Order	Prohibiting the feeding of Game Birds with Wheat, Pulse, or other Grain or Foodstuffs.
The Sugar (Confectionery) Order	As to retail prices of Chocolates and Sweetmeats, and prohibiting the use of Sugar and Chocolate for covering Cakes.
The Bread Order	Prohibiting the sale of New Bread, and as to the shape and weight of Loaves.
The Swedes (Prices) Order	Limiting the price of Swedes and Swedish Turnips to 1½d per lb, including cost of bags or other packages.
The Food (Conditions of Sale) Order	Prohibiting, in regard to the sale of any article of food, the imposition or attempt to impose any condition relating to the purchase of any other article.
The Tea (Net Weight) Order	Prescribing that on and after the 1st July 1917, all Tea sold by retail, whether contained in a package or not, shall be sold by nett weight (except Tea sold in a quantity of less than 2 ounces).

The Manufacture of Flour and Bread Order (No. 2) (Clause 5)	Prohibiting the sale or manufacture of Bread or any other article of food for which wheaten flour is used, unless the wheaten flour used therein has been manufactured in accordance with this order.
The Public Meals Order	Prescribing regulations as to Foodstuffs to be observed in every Inn, Hotel, Restaurant, Refreshment House, Club, etc.
The Cake and Pastry Order	Prescribing conditions as to the making for sale and sale of Cakes and Pastries, and as to the Rationing of Tea Shops.
The Wheat, Rye and Rice (Restriction) Order	Imposing restrictions as to the use of Wheat, Wheaten Flour, Rye Flour, Rice or Rice Flour except for the manufacture of articles for human food, and in the case of Wheat for Seed.
The Maize, Barley and Oats (Restriction) Order	Imposing restrictions as to the use of Maize, Barley, Oats, etc., except for seed, human and animal food and the manu- facture of articles of Food.
The Horses (Rationing) Order	As to the rationing of Cereal Foodstuffs to Horses, and prescribing the quantity of Oats which may be given to certain classes of Horses.

| The Oats and Maize Products (Retail Prices) Order | Prohibiting the sale or purchase or the offering for sale or purchase of Maize Flour, Maize Flakes, Maize Semolina, etc., at a retail price exceeding 4d per lb., and of Oatmeal, Rolled Oats, or Flaked Oats, including Proprietary Brands, at a retail price exceeding 5½d per lb. |

Notice is hereby further given, that the Town Council in pursuance of the powers and duties conferred on them will take legal proceedings against all persons acting in contravention of the above mentioned Orders.

Although rationing is mentioned in these Orders, the main emphasis at this time was economy and price control. In August, however, International Tea Company Stores (with shops at 19 Tindal Street and 26 Moulsham Street) took out an advertisement notifying their customers about changes to sugar distribution; specifically, that after 30 December 1917 sugar would only be sold to members of the public holding Sugar Cards and who have registered with the shop. These cards were to be issued by the Local Food Committee, which in Chelmsford had not yet even been formed. Perhaps this spurred the Council into action, because a Food Control Committee was appointed the following month with the Mayor, Alderman Thompson, in the chair. This committee had wide-ranging powers and membership was drawn not just from within the Council but from a number of outside organisations and groups: there were to be two representatives from the Chelmsford Trades Council, one from the Chelmsford Star Co-operative Society, one representative from the Local Trader's Association, and two women. The membership immediately attracted controversy. By the time the Council met on 29 September, a petition with 1,500 signatures had been received from the Chelmsford Trade Council protesting the appointments of Mrs Hamilton, Mr Blooman (Traders' Association), Councillors Collins, Simmons, and F. Luckin Smith, all of whom were seen to have vested (and not so vested) commercial interests, at the expense of consumer representation. Councillor Luckin Smith was a wholesale provision merchant and grocer, with shops at 76 High Street, 182 Moulsham Street and 149 Springfield Road. Despite the Council recording its confidence in the committee membership, Mrs Hamilton, a member of the Education Committee, resigned and her place was taken by Mrs Cowell, of 35 Anchor Street, a member of the Chelmsford Branch of the Co-operative Women's Guild (the other female member of the Food Control Committee was the Mayoress, Mrs Thompson).

The Food Control Committee had an executive officer, Mr Melvin (the Town Clerk), a staff and an office in order to deal with a rapidly increasing workload. The Local Food Office, at 16 New London Road, opened in the first week of September 1917. Its first job was to manage the Sugar (Registration of Retailers) Order and the sugar card scheme, with registration cards being made available in Post Offices from 30 September, to be completed and returned by 5 October. The Meat (Maximum Prices) Order 1917 required butchers to post 'in a conspicuous position' a price list of all cuts of meat in the shop, and to submit a copy to the Food Control Committee within twenty four hours. Infringements were, of course, summary offences under the Defence of the Realm regulations.

At the same time that the Food Control Committee was finding its feet, the Coal Distribution Committee was created. A letter had been received from the Board of Trade concerning a previous scheme for towns with more than 50,000 inhabitants to make arrangements for the supply and distribution of coal 'for the use of the poorer classes', which was now being extended to towns with populations of 20,000 or more. The Council agreed to purchase a stock of 500 tons of house coal to be sold as necessary over the forthcoming winter (subject to the Retail Coal Prices Order). The committee kept a close eye on fuel supplies and requested weekly returns from the coal merchants such as the Star Co-operative Society, which had a coal depot on New Street (by the railway bridge). Over the winter of 1917-18 coal stocks were at 220 tons in October, and they were down to 160 tons in February, with over 800 tons received and distributed. Although London had a Coal Rationing Order imposed on it, by prudent management of stocks Chelmsford managed to avoid taking this step.

Towards the end of September 1917 the Food Control Committee debated meat prices. A complaint had been received from Mr Cruikshank, of 22 Upper Roman Road, protesting that Chelmsford meat prices were above the Food Controller's limit. One of the duties of the Food Control Committee was to set the prices to be charged in the borough in consultation with the retailers and the consumers. It was learned that the town's retail butchers had already held a meeting to agree and fix their prices; the justification of the pricing was based on the butchers' purchase of live animals for slaughter, rather than the prepared meat itself, which meant that Chelmsford prices were slightly higher than those elsewhere in the county. And although the price was fixed by law, the Food Controller had allowed for a profit of 2½d per pound, but this still meant that pork, for example, had to be sold over the counter at a price lower than the butcher had paid. An unsympathetic Mr Bence, the Labour Council representative, suggested that the workers should hold a Vegetarian Week to leave the butchers with unsold stock. The Committee adopted the prices and published them in the *Chronicle* on 5th October.

The Chelmsford Trades & Labour Council was deeply dissatisfied with the way in which the Council had set up the Food Control Committee and the way in which it was 'practically packing [it] with traders'. At a heated meeting at Shire Hall the call was for agitation, recognising that there was an undoubted shortage of food but that the workers had no margin for further economy. On behalf of the agricultural workers they adopted the slogan 'those entitled to the best the earth produced were those who produced it', and a resolution was carried protesting the composition of the Food Control Committee and resolving to form instead a workers' Local Food Vigilance Committee. The Council's response was slightly offhand – apparently the public had a 'hazy idea about who are the members of the Trades & Labour Council and [asked] what right do they have to interfere in the affairs' of the Food Control Committee.

Mr Cruikshank wrote another letter, this time to the Ministry of Food and copied to the Council, protesting about the meat price controls being ignored by local butchers and he concluded: 'The interested parties of the Chelmsford Food Control Committee prevent any action being taken', a comment which finally goaded the Council into doing something. Mr Melvin, the Town Clerk and Executive Officer of the Food Control Committee, also received a letter from Mr

Debnam of 50 Primrose Hill, concerning a butcher overcharging him for meat and he wanted a prosecution. The Council appointed Superintendent Mules to be the official inspector of the Committee and requested that he carry out a formal investigation. Mr Debnam promptly withdrew his complaint, but following a comment from Mr Walls, one of the labour representatives, that 'I have been told today by a tradesman that this Committee is nothing, and that orders are only going to be taken from Lord Rhondda', the committee felt that to maintain credibility legal action was the only recourse. On 16 November 1917, Frederick James Underwood, a butcher at 38-39 Duke Street, was summoned to Chelmsford Petty Session, and charged with 'selling meat by retail at a price exceeding the scale prescribed by the Order of the Local Food Control Committee', to which he pleaded guilty. It was a sorry case: the facts of the matter were that Miss Johnson, Debnam's niece, ordered a joint of topside for their Sunday dinner. Underwood charged her 6s 4½d for a 3¾ lb joint, when it should have been 5s 7½d. Debnam was very upset at having to give evidence against his family butcher, who had made no attempt to evade or deny the matter, but in the interests of public confidence the bench fined Underwood £5 with 5s costs.

The Food Control Committee was next vexed by the matter of milk pricing. A letter from Lord Rhondda in October made the first direct threat of rationing if voluntary controls did not work. The Committee fixed the price of milk at 6d a quart, which led to complaints from the Chelmsford & District Milk Retailers' Society and from the Essex County Farmers Union that it was impossible to retail at that level and it was better for them to sell wholesale (to the butter and cheese manufacturers), as there was no price control in that market. Unlike the cost of meat, Chelmsford milk was a penny cheaper than that being charged elsewhere in Essex. Mr Melvin suggested that the milkmen be gently reminded of the Committee's powers, by which they could compel them to deliver to consumers.

At the suggestion of the Food Controller another layer of bureaucracy was formed, this time the Food Economy Committee. With the objectives of encouraging the people to cut down on unnecessary consumption and to minimise food wastage, the membership was to be far more representative than the Food Control Committee. There were to be only two councillors, with two members of the Education Committee, two teachers, and two from each of the War Savings Committee, the Trades & Labour Council, the Star Co-operative Society, the Co-operative Women's Society, and the four church leaders: Rev. Canon Lake, Rev. Pressey, Rev. Mundle, and Msgr. Watson. One of their first tasks, delegated from the Food Control Committee, was the review of the applications from the fifty-seven caterers, twenty-four manufacturers and twelve institutions which had applied for permits to sell or deal with sugar. They then had to consider the matter of dog food – Councillor Collins had complained that although there was rationing of food there was no rationing of dogs, although his colleague, Councillor Simmons, pointed out that dog food was prepared from materials unfit for human consumption.

Sugar rationing commenced in December 1917. With the help of the Springfield Troop of Boy Scouts the cards had been filled in and issued to all households in the borough and the scheme worked. The harsh reality of the first legal restriction on food supply brought to a head a number of rumours and allegations of hoarding, not just of sugar but of tea and cheese, and of preferential treatment, particularly for the wealthy. The town's butchers had to make a declaration that they would undertake to distribute their meat supplies 'equally among their customers of all classes'. Queues began forming outside butchers and other shops as early as six o'clock in the morning, and there was indignation as the best cuts of meat were sent off for delivery 'to rich people'. Butter seemed to have disappeared altogether and the supply of margarine was erratic at best. The School Attendance Officer voiced his concerns that children were missing school because their mothers were making them hold their places in the slow moving queues. In January a terrible rumour circulated that a girl had been crushed to death in such a queue and public feelings ran high. It was the irregularity of the food supply that caused the problems; after spending an hour or so in line it seemed only natural that people wanted to buy as much as they could, without thought for anyone else.

The solution would be to guarantee a fixed amount of a food item and to restrict the amount that an individual could purchase, and yet it seems slightly incredible that even in January 1918 there was no food rationing in the United Kingdom. Sir Arthur Yapp was the national Director of Food Economy and he embarked on a tour of the country to promote the National Food Economy Campaign. He appeared at the

CHELMSFORD BOROUGH FOOD BULLETIN

(Cut this out for reference.)

RATIONS FOR NEXT WEEK:

BUTTER or MARGARINE, 5oz.; SUGAR 8oz.

MEAT: Coupons available next week, No. 17, and No. 16 up to Wednesday only.

Coupons must only be detached by the Retailer at the time of sale, as loose coupons are worthless.

Butchers' Meat (including Pork), 8d. worth per coupon.

(a) Edible Offal: Tongues, Kidneys, Skirt, or Loose Fat, 8d per coupon.

(b) Edible Offal, except above and the kinds obtainable without coupons, 24d. per coupon.

SAUSAGES :—First quality, 67 per cent. meat, 12ozs. per coupon.
Second Quality, 50 per cent. meat, 16oz. per coupon.

BACON :—With bone, 8oz.; without bone, 7oz. per coupon.

HAM :—With bone, 12oz.; without bone, 10oz. per coupon.

Hamhocks, Gammon-hocks, Forehocks, up to 3lb., no coupon.

Sheetribs, ditto, 2½lb., no coupon.

Picnic Hams, ditto, 5lb., 2 coupons.

For every additional pound or part of a pound extra 1 coupon.

Hams or Joints of Bacon may be sold upon coupons current in the three weeks following the week of sale, as also upon coupons current in the week of sale.

SUET :—Beef and Mutton, 8d.; BONES 8d.; DRIPPING, 8oz.

Cooked or Prepared Sausages, Polonies, Brawn, Canned or Potted Goods, containing no meat, but edible offal (except Tongue, Kidney, or Skirt) 24oz. per coupon.

Other Canned or Preserved Goods are at the original coupon rate, e.g., Corned Beef, 4oz. per coupon.

The Food Bulletin was published each week in response to local and seasonal changes in food supply.

Drill Hall in Chelmsford on 31 December and in his introduction the Mayor, J Gowers, emphasised that if food economy was not implemented then they would be rationed 'which would be a terrible thing'. Sir Arthur's talk was pure but effective propaganda: the

Germans had issued 378 million bread tickets in two years, when they had a major shortage of paper. They issued 66 million bread tickets a week. Referring to the submarine campaign he pointed out that the loss of a 5,000 ton ship would mean the loss of enough bread and flour to feed Chelmsford for 127 weeks; at a parochial level he noted that if every person in Chelmsford saved one slice of bread a week it would provide a week's rations for the whole population of Maldon, and a meatless day would save enough to feed Hatfield Peverel for thirteen days. The 'meatless day' was in fact already a reality: starting on 1 January 1918, Lord Rhondda had decreed that on one day each week no meat, cooked or uncooked, was to be sold, and no butcher was to sell in four weeks more than three quarters the amount sold in the four weeks ending 27 October 1917. The Chelmsford Food Control Committee published an order to this effect on 18 January.

But rationing was inevitable and in January, just a couple of weeks after Sir Arthur's speech, the Food Control Committee drew up plans for the rationing scheme that would be implemented in London and the Home Counties. All householders had to obtain an application form from the shopkeeper with whom they wished to register; these forms had to be completed and returned to the Food Office by 28 January, and the cards would be issued up to 13 February. Registration with the shop had to be completed by 18 February and the rationing of butter and margarine would begin on Monday 25 February. The Food Control Committee was empowered to amend the registers for each shop to ensure that businesses were not favourably or adversely affected. The ration card had to be produced each time, it was not permitted to use the card at a different shop and, as the *Chronicle* kindly pointed out, rations must be purchased each week or they were forfeited. Servicemen home on leave would be issued emergency ration cards. A similar but separate scheme was also set up for ration cards for meat, and in the same way households had to register with a specific butcher. The definition of 'meat' was very broad and covered 'everything in the character of animal food, cooked or uncooked', tinned, preserved and prepared meats. 20,638 adults and 4,623 children registered for meat cards. The weekly ration ended up as 8oz of sugar, 4oz of butter or margarine, and 1½ lb of butcher's meat. The population was initially divided into three classes: children (A), normal adults (B) and adolescents (C). Within a month three more classes were formed: for very heavy industrial workers (D); heavy agricultural workers (E); and heavy industrial workers (F), for whom a Supplementary Ration scheme was introduced. Application forms had to be endorsed by employers. Yet another sub-committee had to be formed, to consider appeals. Some two thousand workers in Chelmsford were issued with cards entitling them to the additional allowance, of an extra 50% of meat 'other than butcher's meat, that is, bacon, rabbit, or poultry'. This amounted to 8 oz of uncooked bacon on the bone, or 7 oz off the bone; and the allowance was nearly doubled in June. Non-rationed foods included fish (fresh and preserved), potatoes and all vegetables, fruits (fresh, tinned, dried, and nuts), jam (including marmalade and honey). Bread was not rationed but its ingredients were subject to various controls; and potato flour was a common constituent by late 1918.

The Food Control Committee had exercised its powers over the supply of margarine in mid-January, by requisitioning all stocks in the town, in particular those of the Maypole Dairy at 59 High Street, which was the main manufacturer of margarine in the area. These stocks were to be distributed equally to the other shops and the scheme appeared to work, with a restriction of a maximum of 1 lb per person per week. In early February there was a major outcry when Marconi's, Hoffmann's and Crompton's apparently obtained supplies of margarine and cheese from the Army & Navy Canteen Fund, and sold these on to their workers. Mr Mitchell, the Marconi Works Manager, explained that they had hoped to ease supply problems and reduce queues in town and that there was no question of soldiers going short.

In the last days before rationing

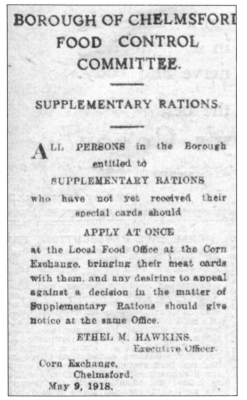

Supplementary rations.

started the Town Clerk announced that 25,000 cards had to be written, checked and sent out. Over one-third of them had been incorrectly filled in. The clerical work for this massive task was undertaken by eight temporary clerks and a team of volunteers, mainly ladies, and boys from King Edward's Grammar School. On 22 February the following notice was published in the *Chronicle*:

Chelmsford Borough Food Control Committee
Important Notice to the Public, to Butchers, and to Pork Butchers
Warning of Monday's Rationing Scheme

Butchers' shops opening times
     Monday – closed   Dinner time – 1 to 2.30 each day
     Tuesday – 9 to 6
     Wednesday – closed
     Thursday – 9 to 6
     Friday – 9 to 6
     Saturday – 9 to 8
     Sunday – closed

Following the big day, Councillor Simmons reported that he was 'pleased to say the streets have returned to normal conditions, and look like old Chelmsford again (hear, hear). There are no queues, the policemen are walking about in pairs with nothing to do, and everybody is happy'. A simple statement in itself but it clearly gives an insight into how bad things must have been in the last few weeks before rationing. Basil Harrison recalled the impact of rationing on his father's grocery business at 9 Duke Street. With the threat of food shortages, customers had to register with specific shops and he found that he was able to convert many formerly occasional shoppers into regular clients with profitable results. Rationing brought with it a lot of paperwork and Basil was able to help his father with this additional chore after school.

One approach to both food and fuel economy was the Communal Kitchen or 'Kitchen For All', promoted by the National Economy Kitchen programme. Rather than having hundreds of homes stoking up their cooking ranges for each meal, it would be much more efficient to prepare and cook food on an industrial scale, for 'workers of all classes'. Mrs Maude Fox, wife of Captain Fox RA, of 76 Baddow Road, 'a lady of great experience', volunteered her services to organise the scheme for the town. This attracted much popular interest and she was successful in securing a location in the Market Place for a marquee, whilst the military generously offered stoves and boilers and erected the kitchen at a cost of £600, with a capacity of 1,000 persons. The service was to be run on sustainable commercial lines and not as a charity, with paid workers; and would be able to repay any loan made to it by the Council or other lender. Following a meeting with the Mayor in late January, Mrs Fox prepared a sample menu (pea soup, roast meat, potatoes, swedes, boiled rice, jam and treacle) and, fired up with enthusiasm and offers of support, she attended the Council meeting on 30th January to explain her request for a grant or loan. To the bewilderment of Mrs Fox and her supporters – including the Mayor – the proposal 'fizzled out' in an unpleasant and prolonged discussion, in which the majority view appeared to be that Chelmsford had no need of such a kitchen. The Food Control Committee came up with its own suggestion for providing cans of baked potatoes and hot soup. In the face of such abject petty mindedness, Mrs Fox publicly withdrew her proposal and resigned from the project.

The communal kitchen issue was resurrected in March when the divisional director of the National Kitchen scheme wrote to the Council in March, offering a grant of 25 per cent of the cost. His letter was passed to the Food Control Committee for consideration, who of course formed a Kitchen Sub-committee, with the initial comment that rationing now meant that everyone got a fair share of the meat and so could eat at home. The chairman, Alderman Thompson, still supported the idea, pointing out that the National Kitchen offered non-rationed food and 'in a very attractive way too', that it 'saved a good deal of labour and fuel at home' and enabled 'women at work to get very cheap meals, well-prepared, nourishing, and hot, and take them home all ready for dinner'. In a final end to the communal kitchen scheme, the sub-committee voted 3 to 2 against the proposal, remarking that the time had not yet arrived to establish such an institution, and, patronisingly, that the women 'would rather cook at home and be saved the trouble of fetching it'.

In March the Food Control Committee received a letter from Mr Ernest Palmer, who had a shop at 43 Moulsham Street, where he specialised in horse meat. Prior to rationing he had been doing good business with people who were not too fussy about the source of the meat in their pot, but now that they were guaranteed meat at the butcher his business had collapsed – from turning over between £7 and £10 a week he was now taking 8s. He requested a special licence to sell horsemeat without coupons. The chairman announced that 'he had had a [horse] steak and never wanted to eat anything nicer', and the Committee agreed that horseflesh should be outside the rationing scheme and they gave him permission to trade for three months. The young Basil Harrison remembered passing this horsemeat shop and he 'shuddered at the thought of eating it'. The horses were obtained from Mrs Shedd's licenced slaughterhouse in Viaduct Road and inspected by the Council's veterinary surgeon before sale.

The Food Control Committee's work over the next few months is summarised in their Annual Report, published in July 1918. In March the committee's membership had expanded as the Food Controller authorised additional worker representation, and they now had members from Marconi's, Hoffmann's, Crompton's, and Clarkson's. They also had a new executive officer, Miss Ethel Hawkins, who had three lady assistants. The report mentions the success of the sugar rationing scheme and the meat price controls, and notes that they had held around forty meetings. Recalling the initial list of seventeen Food Control Orders they had published the previous June, they had since implemented a further *700* orders from the Ministry of Food! They were also rather proud of the fact that there were only four infringements of the orders sent to the courts, resulting in four convictions. One such prosecution was of Fred Luckin Smith, proprietor of Smith's Wholesale & Family Grocers, Provision & Wine Merchants, 76 High Street. He was also a councillor and a member of the Food Control Committee. In April 1918 he was summonsed, along with his former employee, Joseph Clulow, for the offence of supplying 5lb of margarine to a servant without production of a food card. Luckin Smith pleaded not guilty, Clulow guilty. The facts were that they had received a double order of margarine and Clulow, working as the shop assistant, had mistakenly assumed that there was no restriction on its sale. Mrs Lockwood, registered with the Maypole Dairy, was in the shop and saw two other women purchase margarine without cards, so she did the same. Clulow sold her 5lb at 1s 2d a pound, 'that being the proper price'. The sale was made openly and without secrecy. As soon as Luckin Smith heard of the matter he went straight to Alderman Thompson, and the two of them interviewed Clulow about the incident and reported him to the police. The defence case was that of the servant 'acting directly against his instructions, so the Company was not liable'. The bench disagreed, found Luckin Smith guilty, and fined him £5 with 5s costs. Clulow was fined £5. The Council took no action against Luckin Smith, despite his position on the Food Control Committee.

The milk producers had a final run in with the Food Control Committee in October 1918. A decision to fix the price in Chelmsford and district at 8d a quart to the end of December and at 9d a quart from then until the end of April 1919 led to the milkmen refusing to deliver milk to households, although milk could be purchased at dairy shops. The strike began after the milk round on 1 October, but the action was opposed by the Trades and Labour Council, with workers at Clarkson's, Marconi's and Crompton's voting against the strike. The general opinion was that the financial difficulties of the milkmen were caused by the milk producers: the farmers were selling at 2s 3d a gallon, and the public were paying the equivalent of 2s 8d a gallon, with 5d then going to the milkmen themselves. The strike was unpopular and short lived, as the Food Control Committee threatened to apply for an Order compelling the milkmen to resume deliveries. A new business model was developed in which one dairyman would supply the milk for each area and without overlapping territories and by the 18 October deliveries had resumed, so that the application for a Ministry of Food order was withdrawn.

The Milk (Mothers and Children) Order 1918 and the Local Authorities (Food Control) Order No. 1, 1918 required local authorities to arrange a supply of milk and food for expectant and nursing mothers and of milk for infants and children under five. This was not a mandatory provision for all mothers but only applicable to those in particular need. A subcommittee of the Sanitary Committee was formed, of Alderman Thompson, Councillor Gowers and the Town Clerk, to investigate all cases which were brought to the attention of the council and to decide on 'necessitous' cases. The opinion of the Medical Officer of Health was that such provision was unnecessary in the borough and the scheme never progressed.

New ration books were required in the summer of 1918. A request to the Education Committee to close schools early on 24 June to enable the teachers to 'volunteer' to help write up the 20,000 new ration books was resoundingly rejected, probably to the annoyance of their pupils. In September the Council instructed everyone to complete and send in the green reference leaf from the front of their ration books and return to the Food Office by 21 September.

The final meeting of the Food Control Committee during the war dissolved into farce. Following the dispute with the dairymen there was further nonsense about the opening hours for the butchers, with a request to open for an extra hour on Fridays (which was pay day). The Mayor, Councillor Gowers, resigned from the committee over 'shilly-shallying' and that they were at the mercy of the butchers and milkmen. The chairman, Alderman Thompson, accepted his resignation and continued the business of the meeting by forming another sub-committee.

The Local Food Control Committee underwent its final revision on 9 November 1918, with a broad and more representative membership drawn from the Council, Chelmsford Trades Council, Chelmsford and District Cottage Gardeners' and Allotment Holders' Association, the Co-operative Movement, Chelmsford Traders Association, and two women. But their work was almost done. The queues had gone and food supply was regular and reasonably secure. Astonishingly, the Food Control Committee ended up with the oversight of 1,400 Orders. Although the war would finish within eight weeks, rationing of meat continued until 15 December 1919, butter until 30 May 1920 and sugar until 29 November 1920.

CHAPTER 12

The Blighty One

Dear Little Friends,
We thank you very much for your kind gift, which we enjoyed
very much, and we think it very good of you to think of us in this
way. The sponge cake was pronounced excellent by all of us, and
we all think that you must have been instructed exceedingly well
to cook in this manner. Once again thanking you very much.
Yours truly – two wounded Tommies. Chelmsford Red Cross
Hospital
Letter to Misses E Wicker and E Huckle, Trinity Road Girl's
School, June 1915

Private Ernest Charlick of the 9th Battalion Norfolk Regiment had to
have his arm amputated due to wounds received in Flanders in October
1917. After a spell in a General Hospital in France he was evacuated
back to England to recover. He was put on a hospital train destined for
the Colchester Military Hospital, but it also stopped at Chelmsford.
Charlick spoke to the medical officer in charge of the train, from whom
he obtained permission to detrain. Charlick was a local boy and his
parents lived at 5 Phillips' Cottages, on Church Lane in Springfield,
near the Tulip Inn. He was taken by motor car to the Red Cross annex
at the Chelmsford & Essex Hospital and Dispensary on New London
Road. He was just one of several hundred soldiers who were treated in
and around Chelmsford during the war.

As part of the reforms of the territorial and reserve forces before
the war, the concept of the Voluntary Aid Detachment (VAD) was
formulated, 'for the care and transport of the sick and wounded in war
in the home territory', to be made up of men and women with first aid

and basic nursing skills. The organisation was to be run by the British Red Cross Society and training was to be provided by the St John Ambulance, based on the Royal Army Medical Corps training syllabus. In a letter to the *Chronicle* in November 1909 Lady Warwick, wife of the Lord Lieutenant of the County of Essex, announced the formation of the Essex Branch of the Red Cross and its immediate goal of recruiting for the VADs. The following were qualified to join:

1. Registered Medical Practitioners, ladies or gentlemen
2. Fully-trained Hospital Nurses
3. Trained Pharmacists
4. Those of either sex possessing First Aid and Home Nursing Certificates of the St. John Ambulance Association.

A detachment would consist of women and men under their own officers. The officers would be men, but there would be lady superintendents. A fully staffed unit would have sixty six men and twenty two women. Men's detachments would have a commandant, an assistant commandant, two medical officers, a quartermaster and assistant, two pharmacists with assistants, four under-officers, and forty eight men. A women's unit comprised a commandant, assistant commandant, quartermaster (man or woman) and assistant, two lady superintendents and 20 women, of whom two would be fully qualified nurses. Funding would come from a membership fee and from the Red Cross. By December the same year Miss Gladys Nicholas, of Green Close, Springfield, had been appointed as the Organising Hon. Sec. for Chelmsford and was busy recruiting members and arranging 'Ambulance Classes in First Aid and Nursing'. Women were particularly keen to join, and soon Chelmsford had two detachments: Essex No. 40, under Miss V M Kemble, and Essex No. 4, under Mrs. Magor. The Chelmsford VAD was formally recognised by the War Office in April 1910. In November the men's detachment, Essex 3, met for the first time, and with the majority of men already holding qualifications the evening was spent on stretcher drill and bandaging exercises. Unfortunately the men appeared to lose interest and the Chelmsford Men's VAD had to be 'resuscitated' in April 1914. The local president, Major Hilder accepted the blame – he had made a speech in Braintree a few years before in which he had criticised the

Territorial movement and had thought that there was no possibility of an invasion and so had let the VAD lapse. He had now realised that the Regular Army had the Royal Army Medical Corps to provide medical services to the sick and wounded but that no such provision was available to the Territorials. Captain Wenley was appointed as commandant of the Chelmsford Men's VAD and he managed to increase numbers to fifty four by the outbreak of war in 1914. Membership across the county membership stood at around 2,000, with seventy three VADs.

A Red Cross county depot was set up in Chelmsford in August 1914, for the collection of stores and clothes which could be sent to the office at 74 Duke Street, and a house at 67 High Street (above Halford's Cycle Shop, now Clinton Cards) was taken for storing goods. Sheets, towels, dusters, cotton wool, boracic wool, gauze, slippers, and dressing gowns were given generously by the people of Chelmsford; and later the county store moved to 84 High Street. The Volunteers themselves, soon simply known as VADs, began their war duties by providing refreshments to the many troops arriving in the area, initially at the Corn Exchange.

The opening days of the war brought about a number of generous offers of large houses and stately homes to be used as hospitals. Fairfields was offered by Dr Newton, whilst the Society of Friends were willing to give up their Meeting House on Duke Street. Mrs Shaw offered Skreen's Park in Roxwell as a convalescent home and Major Hilder, already involved in the Red Cross, offered his home, Huskards in Ingatestone. Sir Daniel and Lady Gooch offered Hylands.

By the end of August 1914 Hylands had been transformed. Sir Daniel was at the time in Buenos Aires where he was managing the dogs that Sir Ernest Shackleton would be using for his forthcoming transantarctic expedition, but on his behalf Lady Gooch made the following proposal to the Red Cross:

> To provide a hospital in their house for about one hundred beds, for either urgent or convalescent cases.
> To find twenty beds complete; all the necessary cooking; electric light, coals and water; all vegetables, fruit, etc.; all partridges, pheasants, rabbits, etc.; laundry and staff; and resident medical officer.

To guarantee £100 a month to the general fund.
To provide a nursing staff, assisted by the VAD, under the Hon.
Mrs AHF Greville.

Sister Rosling was engaged as the first matron, with Drs Alford, Gimson, Newton and Martin (an anaesthetist), and began by converting most of the ground floor rooms into hospital wards. The house was well positioned to receive casualties, as the Hylands estate had a railway siding, the ramp to which can still be seen at Elm Cottages. The initial estimate was that they would be able to take up to a hundred wounded in five wards, with an operating theatre and an X-ray machine. The 2nd and 3rd South Midland Field Ambulances of the RAMC set up their tent sections in the ground and began taking in the sick and injured from the South Midland Division quartered in the area. However they were under a twenty-four hour notice to quit should the hospital be required for the reception of wounded. By October 373 Territorials had been treated at the hospital. At 10.30 pm on 10 October the War Office telephoned Lady Gooch to warn her to be prepared for a party of wounded Belgian soldiers. The RAMC left as agreed and moved into Oaklands House on Moulsham Street, so that on the day that the King visited Hylands (14 October) there were only five soldiers remaining, one of whom was Private Baker, the son of the caretaker of the Public Library of Chelmsford, who had been wounded in the thigh by shrapnel at Mons. These men were then evacuated to Chelsea Hospital. Despite that advance notice, the first Belgian soldiers did not arrive until 24 October 1914.

The first British wounded arrived in Chelmsford on 30 October 1914 at 2.15 pm, on a train from Harwich. About thirty members of the local detachment of the Men's VAD worked with the men of the RAMC to transfer the wounded from the train to the ambulance wagons and motors. These were drawn up on what was known as the 'milk van siding' which is a ramp which runs from the end of the modern Platform 2 across to Mill Road and can still be seen. There were only five stretcher cases, and most of the wounded appeared to be in an advanced convalescent stage and able to walk, some with the aid of sticks. It was noted that the wounds were principally of the feet, legs, hands and, in a few instances, about the head. The stretcher cases were accommodated in a motor van, which Mr JW Austin, of Austin's

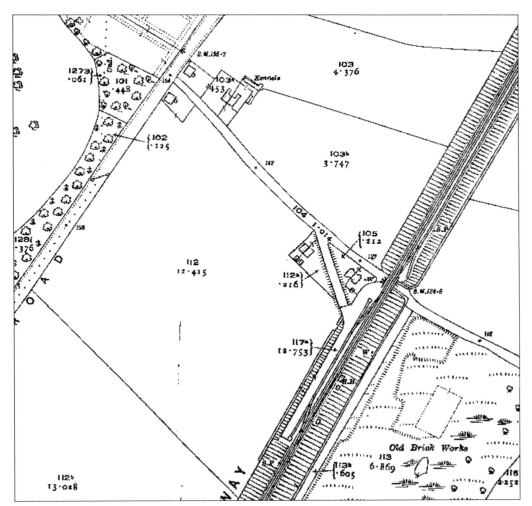

The Hylands railway siding at Elm Cottages.

County Motor Works, had fitted up 'in a clever manner to take six or seven patients, novel racks holding the stretchers'. It took only fifteen minutes to move the wounded into the vehicles and they departed for Hylands and Skreens. Although the arrival of the hospital train had been kept a secret, a large crowd of onlookers and well-wishers gathered in Mill Road and Railway Street to cheer on the wounded men.

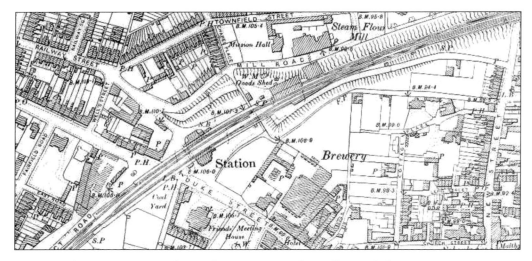

The two ramps at the Railway Station. The Milk Van Siding ramp runs down to Mill Road.

The role of the VAD in providing valuable, trained assistance to the medical authorities was apparent and there was much interest in their work. As with all of the voluntary services, funding was a continuing issue, although the Red Cross was fortunate in having not only a high profile but was already the beneficiary of grants from the Prince of Wales' War Relief Fund and other established sources. Initially there was no funding for a uniform and, although the women wore a pinafore and a linen cap, the men had to make do with a small metal Red Cross badge; but by the spring of 1915 they were in khaki. The military were also interested in this pool of qualified first aiders and within the first few months of the war the Chelmsford men's detachment lost twenty five men to the RAMC in Ipswich and several others went to serve as Red Cross orderlies in France. One man even went out to the Red Cross hospital in Serbia.

The use of the Red Cross emblem was strictly controlled. In March 1915 the Home Office sent out a letter reminding the Local War Emergency Committees and the branches of the Red Cross of the restrictions:

According to Article 27 of the Annex to the Hague Convention of 1907, hospitals and places where sick and wounded are collected, buildings dedicated to public worship, art, science or charitable purposes or historic monuments, are to be spared, as far as possible, in bombardments, provided they are not being used for military purposes… the only hospitals entitled to the Red Cross emblem are those exclusively under Military or Naval control. The fact that a hospital or other building is used for accommodation of wounded soldiers or sailors does not in itself justify the use of the Red Cross.

British soldiers wounded in France and Belgium were shipped across the Channel to various ports along the south coast (the use of Harwich was discontinued very early in the war after a number of German submarine attacks on shipping in the North Sea). One major centre for the reception of casualties was the military and Red Cross hospital at Netley, on the Solent near Southampton. In November 1914 the Essex Branch of the Red Cross paid for an 'Essex Hut' at a cost of £960 per year, staffed by Essex nurses. A letter was published in the *Chronicle* on 16 April 1915 from the unnamed Sister-in-Charge of the Essex Hut in which she described the first intake of patients, a group of twenty Indian soldiers who could speak little English. She now had British soldiers, but was working with a staff of Japanese nurses. She would be delighted to receive gramophone records for the men.

The Essex Hut at Netley. [Reproduced by courtesy of the Essex Record Office ERO D/DU 787/4]

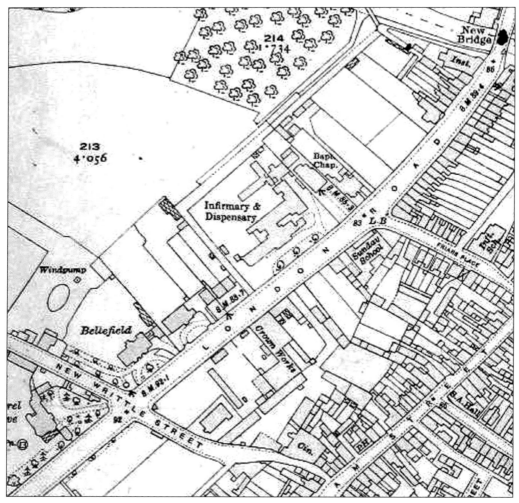

Chelmsford Hospital on New London Road. The buildings at the rear of
the hospital and chapel were used by the Red Cross, as was Bellefield.

The Essex Red Cross Committee, under the Hon. Mrs Greville formulated a strategic plan to provide three hospitals on the Colchester mainline: at Hylands; Coombe Lodge, Brentwood (a sixty-five bed facility); and a new one at Chelmsford. The existing civilian hospital on New London Road had all the necessary operating theatre facilities,

X-ray apparatus, and medical staff. It was decided to build an annex at the rear of Chelmsford Hospital 'in the shape of a Furley Fieldhouse hut on the Nissen pattern' (a patent design for a Portable Barrack Hospital hut) and, following Chelmsford Council approval of the plans in January 1915, construction took place over the winter months at a cost of £300, of which £50 was contributed by Mr Ridley and another £50 from the War Relief Fund. It officially opened on 11 May 1915 and offered accommodation for forty patients, ten of whom were shortly sent off to recuperate in Eastbourne. Miss VM Kemble, Commandant Essex 40 VAD, was in charge of the hospital, with two trained sisters and ten Red Cross nurses and two orderlies from the men's detachment.

A *Chronicle* article on 14 May 1915 painted a picture of the work of the VAD and the Red Cross hospitals:

Wounded from the Front.
The local VAD of the Red Cross are now able to put to most practical use their knowledge, gained by months of patient training, for 30 soldiers from the Front arrived early on Tuesday morning, and are being treated at the Red Cross Hut, erected at the rear of Chelmsford hospital. Last Friday the VAD, the male members of which look smart in their new khaki uniforms, were notified that wounded soldiers were to be expected. On Monday morning they received notice that wounded had been landed at Dover, and after standing by a hospital train arrived just after 2 o'clock in the morning. All but one of the wounded were 'sitting' cases, but some were in a bad way, and there was one case of gas poisoning. They were in the trenches on Sunday, and had been only temporarily attended to, and still wore their mud-stained clothes. The male section of the VAD, under Quartermaster H. Gripper and Pharmacist T Bellamy, carried the men to motors, conveyed them to the hut, undressed and bathed them, tended the wounds, etc., and put them to bed. In this work the female section, the Essex 40, under Miss Kemble, commandant, were able to render great service. One of the wounded soldiers, when placed in his brand new bed, remarked 'this is like dropping out of hell into Heaven'. The men of the VAD are providing the orderlies, and the ladies, with the

assistance of sisters and the medical staff at the hospital, are doing the nursing, etc. A few of the cases are being treated at the general hospital. The hut is splendidly fitted on up-to-date lines, and close by is a bungalow, where the nurses do cooking, etc. The men's section have also supervised the detraining of batches of wounded for Hylands and Budworth Hall, Ongar.

The Marconi worker, Herbert Bohannan, whose brother Stanley was serving in the RAMC in France, recollected taking out stretchers as a member of the Red Cross at this time. The first wounded in Chelmsford were sent to Hylands, and the later ones went to the temporary hut with forty beds at the back of the Chelmsford hospital. He worked there in his spare time and often at night.

Following the King's visit the previous year, in August 1915 Lord Kitchener, the Secretary of State for War, paid a visit to Hylands to inspect the troops of the 2/1st South Midland Division in Hylands Park.

The Hylands and Chelmsford Red Cross Hospitals were officially described as Auxiliary Hospitals and they were administratively grouped with a military or general hospital, in this case the Colchester Military Hospital and the Middlesex War Hospital, Clacton-on-Sea. Theoretically, wounded soldiers were meant to travel to the main hospital first but in practice they were often sent directly to the Red Cross facility. Many of the subsequent newspaper reports of casualties arriving at Chelmsford were those destined for the Red Cross annex; Hylands cases appear to have been collected directly from the Hylands railway siding. Each auxiliary hospital recognised by the War Office (and deemed Class A) received a grant of 3s per bed per day; with the Class B convalescent homes receiving 2s per bed per day. It should also be remembered the Chelmsford & Essex Hospital was still functioning as a civilian hospital. In the Chelmsford Joint Hospital Board annual report for the period to March 1916 it was noted that in the previous twelve months they had treated 941 patients, of whom 400 were military personnel; the total in previous year was 641.

In February 1916 in was announced that the Red Cross Hospital was being closed until March for cleaning and for further work, which included the addition of two bathrooms, lavatories, cupboard accommodation, funded by an additional £150 grant from the War Relief Fund. There would also be a further ten beds in a former schoolroom in the adjacent Baptist Chapel. The hospital, chapel and the schoolroom are still standing, on New London Road, with the rear area now occupied by the County Place development. Hylands was also closed for the customary cleaning and patients from both hospitals were distributed to Colchester and the other military hospitals.

In those pre-antibiotic days the risk of infection in wounds was significant but an unusual and unfortunate accident occurred at Hylands. Miss Hilda Ayre Smith was a trained nurse at the hospital; in February 1916, whilst changing infected wound dressings, she contracted septicaemia, or blood poisoning. Despite receiving every attention from Dr Gimson and from a London specialist, nothing could be done to save her, and she passed away in forty-eight hours. She was buried at home in Dulwich.

By this time some 505 patients had been through the Red Cross hospital and there had been no deaths, here or at Hylands. In part this was because of the nature of the casualty evacuation chain, which moved men rapidly away from the front line areas provided they were assessed as fit to withstand the rigour of the next stage of their journey. This meant that the most serious cases were retained in the great base hospitals in Rouen and elsewhere and return to the UK only followed recovery. This was to change in the great medical evacuation disaster at the opening of the Battle of the Somme on 1 July 1916. Tremendous numbers of casualties were passed rapidly through the system, in which the casualty clearing stations behind the front line were under pressure to move their patients back so that they had beds available as quickly as possible; and the base hospitals adopted a similar policy. For one of the few times in British military medical history, wounded men were returned directly to the United Kingdom having received little other than cursory medical attention and the home hospitals had to deal with soldiers still wearing their first field dressings and covered in the mud of battle. On Saturday 22 July Essex 3 received a sudden call to detrain twenty wounded soldiers straight from the dressing stations in France. In the small hours of the morning and with a shortage of motor ambulances, the casualties were collected and taken to the Red Cross Hospital. All were stretcher cases and were by far the most serious seen so far in Chelmsford. Private John William Hanstock, of 62nd Company Machine Gun Corps, aged 25, had gangrene in a leg wound and by the afternoon he was dead – the first death at the hospital since it had opened. He came from Shirebrook, in Mansfield, Derbyshire, and his body was sent home by train on the following Monday. Convalescent soldiers from the hospital carried the Union Jack-draped coffin to the gun carriage and marched behind it to the station, while the pipers of the 7th Royal Scots led the procession.

Most of the time the military hospital patients had received medical attention in France. Once at the base hospitals they were stripped of their khaki uniforms and, if not restricted to bed, were issued with a new outfit of a blue jacket and trousers, with a white shirt and red tie. This gave them the nickname of the 'Boys in Blue' and invariably made them the centre of attention when out and about. Both Hylands and Chelmsford Red Cross hospitals laid on motor car excursions, trips into town and to local sights, and the distinctive uniform ensured that they did not have to pay for theatre or cinema tickets and would often find their refreshments paid for. However, it did not entitle them to free drinks and the local police would be on the lookout for any Blues in the vicinity of a pub; and landlords were under strict orders not to serve these patients. Needless to say, an order under the all-encompassing Defence of the Realm Act had already made it an offence to stand a soldier a pint, wounded or otherwise.

Wounded soldiers at the Essex Hut. [Reproduced by courtesy of the Essex Record Office ERO D/DU 787/4]

The military medical services were provided by the officers and men of the Royal Army Medical Corps (RAMC). Although there were permanent military hospitals around the country, the RAMC Field Ambulance provided routine healthcare for soldiers in billets and camps. This unit comprised about 220 men, and each division had three field ambulances (note that ambulance in this sense means a military unit, not a vehicle). The 2nd and 3rd South Midland Division Field Ambulances (SMFA) were initially set up at Hylands but subsequently moved to Oaklands and this then became the Main Dressing Station or medical headquarters of each division that moved into the area. The field ambulances were not responsible for the war wounded, as these were treated in the Red Cross hospitals and elsewhere, but provided medical care for the sick and injured – the coughs and sneezes and the sprained ankles - of the division, with an additional responsibility for the sanitary arrangements, such as water supply and waste disposal, and the cleanliness of cooking and billeting facilities. At the front the field ambulances operated the Advanced Dressing Stations (such as Essex Farm, north of Ypres), which were usually primitive medical posts designed for casualty collection and evacuation away from danger. At home they set up dressing stations in buildings such as Oaklands, as well as tents and marquees in the grounds, which included operating theatres and surgical and medical wards. A soldier feeling unwell, for example with an upset stomach, would initially report sick to his regimental medical officer, who would then refer him to the field ambulance and he would probably get admitted to the dressing station. A serious case might then be transferred to the local civilian hospital. To confuse matters slightly, both the military and civilians used the term 'hospital' to describe the RAMC dressing station. In addition to the Oaklands hospital, there was a similar unit run by 1st SMFA at Eves Corner in Danbury. The three field ambulances would have rotated between the sites, as did the units of the Lowland Division, which replaced the South Midlands Division in March 1915.

The Medical Officer of Health for Chelmsford, a civilian doctor who oversaw medical matters in the borough on behalf of the Council, was Dr Henry Newton, and he was singularly unimpressed with the RAMC men he encountered. He complained, repeatedly, that medical officers were not visiting sick soldiers in their billets and so the host families were bearing the brunt of caring for them. Over the winter

Men and patients of the South Midland Field Ambulance at Hylands House. [author's collection]

months 1914-15 there was an outbreak of influenza amongst the troops billeted in the town and on 20 January 1915 Newton raised his concerns with the Council's Sanitary Committee. The military authorities had made no provision for nursing such troops or providing them with a suitable diet, and Lieutenant Colonel Raywood, Assistant Director of Medical Services (ADMS) for the Division, was apparently not prepared to take action. The Town Clerk, George Melvin, took up the matter and was able to report to Council the next week that all military sick were to be visited in their billets each day by their own regimental medical officer, and that every courtesy and consideration was to be shown to the householders. Milk would be supplied daily to those who were confined to bed in their billets, and all serious cases were to be admitted to Oaklands field hospital.

Then came an outbreak of 'Spotted Fever', also known as cerebro-spinal fever or meningococcal meningitis. Although the causative bacterium had been identified and the association with crowded living conditions was known, the exact mode of transmission had not been

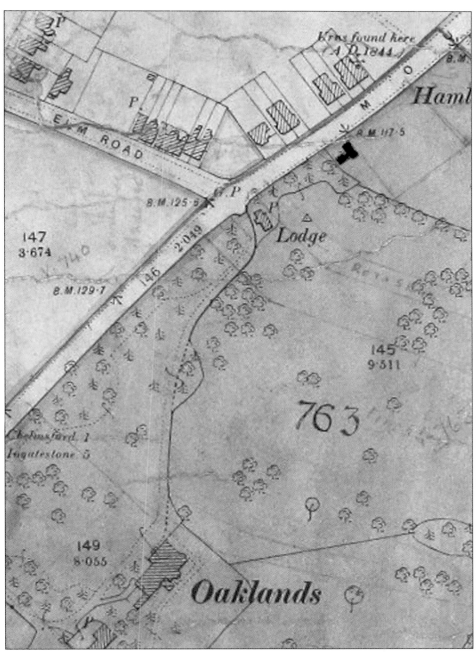

Oaklands House military hospital and Kenilworth isolation house (to right of Lodge).

identified. With men sharing rooms in billets, the disease spread rapidly. Private Frederick Sims, of the Gloucester Royal Field Artillery Ammunition Column, felt unwell on 9 February but did not feel he needed medical attention. A comrade called on him the next morning at his billet at 35 Primrose Hill, as he had not appeared for breakfast, and found him dead in his bed. Another death followed and on 17 February 1915. Dr Newton reported this to the Council's Sanitary Committee, and he also alerted the Local Government Board and the ADMS and his staff. Infectious diseases of this nature in the civilian community were treated at the new Isolation Hospital off Baddow Road (now the area of Goodwin Close), which had twenty beds. However, at this time the hospital was nearly full, due to a number of cases of scarlet fever. An urgent meeting was held in mid-February, attended by Dr Newton; the Mayor; Dr Thresh (the County Medical Officer of Health); Captain Dale, the Sanitary Officer of the South Midland Division; Colonel Wilkinson and two officers from the 3rd Army Headquarters. It was decided to take over 'Kenilworth' (103 Moulsham Street) and equip it as an isolation hospital, with nursing staff provided by arrangement with the Joint Hospital Board from the civilian Chelmsford Hospital, and medical staff and orderlies from the field ambulance. This Special Hospital would take in military and civilian patients. Matthew German, an orderly with 1st South Midland Field Ambulance, recalled cleaning and preparing Kenilworth with the company sergeant major, a lance corporal and three comrades. The Army also erected a number of huts at Oaklands for the quarantine of those who had been in contact with the disease, where they could be kept under observation until the danger passed. Unfortunately the orderlies were at great risk themselves; Private Ernest Stone died of meningitis on 9 February and his colleague, Private Harry Edmondson, who was one of the RAMC orderlies who actually worked at Kenilworth, contracted the disease and died on 19 February. German was too upset to attend the funerals. Both are buried in Writtle Road Cemetery.

The military authorities also erected a wooden pavilion at the Isolation Hospital, which added a further twenty-two beds. The Council set up a mortuary in Viaduct Road. The warm weather in the spring brought the outbreak to an end and at the start of May the Town Council was able to report that there had been no further cases notified. In total there were twenty-seven cases, with sixteen deaths, ten of whom were soldiers.

Military funeral procession passing the Shire Hall. [Spalding, author's collection]

With the Chelmsford & Essex Hospital, the Isolation Hospital, Kenilworth Special Hospital, Oaklands and Danbury Military Hospitals, and the two auxiliary hospitals, it would appear that there was a wealth of medical provision in the area. Additionally, Mrs Edward Upton, of Coptfold Hall, maintained eight beds for convalescents from Hylands Hospital, with a fully trained nurse in charge, throughout the whole war. The stately home of Skreens (long since demolished but the estate, Skreens Park, in Roxwell, is still there), was the home of Mrs Shaw, and she ran it as a convalescent home in the first year of the war, before getting into financial and staffing difficulties. In October 1914 she received a party of twenty-five wounded Belgian soldiers from St Bartholomew's Hospital. The men arrived at Chelmsford Station and were conveyed in motors to Skreens. Mrs Shaw had a staff of four nurses in attendance and defrayed all the costs incurred and a number of men stayed at the house until she closed in November 1915.

Major, now Colonel, Hilder, the pre-war invasion sceptic who had nearly put paid to the early Chelmsford Men's VAD, was completely converted to the VAD cause and his house, Huskards, Back Lane, Ingatestone became a fifty-five bed hospital. Although close to Hylands and Chelmsford it was not included in the Essex District of the Red Cross and instead came under the London region, and was classed as an Auxiliary Hospital to the 3rd London General Hospital at Wandsworth. Over 1,500 patients passed through the hospital during the war, including a large number of Australians, which merited a visit from the Rt Hon Andrew Fisher, High Commissioner of Australia, in August 1917. Huskards closed on 19 January 1919 and the final patients were collected in a motor bus from Chelmsford and driven to Ingatestone railway station.

In 1917 the Essex Branch of the Red Cross published a 'few facts' about their work in the war so far. 242,315 garments had been sent from the county store to hospitals at home and abroad; 1,568,770 cigarettes had been sent to units of the Essex Regiment; two motor ambulances had been sent to the Front; there were ninety-one VAD detachments in the county with 3,000 members; and they had a complete system for the transport of wounded in the case of air raids.

Following the death of the architect and alderman, Frederick Chancellor, in January 1918 his house, Bellefield, was left empty. The War Office managed to secure a rental agreement, with an anonymous gentleman paying the rent for the first year, and the property was offered to the Red Cross, adding a further eighty beds to the auxiliary hospital. The official opening of Bellefield by Lady Gwendoline Colvin took place on Saturday 21 September 1918. There was an inspection of VADs from Huskards, Hylands and Chelmsford by Mr Wythes, the County Director of the Red Cross for Essex, and a display of stretcher drill by C section, Essex Field Ambulance RAMC(T), whilst the Hoffmann's band played in the garden. Bellefield is still standing on New London Road.

In April 1919 Hylands Auxiliary Hospital was demobilised. From opening in August 1914 it first dealt with the sick and injured of the South Midlands Division and handled over 500 cases. In October 1914 it received its first war wounded, and subsequently treated fifty-nine Belgians and 901 British casualties, giving a total of 960. 160 operations were performed, although it was noted that far fewer operations took place later in the war as the surgical facilities in France improved. The average residence of each patient was seventy days and the Essex Branch of the Red Cross calculated that the cost per patient was between £4 14s 1d to £12 10s 7d, depending on the length of stay. When the hospital opened the staff were assisted by VADs Essex 4 and 40, but after a few months these were sent to run the Chelmsford Auxiliary Hospital and probationers were employed to fill their places. The full-time staff consisted of five trained nurses, five probationers, two orderlies, and two ward maids. All the expenses of running and equipping the Hospital were borne by Sir Daniel and Lady Gooch, without any outside assistance whatever (other than the capitation grant), and doctors WD Gimson, HW Newton, and JL Martin (as anaesthetist) gave their services voluntarily during the war. The Chelmsford War Work Depot sent a much appreciated weekly supply of bandages and dressings. The closing of the Hospital was celebrated by a 'Demobilisation Dance' at which a fine jazz band performed (interestingly this is the first reference to this form of music in Chelmsford!). On behalf of the staff and patients a presentation of a silver cigarette case was made to Lady Gooch by Private B Galloghly, 6th Camerons, from his bedside, the last patient to be evacuated.

From 1917 onwards a number of the Red Cross nurses and VADs had their work recognised; in the *Chronicle* for October 1917 a notice appeared:

The undermentioned are included in a long list of those who have been brought to the notice of the Secretary of State for War for valuable services rendered in connection with the war:

Callingham, Miss M, Nurse, Hylands Auxiliary Hospital
Gooch, Lady MW, Commandant, Hylands Auxiliary Hospital
Magor, Mrs FE, Commandant, Hylands Auxiliary Hospital
Meeson, Miss E, Nurse, General and Auxiliary Hospital, Chelmsford
Pitts, Miss E, Nurse, General and Auxiliary Hospital, Chelmsford
Poole, Miss D, Nurse, Hylands Auxiliary Hospital
Smith, Miss FM, Matron, Hylands Auxiliary Hospital

Miss Ethel Charlton, sister at Chelmsford Auxiliary Hospital, and Miss Ethel Craig, a nurse and quartermaster at Writtle (Hylands) Auxiliary Hospital were made Associates of the Royal Red Cross in 1917. Miss EM Boake, assistant quartermaster and VAD nurse at Chelmsford Auxiliary Hospital, and Mrs Evelyn Hilder, of Huskards, received the Royal Red Cross, 2nd Class, in April 1919.

It is remarkable to note that of the two thousand or so wounded soldiers who passed through the Chelmsford hospitals during the war, so few of them died – so few that the sad event was usually newsworthy. Some of them were sent to their own home towns. The others were buried locally. They all have the standard Commonwealth War Grave Commission headstone.

CHAPTER 13

Coming Home

On the morning of 11 November 1918 Miss Bancroft, the headteacher of the Chelmsford County High School for Girls, summoned the School Captain. She was told that the prevailing rumours of an armistice had not been confirmed, but if they were, hooters would sound. And at 11 am they did. Miss Bancroft continued giving a Scripture lesson to the Sixth Form and '… she then assembled the whole school, which sang "O God our Help in Ages Past"'. Afterwards the girls were given a half-hour break – most of it spent leaning from the windows and waving at the flag-bedecked traffic streaming along Broomfield Road'.

The Signs of the Times columnist in the *Chronicle* captured the arrival of the news:

The wonderful news of Peace and an end to the great war came with almost tragic suddenness on Monday morning. True it was expected, but not for an hour or so before it arrived. Chelmsford, for instance, was busy preparing for the opening of its 'Feed the Guns' week at 10 am, when, at 9.30, the great news reached the head office of the Essex County Chronicle from a private source. It was confirmed from the same source, but we thought it proper to wait for the Prime Minister's official confirmation before publication was made. How anxious an hour as that which followed can be better imagined than described. At 10.25, however, the pent-up feelings were released, for there came the message: 'Mr Lloyd George is now announcing armistice signed at 5 am; hostilities cease at 11'. Within five minutes this was in the windows of the office.

The end of the war meant that the men were coming home. There was still work to do – on 3 December the British Army crossed the Rhine and occupied the area around Cologne, but combat forces were no longer required and men could be released from the Army. Priority was given to the longest serving men and to married men, but the Government was deeply concerned about the possible effects of releasing large numbers of men into the civilian labour market. One way to speed up the process was for an employer to request the services of a previous employee; Mr Young, the secretary of the Chelmsford Star Co-operative Society (forty-nine of whose staff had either volunteered or been conscripted), received a number of letters from former employees asking him to help. The official procedure was to write to the secretary of the Local Advisory Committee at the Employment Exchange at 221 Moulsham Street, and Mr Young used the following format:

Dear Sir,
We, Chelmsford Star Co-operative Society, hereby declare that [number] [rank] [name] [unit] was in our employment before [date] and that we are prepared to offer him employment as [job title] immediately on his return to civil life, and shall be glad if his early release can be obtained.
Yours faithfully

The soldier had to complete Civil Employment Form Z16, naming the intended employer, which would then be matched up with the employer's letter. Mr Young received dozens of letters from former employees asking and, in some cases begging, to return. Quickest off the mark was Private Stanley Bohannan (Herbert's brother), RAMC, who wrote to Young on 20 November 1918, whilst recovering from an operation in No. 5 Convalescent Depot in France. He had been seriously wounded in April 1917 and suffered from shell shock. Clearly impatient to get out of uniform, he wrote again on 20 December. By February he was again a warehouseman. On 4 December 1918 Corporal Pilgrim wrote, reminding him that he had been called up to the Colours on 4 August 1914. He had served in France for a few weeks but contracted rheumatic fever, which kept him unfit for further foreign service. He gave his address as a guard at the prisoner of war camp at Rickmansworth. Bandsman Harry Stevens was also called up as a Territorial at the outbreak of the war and was now a 'time-expired man, having served my five years with over two in France', and wanted to come back to the Wells Street bakery he had left so long before. In January Private Thomas Jarvis wrote an indignant letter, having apparently been refused his old job for 'reasons you state are very poor and not well thought out'. He predicted that furnishing and hardware would boom tremendously, and hoped that his position would be filled by 'someone who has served their Country'. His truculence paid off and he was re-engaged as a shop assistant. Mrs Cooper, of 10 Rochford Road, wrote on behalf of her son Private Cyril Cooper, who was serving in India.

The men came back, bringing with them their stories. And there were so many of them. Chelmsford did not produce great heroes or great exploits but there was enough to be proud of. There was a Chelmsford Victoria Cross, the highest military decoration, but the link to our town was tenuous as it was awarded to Corporal Charles Jarvis, a Scotsman who had worked at Hoffmann's before the war. While serving with 57 Field Company of the Royal Engineers during the withdrawal of the British Expeditionary Force at Mons he managed to lay explosive charges and blow up a bridge. His citation reads:

'For great gallantry at Jemappes on 23rd August 1914 for 1 ½ hours under heavy fire in full view of the enemy, and in successfully firing charges for the demolition of a bridge.'

Originally from Aberdeenshire in Scotland, Jarvis served in the Royal Engineers as a regular for several years and on discharge had lived in London and then Chelmsford for nearly two years before the war. Apparently he was a well known character, nicknamed 'Scotty' or 'Mac'. He was employed at the Hoffmann Works and was an active trade unionist, as a member of the Amalgamated Society of Engineers. He also founded the Chelmsford City Sea Angling Club and served as its secretary. Jarvis was wounded and hospitalised shortly after his exploits. It was reported that he was Mentioned in Dispatches in late

Lance Corporal Jarvis VC blowing the bridge at Jemappes

October 1914. By 20 November he was in the London Hospital when it was announced that he had been awarded the Victoria Cross. He never fully recovered and was discharged from the Army; as a skilled mechanic he agreed to be drafted into munitions works at Portsmouth Dockyards, where he spent the rest of the war.

Seaman Gunner H Elliott, of 23 New London Road, was on board HMS *Cressy*, torpedoed and sunk in the naval fiasco in the North Sea on 22 September 1914, one of the first actions of the war. He survived.

Major Merriman, formerly adjutant of the 5th Essex – the Chelmsford Battalion – of Old Court, Arbour Lane, transferred to the regular army at the start of the war and joined the 1st Battalion Royal Irish Rifles. He took part in the Battle of Loos in September 1915, in which he lost his left arm. He was awarded the Distinguished Service Order and was appointed as Brigade Major of the Tyne Garrison, where he spent the rest of the war, and survived.

The Military Cross (for officers) and the Military Medal (for men) were the two commonest awards during the First World War. It took until January 1917 before Second Lieutenant Edward Hamilton King, Intelligence Corps, of Springfield Dukes, became the first man in Chelmsford to win the Military Cross. He survived.

Captain Ernest Aylett, 1st Battalion Northamptonshire Regiment, lived at Alton, 6 Swiss Avenue and originally worked in the finance department of the Essex Education Committee. He joined Kitchener's Army, went out to France as a sergeant and was commissioned in the field. On 24 January 1917 he received a Military Cross from the King for bravery in the operations on the Somme the previous summer. He survived.

The Military Medal was given to the men, and it was relatively unusual to be awarded it twice (a bar). Private Mark Butcher, 9th Essex, the son of Mr and Mrs Butcher of 17 Coval Road and a former *Chronicle* employee, was awarded the Military Medal and bar at a parade at Widford Camp in May 1917. His exploits included rescuing wounded under heavy fire at Pozières in August 1916 and the bar for carrying wounded out of No Man's Land under heavy fire to a dressing station, a distance of 1½ miles. He joined the Army at the outbreak of the war and was invalided out in late 1917. He survived.

The Distinguished Service Medal was awarded to submariner A G Ward, of 6 Upper Bridge Road, for bravery while operating in the submarine E11 in the Sea of Marmara during the Gallipoli campaign. He survived.

Ernest Spalding, the younger of Alderman Spalding's sons, enlisted under the Derby scheme and served with the 15th Battalion London Regiment. In September 1916 he earned himself a lance-corporal's stripe but the following month he suffered shell wounds to his face and right hand and was sent back to England to recuperate. After several periods in hospital he was eventually discharged on 4 September 1918 as 'No longer physically fit for war service'. His brother, Fred Spalding junior, joined the Artists Rifles in January 1917. In April he was accepted for flying training and trained as an observer. He was injured in a flying accident in August 1917, but was subsequently commissioned into the Royal Air Force in April 1918. Both Spalding boys survived.

Flight Lieutenant Fred Spalding.

A former Marconi man, Private Benjamin Driscoll, a reservist called up at the outbreak of the war, had a classic narrow escape story. On arriving in France in December 1914 he needed a cigarette case and his brother, John Driscoll, also at Marconi's, sent him a fine nickel-plated case, which Benjamin carried in the left breast pocket of his tunic. During the attack on Neuve Chapelle in March 1915 he was struck by a bullet which hit the cigarette case and was deflected down to his legs, causing minor injuries only. His relief was short lived as, while waiting for medical attention, he was hit again in the right arm and was finally evacuated back to the 3rd London General Hospital in Wandsworth. While he was there the bullet 'dropped out' when, in a story surely calculated to scare his future grandchildren, an artery burst in his arm and he lost a large quantity of blood. Blood poisoning set in but he survived.

Sergeant Reginald Marshall of the Queen's Bays, and son of Police Sergeant Marshall of the Police Headquarters, Chelmsford, had a great story about having his horse shot from under him at Mons. Later he was ordered with his section to take a house lying between British and German trenches near Ypres. When they entered the house they found it full of dead and wounded men, including one lad who had been pinned under rubble for two days. He remembered Christmas at the front and being one of eight men in the company who managed to get home leave, arriving back in Chelmsford on Boxing Day. He survived.

Private Stanley Roper, Lincolnshire Regiment, of 3 Mildmay Road, came home from a French hospital with his left arm amputated in October 1917. He survived.

Private Bertram Hazell, the Chelmsford postman from Beehive Lane called up with the Reserves at the outbreak of the war and sent to the front in the 4th Middlesex, was invalided home just a few weeks later. Involved in the Retreat from Mons, he 'passed through the serious fighting scatheless, but his false teeth gave way under the hard biscuit ration, and this, combined with the heavy fatigue of the campaign, undermined his health for a time'. He survived.

Private Armon Prior of the 6th Buffs, 6 Siding Cottages, Widford, arrived home in December 1918 after a year in a German prisoner of war camp.

Mr William Rice, of 31 Regina Road and an engineer at the Chelmsford Steam Laundry in Victoria Road, had all five of his sons serving the King. William Rice junior was a mechanical transport driver, Able Seaman Philip Rice served on HMS *Monarch*, Driver Albert Rice was in the Royal Field Artillery, Private Fred Rice was in the Duke of Cornwall's Light Infantry, and Private George Rice served with 3rd Essex. They all survived.

These are just some of the survivors and they deserve to be remembered as much as those who lost their lives. The idea of a memorial to the dead of the Great War was addressed by the Bishop of Chelmsford as early as November 1916, when he wrote an article in the *Diocesan Chronicle* expressing concern that any such memorial must be of sufficient artistic merit to make an impression on worshippers 'in the year 2000 AD', and he cautioned against individual memorials in churches, recommending instead a Roll of Honour at the end of the war.

The Mayor, Alderman W Cowell, first proposed a war memorial for Chelmsford at the Town Council meeting on Wednesday 27 November 1918 and a public meeting was held on Monday 16 December 1918 at which, following discussion, the council reacted in its usual way by appointing yet another sub-committee. A Mr E P Bucknall submitted a plan for a monument which he had prepared, which would cost around £3,000 if built of marble. The War Memorial Sub-committee first met on 20 January 1919, at which it was decided that the primary purpose of the memorial 'should remind the present and future generations of the supreme sacrifice made by Chelmsford officers and men in the war'.

In March four memorial schemes were selected from twelve proposals, including a 'Victory Ward' at the Chelmsford & Essex Hospital; a Town Hall and Memorial Hall; a monument in the lower part of Duke Street; and a memorial playing field. By early March the Town Hall and Memorial Hall plan had been chosen, and the public were invited to contribute funds. The Memorial Hall was to be 'an inspiring building, with organ, gallery, platform, pillars, stained glass windows, statues, pictures and so on...' By July a £500 gift had been received from Mr George Courtauld, of Halstead, towards the proposed 'War Memorial Hall' and concerns were raised that the fundraising for the hall would conflict with a campaign by the hospital, which was seeking £20,000 for an extension.

A heated council meeting in September 1919 saw the approval of a site for the new municipal buildings and memorial hall at the corner of Rainsford Road and Coval Lane, on 2 acres and 320 square yards of land for £2,700. Criticisms of this site included that for Springfield and Moulsham councillors this was at the 'extreme [north] end of the borough' and the proposal was rejected at the October meeting. In December it was announced that the War Memorial Sub-committee were to look at two further sites. In February 1920 they reported that they had identified a site on London Road between the Manse and the Cloisters (now under the Parkway) which was suitable for the joint building (£750), and also that Rainsford House, on the corner of Duke Street and Coval Lane, would be a good site for the municipal offices.

By April 1920 there were complaints from the public about the lack of progress with the Chelmsford memorial, when memorials had been erected by villages and hamlets throughout the land. This appeared to galvanize the council, and then it was announced that the London Road site would be acquired and an appeal for funds was launched on the 9th June. By July the whole idea of a memorial hall was dropped, following the poor response from the public (the hospital appeal had by now raised nearly £20,000 and was looking to continue with further fundraising).

In October 1920 the whole process of the Chelmsford War Memorial was re-started; and in November, in the absence of a borough memorial, the first Armistice Day ceremony was marked with a service of commemoration at the Cathedral.

The sub-committee continued its deliberations and by March 1921 they were considering some form of monument, to be sited either in place of the Sebastapol Gun in front of the Shire Hall, or in place of the statue of Judge Tindal (to be moved inside the Shire Hall). In July the decision was taken to move the Tindal Statue to Bell Mead and that the Chelmsford War Memorial would be erected in Tindal Square. There would be an open competition for designs. The competition was arranged under RIBA guidelines and eighty-seven designs and models were considered. Incredibly, at the September council meeting it was announced that the winner was Mr W Hamilton Buchan, of Battersea. It was to be 27' 3" in height, made out of Portland stone, and would cost £2,750. His prize was ten guineas. An appeal was made for £2,300 from the public.

£1,606 had been raised by the end of March 1922, and there was an increasing feeling that the Tindal Square site was not satisfactory. The sculptor wrote to the council offering to reduce the height from 27' to 24' 9", which would cut the cost to £2,745; and that once given permission to start it would take him ten months to finish.

Meanwhile the plans for new council offices at the Rainsford House site had been approved and so there was little surprise that at the September council meeting it was announced that the Tindal Square plan had been abandoned and the memorial would be erected on the east side of the new council chambers. A cenotaph-type design was suggested, which would keep costs within the £2,000 or so that had been raised. It was further suggested that a semi-circular portico would be set up at the entrance to the council building, with the names of the fallen inscribed on panels and, funds permitting, a stained glass window. March 1923 saw a decision to press ahead with the cenotaph monument, noting that the portico and panels were a separate project, and in June the Borough Engineer, Mr Ernest J Miles, produced a model of the monument to be erected in Duke Street 'ready for unveiling on Armistice Day'. Names of the fallen were to be placed on bronze panels, and families were asked to submit names to the Town Clerk's office. In August the local masonry firm of Wray and Fuller were invited to construct the memorial for £990, employing ex-servicemen for the work. The bronze panels would cost £250, and the balance of the fund would be used for a window. Work began quickly.

On 1 October 1923 the Mayor, Alderman Fred Spalding, led a ceremony involving members and officials of the council, in which a

The unveiling of the Chelmsford Cenotaph.

casket of Portland stone lined with lead and filled with 'records of local and national interest, specimen war medals, etc.' was lowered into a cavity at the base of the unfinished memorial.

Finally, on Sunday 11 November 1923, Vice-Admiral Sir Roger Keyes unveiled the Chelmsford War Memorial, in front of a number of distinguished guests and civic dignitaries. The guard of honour was provided by 5th Battalion Essex Regiment, and a large crowd witnessed the ceremony. Wreaths were laid by ex-servicemen and voluntary groups including the Girl Guides and the Boy Scouts.

In the 1911 census the population of Chelmsford was given as 18,008. Excluding the soldiers billeted or camped around the town the wartime population was estimated at around 20,000, the increase due largely to the arrival of munitions workers. In 1918 the electoral register was revised and provided a list of those entitled to vote at the local and general elections and included those absent on naval or military service. Across the three wards of the borough there were 1,791 men marked as absent, or nearly ten per cent of the pre-war population. Figures from the Office of National Statistics indicate that in 1918 men of military age (between eighteen and forty one) comprised about twenty per cent of the national population, which suggests that about half the eligible men in Chelmsford were away in the services. The exact figure is unknown, but around 400 Chelmsford men never returned. The Chelmsford Civic Centre War Memorial has 357 names listed, although a number of eligible men appear to have been missed. The Moulsham War Memorial can be found in front of St John's Church in Moulsham Street, the Springfield War Memorial is in All Saint's Church, Springfield, and the Widford War Memorial is in St Mary's Church, Widford. Several memorials can be found in the Cathedral, commemorating the

Commonwealth War Graves Commission headstones in Writtle Road Cemetery. [courtesy Paul Maclean]

Essex Yeomanry, Hoffmann's employees, Essex Constabulary, parishioners, and individuals. Other war memorials can be seen in the Essex Regiment Museum, the Police Headquarters, the Conservative Club, County Hall, Shire Hall, King Edward VIth School, Marconi's, and the Church of Our Lady Immaculate and the United Reform Church. The recently rediscovered and renovated Chelmsford School of Science and Art memorial plaque can be seen in the entrance to the Sawyer Building at Anglia Ruskin University.

There are sixty war Commonwealth War Graves in the cemeteries in the borough, with thirty-eight in the Writtle Road Cemetery, two in the London Road Cemetery, three more in the Rectory Lane Cemetery, eight at Springfield Holy Trinity churchyard, five at St Mary's Church in Widford, and four at the All Saints' Churchyard in Writtle.

Epilogue

The Great War was but a small part of the history of Chelmsford. Compared to the extensive damage suffered in the Second World War or the more deliberate changes brought about through post-war reconstruction and development, our town – city – had little to show for the four years of conflict. But a town is a living community, and in researching and writing this book this has become more and more apparent. I have spoken to many people about my work and although, of course, no one now remembers the Great War, I have been constantly surprised by memories of the landmarks and features written about in this book.

In late 2013 I read *A Celebratory History of Anglia Ruskin University 1858-2008*, by Anthony Kirkby, to learn about the Chelmsford School of Science of Art, one of the university's predecessor institutions. There was nothing relating to the war, but there was an intriguing comment about a 'memorial unveiled in the School after the war'. I immediately referred to my copy of *The Impact of Catastrophe* (Essex Records Office), Paul Rusiecki's great book about Essex in the First World War, which has a comprehensive listing of all war memorials in the county. It did not include the School of Science and Art. The School was originally located in the Chancellor Building on Market Road (now Victoria Road South) which had been sold by the university to the Genesis Housing Association for redevelopment. They were unaware of any memorial, so I contacted Stephen Bennett, the clerk to the university, and it was with some relief that he informed me that not only did he know about the memorial but he was 'looking at it right now' in his office. Subsequently I visited him and was shown a very impressive bronze plaque, which commemorated ten staff and students who gave their lives in the war.

It was then suggested that the memorial should be rededicated. I did some research into the names on the memorial and had an article published in the *Chronicle*. In a subsequent interview I was asked if any one name stood out, and with no disrespect to the others, I had to mention Alick Horsnell. As Second Lieutenant Horsnell of the 7th Suffolk Regiment he was killed, aged 33, on 3 July 1916 and his body was never found. But this man was one of the outstanding architects of his generation – from humble origins in South Primrose Hill, he went to school at St Peter's on Rainsford Road and then went to the School of Science and Art. He won many prizes for his art work, and was taken on as an apprentice at Frederick Chancellor's architectural firm in Duke Street. Whilst here he won further awards, including recognition from the Royal Institute of British Architects. He set up his own practice in London, but at the outbreak of war he volunteered for military service.

Anglia Ruskin University kindly organised the rededication of the beautifully restored memorial on 4 November 2014. Guests of honour included members of the Horsnell family, including his niece, Yvonne, and his great-nephews Bryan and Michael. The memorial is now mounted in the Sawyers Building, opposite the old Hoffmann's building which is where Yvonne spent much of her working life. Although they had never met him, they were justifiably proud of his reputation and achievements and brought with them the Silver Medal Alick had been awarded in 1903.

In memory of Alick Horsnell.

Alick Horsnell.

The Borough of Chelmsford

NORTH WARD	SOUTH WARD	SPRINGFIELD WARD
Admiral Road	Anchor Street	Arbour Lane
Bishops Road	Baddow Road	Brockley Road
Broomfield Road	Baker Street	Gainsborough Road
Burgess Well Road	Bouverie Street	Hill Road
Cedar Avenue	Bradford Street	Navigation Road
Church Square	Braemar Avenue	Queen's Road
Church Street	Crompton Street	Sandford Road
Cottage Place	Elm Road	Springfield Green
Coval Lane	Friars	Springfield Road
Coval Road	Black Friars	The Wharf
Cramphorn Road	Galleywood	Trinity Road
Duke Street	George Street	Weight Road
Fairfield Road	Goldlay Road	
Glebe Road	Grove Road	
Henry Road	Hall Street	
High Street	Hamlet Road	
King Edward's Avenue	Lady Lane	
Legg Street	Lower Anchor Street	
Maltese Road	Manor Road	
Mill Road	Marlborough Road	
Nelson Road	Mildmay Road	
New London Road (2-18)	Moulsham Street	

NORTH WARD	SOUTH WARD
New Street	New London Road
Park Avenue	New Writtle Street
Primrose Hill	Nursery Road
Railway Street	Orchard Street
Rainsford Avenue	Parker Road
Rainsford Lane	Queens Street
Rainsford Road	Redcliffe Road
Rectory Road	Rochford Road
Regina Road	Roman Road
School View	Rosebery Road
South Primrose Hill	Rothesay Avenue
Springfield Road (1-18)	Seymour Street
Swiss Avenue	Southborough Road
Threadneedle Street	St John's Road
Tindal Square	Upper Bridge Road
Tindal Street	Upper Roman Road
Tower Avenue	Van Dieman's Road
Townfield Street	Vicarage Road
Victoria Road	Waterhouse Lane
Waterloo Lane	Waterhouse Street
	Widford End
	Wood Street
	Wolseley Road
	Writtle Road
	York Road

Index